C000146676

Entrepreneurial Excellence in the Knowledge Economy

Entrepreneurial Excellence in the Knowledge Economy

Intellectual Capital Benchmarking Systems

José Maria Viedma Marti

and

Maria do Rosário Cabrita

First published 2012 by
PALGRAVE MACMILLAN

Palgrave Macmillan in the UK is an imprint of Macmillan Publishers Limited, registered in England, company number 785998, of Houndmills, Basingstoke, Hampshire RG21 6XS.

Palgrave Macmillan in the US is a division of St Martin's Press LLC, 175 Fifth Avenue, New York, NY 10010.

Palgrave Macmillan is the global academic imprint of the above companies and has companies and representatives throughout the world.

Palgrave® and Macmillan® are registered trademarks in the United States, the United Kingdom, Europe and other countries.

ISBN: 978–1–137–02406–0 hardback

This book is printed on paper suitable for recycling and made from fully managed and sustained forest sources. Logging, pulping and manufacturing processes are expected to conform to the environmental regulations of the country of origin.

A catalogue record for this book is available from the British Library.

Library of Congress Cataloging-in-Publication Data

Viedma Marti, José Ma. (José Maria)
    Entrepreneurial excellence in the knowledge economy : intellectual capital benchmarking systems / José Maria Viedma Marti and Maria do Rosário Cabrita.
        p. cm.
        ISBN 978–1–137–02406–0
        1. Entrepreneurship. 2. Knowledge management. 3. Intellectual capital.
    I. Cabrita, Maria do Rosário. II. Title.
HB615.V448 2012
658.4′21—dc23   2012022125

10 9 8 7 6 5 4 3 2 1
21 20 19 18 17 16 15 14 13 12

Printed and bound in Great Britain by
CPI Antony Rowe, Chippenham and Eastbourne

We dedicate this book to all the active members of the
Knowledge Management and Intellectual Capital Community.
They were our main source of inspiration.

Living with high-level intangibles such as equity, integrity, honesty and human dignity-principles give us the courage to innovate and take advantage of the opportunities
Jose Maria Viedma Marti, Maria do Rosário Cabrita

Contents

List of Tables

List of Figures

Foreword

John S. Edwards

Intellectual capital, once thought of as the preserve of theoretical economics and management scientists, has now come of age as a field of both research and practice. Indeed, one of its great strengths is its status as an exemplar of research-based practice, with a growing group of research-engaged practitioners and practice-aware researchers who contribute to a virtuous cycle in which research improves practice and practice improves research. There is now a widespread recognition that intangibles – particularly intangible assets – need to be measured and managed just as much as an organization's more tangible resources such as machinery and equipment.

A better understanding of intellectual capital is vital in guiding the continuing growth of the knowledge economy, which constitutes so much of the environment of 21st century life. Jose Maria Viedma Marti and Maria do Rosário Cabrita have put together a book that takes the reader from the basics of intellectual capital and the knowledge economy through to detailed advice about how to use the concepts in a particular business, city or region. It is well known from the closely related field of knowledge management that the hardest step for any organization is going from an understanding of the concepts to devising some implementable initiatives in a particular context.

The authors are well qualified to write this book, combining practical wisdom with a rigorous research track record. Jose Maria Viedma Marti is president of Intellectual Capital Management Systems, which has devised a range of Intellectual Capital Benchmarking Systems for every level, from that of a region down to individual organizations, and even their operations. He is extensively involved in research journals and conferences in intellectual capital and knowledge management, and with professional associations in Spain, across Europe and worldwide. Maria do Rosário Cabrita is also an active researcher and teacher in intellectual capital, with practical experience in the consultancy and healthcare sectors and an active interest in the banking sector.

Although the authors have academic affiliations, the spirit of the book is entrepreneurial – governments do not create worth, only organizations (and specifically the people in them) do that. The approaches set out here can be applied in organizations large or small but there is a particular emphasis on how to use them in organizations which are small and intend to grow. It is well known that small- and medium-sized organizations (SMEs) are the main drivers of innovation and economic growth, especially during the recovery from a period of recession.

The authors begin by setting out ten principles for wealth creation in the knowledge economy. Probably the most important of these principles are that *sustainable* competitive advantage is mainly based on intangibles (tangible assets being easier to imitate) and that success, especially exceptional success, depends on collaboration. The philosophy behind these principles pervades the entire book.

At its heart of this volume is the ICBS (Intellectual Capital Benchmarking System), which has been developed on the basis of extensive research carried out by Jose Maria Viedma Marti and his team over many years. The ICBS consists of three linked elements: the Operational Intellectual Capital Benchmarking System (OICBS) that considers the operations core activities and core knowledge; the Innovation Intellectual Capital Benchmarking System (IICBS) that refers to innovation core activities and core knowledge; and the Social Capital Benchmarking System (SCBS) that focuses on the social capital existing in a cluster or geographical location. Thus we see that two of the elements have an internal focus, while the third has an external focus – looking not at the organization itself, but at the other organizations with which it is associated, either through business or 'neighbourly' relationships. The latter is a very good example of the 'weak ties' that are so vital for organizational learning, a phrase coined by Granovetter (1973). Granovetter suggested that sometimes we learn better from our weak ties (those that extend beyond the boundary of the organization) as people who are relative strangers to us introduce novelty to our stable world. The benefits for innovation are clear, and this speaks to the principle of the need to collaborate.

The authors discuss why existing approaches to strategy formulation such as SWOT and the value chain are no longer adequate on their own in a world where intangibles have such an influence, and explain in detail why benchmarking is so important, thus setting the context for the use of the ICBS. The three components of the ICBS are then explained at length, with detailed practical examples.

Overall, the book achieves its aim, delivering a new approach to strategy formulation and competitive advantage that is fit for the knowledge economy of the 21st century, and one that can readily be put into practice by any business leader or leadership team.

John S. Edwards
Executive Dean Aston Business School

Foreword

Leif Edvinsson

'What did Steve Jobs essentially do in Apple?' asked Bhaskar Prasad in *International Business Times*, October 2011. He concluded that Steve Jobs managed its *Intellectual Capital*. For him, managing Intellectual Capital involved the capacity to give proper direction to the knowledge assimilated by the organization, in order to generate innovative ideas and develop them into final products.

In the early 1990s, I had already started to call this approach 'Knowledge Navigation for Intellectual Capital Development'. When, at that time, I developed the now well-known Skandia Navigator to support the strategic process of leveraging hidden assets, I came to know Dr. Viedma and his work on Intangibles. This new book about ICBS is a very good summary of the refined process of strategy formulation based on IC knowledge navigation. It highlights the approach to systematized knowledge work not only on benchmarking but implicitly also on bench learning about the unknown, and perhaps invisible, strategic opportunity space for the strategy formulating process.

In the modern knowledge economy we all have to pay more and more attention to invisible opportunity spaces. One of the most fascinating ones is the understanding and development of the value of networks, also called Relational Capital in the taxonomy of IC. Therefore, the growth of mobile broadband nodes from about 1 billion nodes in 2011 to 5 billion in 2015 is re-shaping the global business landscape. Just look at the tremendous network development by, among others, Facebook and Google but also by Baidu in China. For Apple, this resulted in shaping a most successful strategy called App Store. Apple is now making more revenue out of the network than its tangible devices. It has also resulted in Apple being one of the highest valued stock listed enterprises in the world, in mid March 2012 valued at almost 600 billion USD.

It can also be seen as a strategic ecosystem, like the Knowledge Tree that I was already using to visualize concepts in the early 1990s. It is about an approach of cultivating the roots for the benefit of the financial fruits. So, the systematized approach to ICBS described in this book, as well as in the systems dynamics-based approach, by Jay Forrester at MIT, and applied in the successful http://www.incas-europe.org is at the core of the Knowledge Economy. The value creating process is in the strategic interdependencies and the knowledge flow between various stakeholders. This often invisible dimension has to be visualized, assessed, and navigated as a dynamic process.

Many people are over-focusing on the metrics and measurements, when the real strategy process is about 'me-assuring'; in other words, assuring the knowledge navigation of more and more intangible dimensions or components of Intellectual Capital. This strategy formulating process can also be seen as an extended dimension over time of the enterprise, or a third dimension. It can then be called the longitude, and seen in combination with altitude and latitude. For an enterprise perspective, see more at www.corporatelongitude.com. The major thrust for knowledge innovation, and IICBS is touched upon, in this book, in Chapter 6.

One of the increasingly important understandings of the modern knowledge economy is in the above-mentioned Relational or Network dimensions. In Asia knowledge is perceived as a relationship in this in-between space while, in the Western perspectives, knowledge is often constrained into an object. So leadership and management have to be more and more focused on the interdependencies of the in-between dimensions.

Furthermore, a more holistic ecosystem perspective might call this 'Social Capital' including the citizenship and growing global brain-power. Sometimes, this is referred to as Crowd Sourcing for the emerging new phenomena called Crowd Funding. For this, the knowledge navigating SCBS approach in Chapter 7 will be an inroad into a new wealth creating approach.

So, for the successful Ecosystem of IC, remember that the most dynamic component is Human Capital but the value creating multiplier function lies in Organizational Structural Capital, together called the IC multiplier ($HC \times SC > 1$).

Happy reading of this valuable and practical ICBS book.

Leif Edvinsson
The world's first director of Intellectual Capital
President of the New Club of Paris

Acknowledgements

The advent of the knowledge economy has fundamentally changed the basis of wealth creation in modern social communities and knowledge and other human-based intangibles have become the fundamental resources of wealth creation.

As a result of this new basis of wealth creation, a new theory of entrepreneurial excellence has been developed. In summary, this new theory supports the fact that entrepreneurial or business excellence is still achieved through good strategy formulation and superior strategy implementation, but its foundations rely on sustainable competitive advantages based on intangibles.

The main contribution of this book resides in its practical research on successful strategy formulation in the knowledge economy context, which has crystallized in ICBS methodologies and frameworks.

I started the development of ICBS methodologies and frameworks at the beginning of the nineties and since then I have improved it with my collaborators and PhD students at the UPC (Polytechnic University of Catalonia).

In any work of this scope, it is impossible to acknowledge all of its many individual contributors. However, we would like to thank those particular individuals and organizations who were especially inspiring, generous and helpful.

First of all, I would like to give many thanks to the presidents and managers of the entrepreneurs' associations, and particularly to Xavier López (ASCAMM), Antonio Saenz and Joaquin Trigo (Fomento) and Júlian Lázaro (Gremio de industrias de la confección de Barcelona). They made it possible, across different public projects, to test, modify and improve the ICBS initial version in more than fifty small and medium sized companies. The executives of these companies who generously offered their time for interviews also deserve special recognition. As representative of them, I would like to mention Joaquin Badrinas (FINSA, where the final version of OICBS was tested) and Juan Aguilar (Ermenegildo Zegna, where the final version of IICBS was tested).

Other relevant contributors to the ICBS project were the members and friends who belong to the KM and IC Communities. In one way or another, they inspired the substantial improvements that have been implemented in the system during the development of the project.

Among them I would like to mention Nick Bontis and Christopher Bart (McMaster University); Rory Chase and Jay Chatzkel (Emerald Group); Patrick H. Sullivan (ICMG LLC); Klaus Tochtrermann (IKNOW); John Edwards (KMRP Journal); Leif Edvinsson, Günter Koch, Ahmed Bounfour, Aino Kianto, Sumita-Takayuki, Pirjo Ståhle, Edna Pasher, Ante Pulic, Karmen Jelcic, David O'Donnell, Kay Alwert, Giovanni Schiuma, Waltraut Ritter, Yasuhito Hanado, Charles Savage, Peter Pawlowsky, Stefan Gueldenberg, Anssi Smedlund, Gunther Szogs, Hank Kune (The New Club of Paris); Daniel Andriessen (Inholland University); Manfred Bornemann (Intangible Assets Consulting); Karl Erik Sveiby (Hanken School of Economics Finland); Göran Roos (IC Services); Baruch Lev (NYU Stern); Bernard Marr (IC Group); Jan Mouritsen, Jan Annerstedt (Copenhagen Business School); Stefano Zambon (University of Ferrara); Dan Kirsch (KMPro); Klaus North (University of Applied Sciences Wiesbaden); Dan Remenyi, Sue Nugus (ECKM); Hubert Saint-Onge (SanitOnge Alliance Inc.); Debra M. Amidon (Entovation); Francisco Javier Carrillo, Fernando Casado (CISC); Pedro Escorsa, José Figuerola, Josep Coll, Francisco Solé Parellada, Miquel Subirachs, Manel Rajadell and Federico Garriga (UPC); Eduardo Bueno, Mari Paz Salmador (Foro Intellectus); Paloma Sanchez, Leandro Cañibano, Cristina Cheminade (Universidad Autónoma de Madrid); Jose Luis Hervas, Juan Ignacio Dalmau (Universidad Politécnica de Valencia); Alfonso López (UNIZAR); Nekane Aramburu, Olga Rivera, Josune Saenz (Universidad de Deusto) W.B. Lee, Cuby Chow (Hong Kong University); Carol Yeh-Yun Lin (National Chengchi University) Paloma Portela (CEDE); Ramón Bastida, Salvador Guash, Oriol Amat, Enric Serradell (ACCID); Ramon Forn, Juan Alberto Prats, Albert Moreno (ACAV); Ramón Adell, José María Jordá, Xavier Gangonells, Joan Baiget, Agustí Casas, Iban Clot, Felip-Neri Gordi, Franz Revollo, Xavier Toll, Albert Pèlach (AED) and Daniel Marti (www.gestiondelconocimiento.com).

Some valuable ideas and reflections for the project came from the following partners and collaborators at the InCaS European Project: Stefan Zickgraf (CEA-PME); Kai Mertins, Markus Will, Wen-Huan Wang, Cornelia Meyer (Fraunhofer IPK); Patrick Humphreys, Charles Kiasides, Lucia Garcia, Thorsten Roser (LSE); Marjan Leber (University of Maribor); Karl-Heinz Leitner (ARCS); Mart Kivikas (WEKE) Jesús Jorcano (FOMENTO) and Roger Pou (SIDASA).

A work of such nature comes into being only through a systematic research approach. In this particular case, it was essentially carried out with my PhD students, and research associates at the UPC (Polytechnic University of Catalonia). I would like to thank the following PhD

Students: Luis Alvarado, Carlos Fernando Alonso, Eduardo Mindrau, Teresita Arenas, Tania Alvarez, Marisol Hurtado, Oscar Magna, José Miguel Valenzuela, Assia Gouza, Jordi Ming, Cristina Maldonado, and Francisco Guarda. Professor Blanca Martins deserves special recognition. She collaborated in many relevant research projects and publications, and her advice was essential in order to review the theoretical foundations of the ICBS methodology.

This book will be launched together with a software package that has been modernized and technically improved by a team from Quidgest-Consultores de Gestão SA. As significant members of the team, I would like to give special thanks to Andrea de Jesus, Cristina Marinhas, João Paulo Carvalho, Carlos Marques, João Araújo, Miguel Marinhas, Rosa Rodriguez, Kim Lembeck and Xavier Navarro.

A special debt of gratitude goes to Laura Jenkins from Emerald Group Publishing Limited, to Sue Nugus from Academic Publishing Limited, to Stephan Zigkgraf from Confédération Européenne des Associations de Petites et Moyennes Entreprises (CEA-PME), to Leif Edvinsson, to Daniel Andriessen and to Erik Saveiby who granted permission to reproduce their figures/tables in our book.

We also appreciate the genuine help and intellectual support of the team at Palgrave Macmillan. We specifically would like to mention Virginia Thorp (Senior Commissioning Editor), Keri Dickens (Editorial Assistant), Vidhya Jayaprakash (Newgen Knowledge Works Pvt Ltd).

Finally I would like to acknowledge the extraordinary work done by my co-author, Maria do Rosario Cabrita. Her dedication and enthusiastic collaboration has made the birth of the ICBS book really possible.

I met Mª do Rosario in 2005 at the World Congress on Intellectual Capital and Innovation that was held in the McMaster University (Hamilton, Ontario, Canada) and since then we have collaborated together not only on the writing of the book but also in the refinement of the ICBS software in order to produce an up-to-date version that includes the latest developments of modern information and telecommunication technologies.

To all of the above, I express my deep gratitude.

José María Viedma Marti
Barcelona, Spain

List of Abbreviations

ABV	Activity-Based View
APQC	American Productivity and Quality Center
ARCS	Austrian Research Centers Seibersdorf
BCG	Boston Consulting Group
BP	Business Process
BS	Business Success
BSC	Balanced Scorecard
BU	Business Unit
CICBS	Cities' Intellectual Capital Benchmarking System
CIV	Calculated Intangible Value
CoP	Communities of Practice
CWP	Citation Weighted Patents
DATI	Danish Agency for Trade and Industry
DCF	Discounted Cash Flow
DIC	Direct Intellectual Capital
EC	European Commission
EFQM	European Foundation for Quality Management
EU	European Union
EVA	Economic Value Added
FASB	Financial Accounting Standards Board
FDI	Foreign Direct Investment
GAAP	Generally Accepted Accounting Practice
GDP	Gross Domestic Profit
HVA	Holistic Value Approach
HRA	Human Resource Accounting
HRCA	Human Resource Costing and Accounting
IAM	Intangible Assets Monitor
IAMV™	Investor Assigned Market Value
IAP	Intellectual Assets Portfolio
IAS	International Accounting Standards
IASB	International Accounting Standards Board
IC	Intellectual Capital
ICBS	Intellectual Capital Benchmarking System
ICS	Intellectual Capital Statement
IICBS	Innovation Intellectual Capital Benchmarking System

InCaS	Made in Europe – Intellectual Capital Statement-Made in Europe
ICT	Information and Communication Technology
IFAC	International Federation of Accountants
IO	Industrial Organization
IP	Intellectual Property
IVM	Inclusive Value Measurement
KBV	Knowledge-Based View
KE	Knowledge Economy
KPP	Key Professional People
MAGIC	Measuring and Accounting Intellectual Capital
MC	Market Capitalization
MCICF	Microclusters' Competitiveness Intellectual Capital Framework
MERITUM	Measuring Intangibles to Understand and Improve Innovation Management
MS	Measurement Systems
MVA	Market Value Added
OECD	Organisation for Economic Cooperation and Development
OICBS	Operations Intellectual Capital Benchmarking System
WBI	World Bank Institute
PDCA	Plan, Do, Check, Act
PHCN	Personal Human Capital Navigator
PMS	Proper Measurement Systems
QQS	Quantity, Quality, Systematic
RBV	Resource-Based View
RCICP	Region's Competitiveness Intellectual Capital Platform
RICBS	Region's Intellectual Capital Benchmarking System
R&D	Research and Development
ROA	Return on Assets
SBR	Successful Business Recipe
SBU	Strategic Business Unit
SC	Scorecard
SCBS	Social Capital Benchmarking System
SCIP	Society of Competitive Intelligence Professionals
SEC	Security Exchange Commission
SECITF	Securities and Exchange Commission-Inspired Task Force
SME	Small and Medium Enterprise
STVA	Structural Value Added
SWOT	Strengths, Weaknesses, Opportunities, and Threats

TQM	Total Quality Management
TMT	Top Management Team
TSER	Targeted Socio-Economic Research
TVC	Total Value Creation
VACA	Value Added Capital Coefficient
VAHU	Value Added Human Capital
VBM	Value-Based Management
VCI	Value Creation Index
VAIC	Value Added Intellectual Coefficient
WBI	World Bank Institute

Introduction

The advent of the knowledge economy has fundamentally changed the basis of wealth creation in modern social communities and knowledge and other human-based intangibles have become the fundamental resources for wealth creation.

The theoretical foundations of wealth creation in the knowledge economy are mainly found at the micro level in the modern strategic management discipline and, more specifically, in the three well-known following perspectives: the resource-based view, the dynamic capabilities-based view and more recently, the knowledge-based view.

These theoretical foundations at the micro level are the most important ones but they have to be complemented at the macro level with recent developments on what is called the strategic management of intangibles in cities, regions and nations. These recent developments are based on a complex body of principles and theories, such as institutional and evolutionary economics, cultural and social economics, systems theory, systems and innovation, triple helix, regional science, and more recently knowledge-based development.

Based on the above mentioned theoretical foundations, some basic principles on wealth creation in the knowledge economic context can be deducted. They are the following:

1. The wealth or poverty of a specific nation is strongly dependant on the number of competitive or excellent companies that the specific nation has.
2. Government does not create wealth but does contribute to facilitate or to hinder wealth creation.
3. An excellent or competitive company is the one that achieves long term extraordinary profits due to the fact that it has a business model with sustainable competitive advantages.

4. In the knowledge economy sustainable competitive advantages are mainly based on intangibles. Consequently, the strategic management of intangibles or intellectual capital becomes a fundamental task.
5. In order to achieve business excellence, strategy perspective is the key one.
6. Business excellence is always due to good strategy formulation and superior strategy implementation.
7. Good strategy formulation and superior strategy implementation is always a human task and strongly depends on the quality of the top management team and the key professional people.
8. In a continuously changing environment business models quickly become out-of-date and, as a consequence of that, innovation in business models[i] becomes an urgent need.
9. In any company, the essential activity to perform is always innovation in the business model so that it can be converted into an excellent or competitive business model.
10. Companies alone do not create wealth. They need the collaboration of other companies, universities and research institutes, financial institutions, government, and other organizations and institutions, and especially the existing ones in the cluster, region or nation where the company is located. In other words, they need to be an active part of a territorial open innovation system and of, what some authors like to call, knowledge based ecologies.

Following the criteria of the above principles, this book deals with wealth creation at the firm level in the knowledge economy context but does not consider the knowledge-based ecologies that have been mentioned in principle 10. Because that reason, some details are given on these ecologies.

As it has been said before, in the knowledge economy, firms alone are unable to create wealth. They need to be part of a suitable micro-cluster, cluster, region or nation where innovation is considered a key competitiveness factor and where knowledge and learning capabilities (i.e. technical and learning skills and capabilities, knowledge infrastructure, networking capacity, values systems and attitudes) are the main ingredients that are conducive to innovation systems and inno-

---

[i] We consider, in this particular context, that innovation in business models, encompass all types of innovations, including products, services, processes, marketing, management, etc.

vation processes. That means that governments should play a role, not only in providing macroeconomic stability, adequate incentives, and the technology and financial infrastructure for firms to compete, but also in promoting the types of linkages (across the triple helix of industry, government and universities) and institutions and a collaborative trust-based innovative culture, that are the *sine qua non* conditions for a sustainable economic development.

Having positioned the book in general terms as dealing with wealth creation at the firm level in the knowledge economy context, we will be more specific in their content through the following sections:

a) The specific purpose of the book
b) Their relevance for achieving entrepreneurial excellence in the knowledge economy context
c) The content of the book.

a) The specific purpose of the book

This book is about achieving entrepreneurial excellence in the knowledge economy context through the systematic use of an Intellectual Capital Benchmarking System (ICBS).

ICBS is the output of long-term research carried out by Dr. Viedma and his team in the field of intangibles, or intellectual capital, that are the main sources of sustainable competitive advantages in the context of the knowledge economy.

After a careful review of the theoretical foundations of entrepreneurial excellence, we concluded, as we have stated before, that business excellence is always due to good strategy formulation and superior strategy implementation. The analysis of the practical models and methodologies that contribute to the development of entrepreneurial excellence leads us to realize that the majority of them focus on the process of strategy implementation. This means that strategy formulation is totally left in the hands of the very well-known SWOT analysis.

ICBS is a methodology and a framework for successful strategy formulation in the knowledge economy that tries to improve SWOT analysis substantially and to fill in the existing gap in strategy formulation models and methodologies. It is a kind of strategy check-up that allows enterprises to evaluate their business models and their competitive advantages using as a reference for comparison the world's 'best in class' competitors. For that specific purpose, ICBS relies on competitive benchmarking and competitive intelligence techniques. When using

ICBS in a systematic and reiterative way we obtain ICBS scorecards and balance sheets that will lead enterprises to better decision-making, helping to determine future goals, to innovate in their business models, and to gain and sustain competitive advantages.

We illustrate what has been said in the above paragraphs in Figure 1.

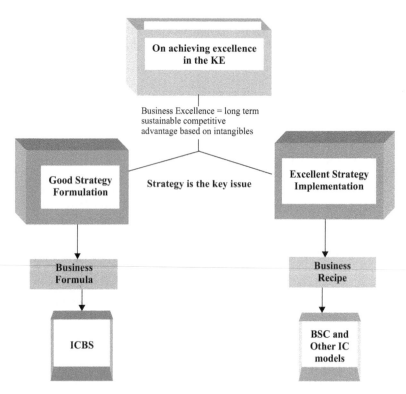

Figure I.1   Formulating good strategies and implementing excellent strategies

b)   Their relevance for achieving entrepreneurial excellence in the knowledge economy context

The process of strategy formulation is mainly on choosing the right things to do or, in other words, it deals mainly on effectiveness. As Peter Drucker (1977) explains, an effective manager is one who selects the appropriate objectives or chooses the right things to get done. At the same time he adverts that no amount of efficiency compensates the lack of effectiveness, which makes effectiveness rather than efficiency so essential to business. Drucker's argument justifies the proposition *doing the right thing (effectiveness) is more important than doing the thing right (efficiency)*. Consequently, effectiveness is more relevant than efficiency.

Hence, ICBS focuses on intellectual capital (intangibles) and strategy formulation which means that it is fundamentally concerned on effectiveness. This makes ICBS more relevant than any other equivalent model or methodology.

c) The content of this book

The content of this book is set out in Figure 2 which guides the reader through the different chapters of the book. Following is a summary content of each one of the different chapters.

Chapter 1. The knowledge economy

After an introduction to the concept and main features of the knowledge economy, where knowledge is stressed as the key resource for economic development, the chapter deals with the new intangible drivers for the future wealth of individuals, organizations, regions and nations.

Chapter 2. Entrepreneurial excellence in the knowledge economy context: the theoretical foundations

After an introduction to the concept of entrepreneurial excellence, the chapter explores the main theoretical foundations of how entrepreneurial excellence is achieved in the context of the knowledge economy. In summary, this is achieved through good strategy formulation (business formula) and excellent strategy implementation (business recipe) where intangibles and intellectual capital have a fundamental role.

The chapter finishes with an attempt to formulate a comprehensive theory of intellectual capital, or, in other words, a comprehensive theory of wealth creation from knowledge and other intangibles.

Chapter 3. The practice of entrepreneurial excellence in the knowledge economy

This chapter considers the different models and methodologies that help organizations to achieve entrepreneurial excellence in the practical contexts of the knowledge economy. After noting the non-strategy focused models,

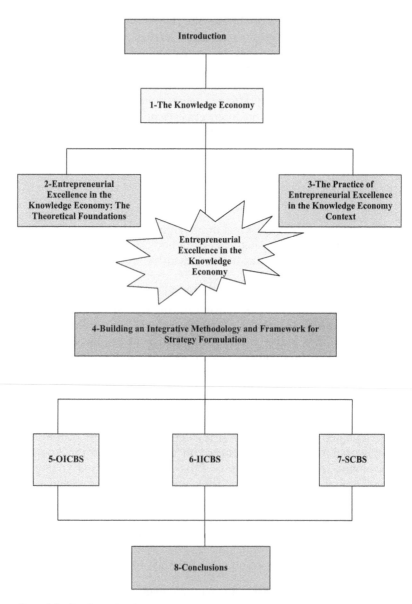

Figure I.2 Book navigation map.

the chapter concentrates on the strategy focused models that fall into the two following categories: a) strategy formulation models which do not break intellectual capital down into its constituent parts, and; b) strategy implementation models that do break intellectual capital down into its constituent parts.

The chapter stresses that in strategy formulation models there is a gap that the existing intellectual capital models do not cover because of their focus on strategy implementation. Consequently, there is a need for an integrative methodology and framework for strategy formulation in order to cover this gap.

The chapter concludes by stating that among the available models the most relevant are the following:

- ICBS for strategy formulation, and;
- BSC and InCaS-Made in Europe for strategy implementation

Chapter 4. Building an integrative methodology and framework for strategy formulation

Chapter 4 mainly concentrates on how this integrative methodology and framework has been built. Starting with some theoretical concepts (the Extended SWOT analysis, business intelligence and benchmarking) it follows with an introduction of the ICBS methodologies and frameworks: OICBS, IICBS and SCBS, which are described in Chapters 5, 6 and 7.

Chapter 5. Operations Intellectual Capital Benchmarking System (OICBS)

In this chapter the reader is invited to know the theory and practical applications of the Operations Intellectual Capital Benchmarking System (OICBS). OICBS, especially designed for operation processes, is a kind of strategy check-up that allows enterprises to evaluate their existing business models and their competitive advantages, using as a reference for evaluation the world's 'best in class' competitors. For that specific purpose, OICBS relies on competitive benchmarking and competitive intelligence techniques. At the same time, OICBS is a strategic information system that allows companies to benchmark against world-class competitors, in terms not only of core competencies but also of the processes, products and services produced by the company's business units. When using OICBS in a systematic and reiterative way we obtain ICBS scorecards and balance sheets that lead enterprises to better decision-making, helping them to determine future goals, to innovate in their business models, and to gain and sustain competitive advantages.

Chapter 6.   Innovation Intellectual Capital Benchmarking System (IICBS)

The book follows up with a description of the Innovation Intellectual Capital Benchmarking System (IICBS). IICBS, especially designed for innovation projects, is a kind of innovation project check-up that allows enterprises to evaluate the competitiveness of their innovation projects, using as a reference for evaluation the world's best-in-class competitors' equivalent implemented projects. For that specific purpose, IICBS relies on competitive benchmarking and competitive intelligence techniques.

At the same time, IICBS is a framework and an information system that focuses on the innovation process and identifies, audits, and benchmarks the core capabilities or key intellectual capital, that the company needs to develop, in their innovation projects, in order to reach its future goals (new products, new services, new processes, new business models) and successfully innovate for gaining and sustaining competitive advantages.

Chapter 7.   Social Capital Benchmarking System (SCBS)

As a complementary component of the ICBS methodologies and frameworks, Chapter 7 describes the Social Capital Benchmarking System (SCBS). It is a new management methodology and tool that identifies, audits, and benchmarks the resources and capabilities, or social capital, existing in alternative cluster locations that are necessary to develop the specific network organization that each particular business model requires.

As has been said when formulating principles of wealth creation, companies alone do not create wealth in the knowledge economy. They need the collaboration of other companies, universities and research institutes, financial institutions, government and other organizations and institutions, and especially the existing ones in the cluster, region or nation where the company is located. Consequently, location matters when a competitive enterprise builds a set of different relationships in a world where vertical integration is practically disappearing. Location matters because first-class competitors in an industry segment are always clustered in cities and regions together with other competitors, suppliers, customers, and other related industries and institutions. In addition, clustering facilitates, through personal contacts, the access to tacit knowledge that is the key ingredient of other companies, organizations and institutions core capabilities, and the one that guarantees long-term sustainable competitive advantages.

Trying to summarize, SCBS is a framework for choosing the right cluster location in order to build the first-class network organization that a specific business model requires in terms of external resources and capabilities.

Chapter 8. Conclusions

The book concludes by stating that in the context of the knowledge economy, entrepreneurial excellence is the main source of wealth. In order to achieve entrepreneurial excellence, the process of strategy formulation is the key one, because it is closely related to effectiveness. Among different intellectual capital methodologies and tools, ICBS is the only one relevant for successful strategy formulation, for innovating and for gaining and sustaining competitive advantages.

1
The Knowledge Economy

1.1 Introduction

Today, there is an emerging view that we are at one of those rare inflection points along the path of world evolution. Some observers describe today's global economy as one in transition from an industrial to a knowledge economy (KE) where investment in intangibles is increasingly recognized as the source of wealth, competitiveness and prosperity. The literature on intangibles exploded throughout the 1990s and many firms, academic institutions and governments, as well as influential organizations (such as, the OECD, the World Bank Institute (WBI), the European Commission (EC), the Brookings Institute, and the International Federation of Accountants) put intangibles discussion into their agenda. At the same time, the popular use of some terms, such as intellectual capital, intangible capital, knowledge organizations, knowledge workers, learning organizations, intellectual assets, intelligent cities, knowledge regions or others has become part of a new lexicon describing new forms of economic value creation and social organization while challenging mental models and business models.

We are now in the 'Age of Revolution' described by Hitt *et al.* (2001) as an age of upheaval and tumult where change is no longer additive and no longer moves in a straight line. As some have said, perhaps more than living through an age of profound and accelerating change, we are experiencing a 'change of age'. It is the argument of new business literature that discontinuous, abrupt and revolutionary change is all around us (Hamel, 2000). Some authors have referred to this momentum eloquently. Drucker (1969) alludes to the 'Age of Discontinuity' to describe the shift from the old order of predictability, involving occasional incremental and linear change, to the new order of rapid radical and discontinuous change. Toffler (1980) dubs the emergent era the 'Third Wave', while Piore and Sabel (1984), facing a revolutionary form of product or process technology, envisage the 'Second Industrial Divide'. Further, Sylvester and Klotz (1983) call our time the 'Gene Age' whilst Galvin (1996) states that we live in the 'Age of Mind', where, in many ways, our future will be limited only by our imagination and ability to challenge the human mind. Whatever the description adopted, we are conscious that what is happening at this time is more revolutionary than it sounds, requiring a change in our attitudes and behaviours. Handy (1989) believes that we are living an 'Age of Unreason', where change is only another word for growth, another synonym for networking and another way of learning. Going further, the author argues that if we change our attitudes, our habits and the ways of some of our institutions it can be an age of true learning, moving towards a new economic and social model.

With this realization has come the need to manage our societies in a new way. Drucker (1993) outlines the vision of a 'post-capitalist society' arguing that the world is witnessing a great transformation in which the basic resource will no longer be the traditional production of input factors, but that the primary resource for both organizations and the economy will be knowledge. The incredible technological advances and the increased importance of knowledge as the source of wealth, has reshaped the global economic environment, changing the logic of business from mass production to knowledge intensiveness (OECD, 1996). New models of business are emerging where the value chain has its hard nucleus in the creation, combination, dissemination, application and leverage of intellectual resources; and this evolution applies to both modern technological industries and traditional ones, requiring continuous innovative efforts strategically combined with a competitive orientation. Adams and Oleksak (2010) define today's business as a knowledge factory based on some knowledge-era equivalents – intangibles as the new raw material, intellectual capital (IC) as the new factory, IC assessment as the new balance sheet, and networks as the new organizational chart.

In particular, the dynamic social and human context within knowledge as it is created today is extremely fluid and complex. Economic productivity models are now based on high value knowledge to be rapidly applied to enhance human well-being. The creation of business value is extremely intangible and socially embedded (Bang *et al.* 2010). The ability to use intellectual capability and create new solutions for human needs is now a central feature in the global KE.

Trends in the environment, such as globalization, technological advances and deregulation, are changing the competitive structure of markets in such a way that the effectiveness of traditional sources of advantage is now obscured. The success, if not the survival, of any nation, region, organization or individual in the KE will come increasingly to depend on the quality of knowledge and the productivity of knowledge. This means that the future will be essentially rooted in our ability to create our knowledge base and use it wisely. This gives us a tremendous and unprecedented responsibility because, for the first time in human history, we all possess the power to influence the evolutionary path of our society.

Looking at the world around us, it is impossible to ignore the more than a billion people around the globe who struggle to survive on less than a dollar a day whilst another three billion live on less than two dollars per day (The World Bank Group, 2005). At the same time, those people remain illiterate, whilst innovation and continuous learning, which are now at the core of a nation's capacity for competitiveness, represent an intangible barrier that has proven extremely difficult for developing countries to overcome. We also know that achieving a more equitable and sustainable socio-economic development implies undertaking a myriad of fundamental changes that demand profound changes both in current institutions and in people's values and mind-sets.

Reducing poverty in developed countries is also a question of shortening the knowledge gaps between the extremes of the economic pyramid on a long-term and sustainable basis. For poverty alleviation and sustainability purposes, a crucial condition is to build learning competencies, namely those that are created as a result of collaboration, because only these will push the poor up toward the top of the pyramid over generations (Martins and Viedma, 2006a). This poses a tremendous challenge for us in providing education, training and, in particular, time in our lives to create global prosperity and wealth in the KE.

All in all, the central issue is that the traditional way of seeing and understanding the world economy is changing. The intention of this chapter is to generate a more nuanced understanding of the KE context, what it is about, how it differs from other paradigms of growth and development, and what the broader economic implications of its rapid growth might be. We are aware that defining KE is a hard, if not impossible task. A number of statistical indicators, fuzzy concepts, questionable methods and different perspectives are included under the KE umbrella. Rather than trying to adapt existing concepts to new situations, we feel that we should aspire to understand a large range of interrelated topics that are emerging as we move toward the KE. As Bertels and Savage (1998) alerted us, despite the fact that we are facing a major transition from the industrial to the knowledge age, industry and agriculture will not die. Agriculture still persisted in the industrial era, although engaging a smaller portion of our population. In the future we will still have industry and agriculture as well. The authors suggested that it is unlikely that industry and agriculture are sustainable in the form we have known them in the past, but we will need to envisage, understand, and manage them from a new perspective, that of the knowledge age. The industrial era focused primarily on people's hands. In the knowledge era, we are working not just with raw materials, but also with raw ideas. The biggest challenge is to be open to learning more about how we can motivate and energize people to use their brains and hearts for wealth creation, and understand what we as individuals, organizations and nations do with what we know.

1.2   Toward a better understanding of the knowledge economy

1.2.1   The concept of a knowledge economy

The Knowledge Economy (KE) concept appears to have emerged in the early 1980s as a description of a state of affairs where wealth creation is increasingly based on the production, distribution, and consumption of knowledge and knowledge-based products (OECD, 1996). The term 'knowledge economy', 'knowledge-based economy' or 'knowledge-driven economy' has become universal, though many still clamour for a clear definition of the term, arguing that it is often used in a superficial and uncritical way. The main argument is that the production, distribution and use of knowledge in an economy is 'everything and nothing because all economies are in some way based on knowledge' (Smith, 2002:6–7).

Indeed, the notion that knowledge plays an important role in the economy is not new. All economies have been based on knowledge about how to farm, to produce or to build and the key to economic success is always linked to the advances in knowledge creation and the ability of a nation to translate knowledge into value to a society. What we see today is essentially more of the same, only differing in the accelerating speed at which knowledge has been created, transformed and, in many cases, has depreciated in terms of economic relevance and value. David and Foray (2003) describe the move to a KE as a 'soft discontinuity' rather than a sharp break from the past.

But while the study of human knowledge has been a central subject of philosophy and epistemology since the time of the ancient Greeks, it is only recently that it has been recognized as a factor of production. In this sense, what is really 'new' is the vision that knowledge is becoming the most important feature of the economy, and what makes it so important today is that it is perhaps the key determinant of our revolution. For the first time in economic history, knowledge is not only an input of products and services found in the market, it is actually embedded in them and this fact defines to a large extent the competitiveness that can give a producer economy its comparative advantage. Consequently, it is not the value of knowledge that has changed but the value that market gives to knowledge.

Part of the problem encountered when searching for a definition of the 'knowledge economy' is that the commodity it rests on – knowledge – is inherently difficult to pin down. Measuring 'knowledge' is a complex, if not impossible, undertaking and relating knowledge to economic effects is still more complex.

Leaving aside such general definitional problems, we may say that the most important application of the concept of KE is to economic growth. Knowledge is actually recognized as the driver of productivity and competitiveness and consequently its role in achieving competitive advantage is becoming an increasingly important management issue in all business and non-business sectors. Arguably, the present emphasis on knowledge has resulted naturally from the economic, industrial and cultural developments which have taken place over time. Based on the Wiig's work, the historic evolution of knowledge importance in the economy is traced in Figure 1.1 providing the reader with a roadmap of today's importance of knowledge management and intellectual capital.

As seen in the figure below, at the transition from the industrial economy to the knowledge economy and more recently to an intellectual capital management approach, the growth basis is not so much influenced by investments in physical factors as by knowledge, which is a key productive factor for application and exploitation of physical capital. The focus thus shifts from individual assets to bundles of assets – in line with the more recent intellectual capital approach – where different types of assets combine and cooperate in the creation of value. In an information and knowledge society the main share of these assets is intangibles. Economic history has proven that in any industry success comes to the companies that have the most creative knowledge or wield it most effectively, and not necessarily those with the most muscle.

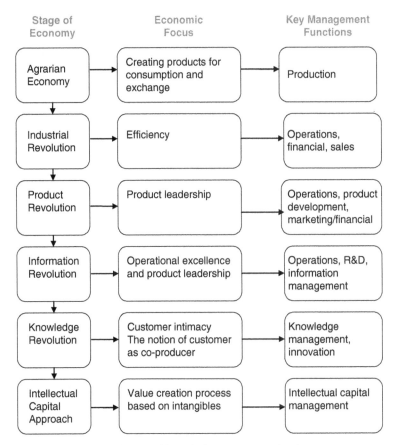

Stage of Economy	Economic Focus	Key Management Functions
Agrarian Economy	Creating products for consumption and exchange	Production
Industrial Revolution	Efficiency	Operations, financial, sales
Product Revolution	Product leadership	Operations, product development, marketing/financial
Information Revolution	Operational excellence and product leadership	Operations, R&D, information management
Knowledge Revolution	Customer intimacy The notion of customer as co-producer	Knowledge management, innovation
Intellectual Capital Approach	Value creation process based on intangibles	Intellectual capital management

Figure 1.1 Historic evolution of knowledge importance in the economy
Source: Adapted from Wiig (1997).

Literature emphasizes the positive association between the production of knowledge and economic growth. However, it is worth noting that long-run historical series are unavailable because neither economists nor statisticians have compiled data on knowledge as an input or output of the economy. As Machlup (1980:9) explains: 'the production of knowledge is an economic activity, an industry … . Economists have analysed agriculture, mining, iron and steel production, the paper industry, transportation, retailing, the production of all sorts of goods and services, but they have neglected to analyse the production of knowledge'. This failure in registering knowledge as a historical factor of production is normally explained by the fact that there is no practical way to isolate the knowledge itself as a phenomenon and, consequently, it is particularly hard to quantify or price (OECD, 1996).

In the course of its efforts to define the KE, the OECD introduced two related concepts that gave it more substance. The first concerned 'investment in knowledge', and the definition is entirely statistical: 'expenditures directed towards activities with the aim of enhancing existing knowledge and/or acquiring new knowledge or diffusing knowledge' (OECD, 2001:19–47). According to the OECD, investment in knowledge is the sum of expenditures on Research and Development (R&D), higher education and software.

The second concept relates to 'knowledge-based industries'. Knowledge-based industries are defined as those that have: i) a high level of investment in innovation; ii) intensive use of acquired technology; and iii) a highly-educated workforce. To measure the KE, the OECD suggests five categories of indicators: inputs, stocks and flows, outputs, networks, and learning.

Another point to stress when defining the KE has to do with our ability to codify knowledge in the economy. In order to facilitate economic analysis, distinctions can be made between different kinds of knowledge, including 'know-what', 'know-why', 'know-how' and 'know-who'. Whilst some types of knowledge, such as know-what and know-why are more easily commoditized, other types of knowledge, in particular know-how and know-who, are more tacit and difficult to measure but often rarer and more valuable. The OECD describes these types of knowledge, as follows:

- *Know-what* refers to knowledge about *facts*, and it refers to information, in so far as it can be broken down into components. Or;
- *Know-why* comprises scientific knowledge of the principles and laws of nature, which underlies technological development and product and process advances. This kind of knowledge is often centered in specialized organizations, such as research laboratories and universities. Or;
- *Know-how* suggests the skills or the capability to do something. This type of knowledge is developed and kept within a company and it is the heart of industrial networks that enable firms to share and combine elements of know-how. Or;
- *Know-who* involves information about who knows what and who knows how to do what. It is internal to the organization and its use is becoming the key aspect in response to the acceleration of the rate of change.

How these different types of knowledge grow and evolve also requires different contexts and channels. While 'know-what' and 'know-why' can be obtained through reading books, attending lectures and accessing databases, the 'know-how' and 'know-who' are anchored primarily in social practice and sometimes in specialized educational environments. The sustainability of knowledge advantage remains in its tacit nature because the difficulty of imitating it allows continuing differentiation.

Because the expansion of KE is mainly based on interactions, building a dynamic community of creators, inventors and innovators to exchange information, resources and experience becomes a fundamental issue. As a consequence, a new kind of organization (knowledge-based communities), and production (knowledge systems) is spearheading the phenomenon. David and Foray (2003:21) define knowledge-based communities as 'networks of individuals striving, first and foremost, to produce and circulate new knowledge and working for different, even rival, organizations'.

Knowledge systems represent a network of knowledge and practice (for example communities of practice (CoP)) that leads to outcomes (for example more knowledge, intellectual property, structural change, employment levels, skill levels, and quality of life) through actors (for example governments, enterprises, public institutions, universities) which are engaged in activities (such as R&D, innovation, diffusion of practices and technologies), and some kind of linkages (for example, networks, alliances, partnerships).

In this sense, the shift from producing indicators of outputs and activity, and moving toward indicators of outcomes, or indicators of linkages, or flows, constitutes a key concern for international organisms involved with understanding the knowledge system, its actors, activities, linkages and its outcomes.

1.2.2   Historical perspective

Theoretical arguments of KE may be found in the classic economic theory (Augier and Teece, 2005). The inclusion of knowledge as a factor in the study of economic growth has played an important role in economic analysis since Adam Smith who, in his *Wealth of Nations,* first published in 1776, compared the acquisition of skills to the construction of a machine. As with the machine, 'much labour and time' are expended, and this must be compensated for by a return on the investment. In order to justify the costs of training, wages must eventually be higher than those for unskilled labour (Smith, 1776 (1910).

Another important contribution to the explicit recognition of the role of knowledge in economic analysis emerged with the neoclassical economist, Alfred Marshall (1890:115), who argued that 'capital consists, in the greater part, of knowledge and organization and knowledge is the most powerful engine of production in organizations [that are] increasingly focused on management'. He also recognized that 'external economies' arising from the interactions between industrial districts were crucial to competitiveness because of the knowledge shared amongst them. Further progress was made by Schumpeter (1934) in introducing the notion of the innovating capitalist entrepreneur into economic theory. From this perspective, the path of long-term growth is the result of 'waves' of innovation, sometimes functionally linked to each other. This produces discontinuities in growth. The introduction of a strategically significant innovation by one entrepreneur leads to the diffusion of knowledge and makes it easier for other entrepreneurs to make decisions about their own production possibilities.

Despite the developments outlined above, economic theory was, in the opinion of Augier and Teece (2005:9), very slow to incorporate this understanding into its frameworks. In this respect, the authors wrote: 'most economists preferred to ignore the subject, as it tended to make economic modelling more difficult'.

The traditional neoclassical growth model (Solow, 1970) does not explain the major determinants of productivity growth. More recently, the 'new growth theory' (Romer, 1986) has focused attention on the nature and role of knowledge in the growth process. Knowledge is then considered the basic form of capital. Probably the most important aspects of the literature on endogenous theories relate to the notion that long-term economic growth is ultimately both constrained and driven by knowledge creation. As explained by Marr (2005), while the crucial elements of Solow's economic model are capital, technology, and labour, Romer added knowledge as another key element that drives the use of capital, technological development, and quality of labour. Emphasizing the notion that things and ideas cannot be separated, Paul Romer (1996:204) described the worldwide view of the new growth theory in this way:

> New growth theorists now start to divide the world into two fundamentally different types of productive inputs that can be called 'ideas' and 'things'. Ideas are non-rival goods that can be stored in a bit string. Things are rival goods with mass (or energy). With ideas and things, one can explain how economic growth works. Non-rival ideas can be used to rearrange things, for example, when one follows a recipe and transforms noxious olives into tasty and healthful olive

oil. Economic growth arises from the discovery of new recipes and the transformation of things from low to high value configurations.

For decades, studies of the economic value of knowledge were almost exclusively linked to the macroeconomic models, focused on the understanding of economic growth. The first attempt to look at what happens *in* organizations may, probably, be attributed to Penrose's (1959) work which envisaged the growth of a firm as a cumulative process in which its members build a stock of useful knowledge through a dynamic learning process in an endogenous process of accumulation and interaction between the productive base of the firm and the opportunity coming from the market. The resource-based view of the firm (Penrose, 1959; Rumelt, 1984; Wernerfelt, 1984) represents a key building block in the construction of an economic theory in which firms may be viewed as a collection of hard-to-copy resources. The optimal growth of firms arises from their unique abilities to accumulate, develop and deploy those resources and capabilities to formulate and implement value-enhancing strategies (Barney, 1991; Peteraf, 1993). However, the analysis of knowledge at the meso and micro levels were explicitly recognized only with works dealing with Japanese experiences (e.g. Nonaka and Takeuchi, 1995; Nonaka and Konno, 1999; Nonaka *et al.*, 2000). More recently, intellectual capital has emerged as a key concept in analysing and evaluating the knowledge dimensions of organizations.

1.2.3 Knowledge as an economic resource

The term 'knowledge' suffers from a certain degree of ambiguity and often requires several adjectives to clarify the sense in which it is being used. Sometimes it is equivalent to 'economic ideas' (Wiig, 1997) or 'intellectual capital' (Stewart, 1997) and is treated in terms of 'object', 'process', 'exchange', 'utilization', and 'capture'. Sveiby (1997) explains that the word 'knowledge' comprises a wide range of meanings (for example, science, experience, talent, competence, know-how, capability, learning, wisdom) depending on the context in which it is used. This has caused a number of controversial positions in the literature. From an economic perspective, knowledge is interchangeably used as 'asset' and 'resource'. The difference lies at the conceptual level, though, with consequences in the strategies chosen for its management. An asset may be traded, stored (physically or digitally) and accounted for with a market value. Because of this, an asset is something relatively static and may be owned by the organization. A resource is an input or a factor controlled by the firm that enables the firm to implement strategies that improve its efficiency and effectiveness (Daft, 1983). On the contrary, knowledge is intrinsically intangible, fluid and dynamic and, therefore, cannot be fully owned by the company: it is not easy to transfer or to imitate, it is context-sensitive and it is observer-dependent (Venzin *et al.*, 1998).

As a productive resource, knowledge has characteristics that are fundamentally different – often termed 'economic' in its content – from all other kinds of resources prevailing in the manufacturing era (land, labour, and even capital). Knowledge is infinite: once produced it can be re-used by others. It is non-excludable: it is difficult to protect once in the public domain. And it is indivisible: it can be aggregated to form a coherent picture before it is applied (Johnston and Blumentritt, 1998). However, knowledge only becomes an economic good when it solves a problem in a way that people are willing to pay for. Once you identify a solution, the only limit to the value of that knowledge is how many people need the solution. Despite the fact that these distinctive characteristics of knowledge have crucial implications for the way KE can be organized, the economics of knowledge are poorly understood.

First, knowledge as an economic resource is conceptually and contextually different from philosophical and scientific knowledge. The societal role of knowledge has moved from a resource for meaning (truth) toward that of a resource to produce. Traditionally, the concept of knowledge has been closely linked to science and often defined as a belief that is true and justified. Today, the concept of knowledge is no longer merely anchored in the notions of truth, validity and reliability. Instead, its value is linked to its ability to generate a superior performance and to sustain a competitive position in the global market which will increasingly depend on the quality and productivity of knowledge. As Spender (1996a:64) wrote: 'knowledge is less about truth and reason but more about the practice of intervening knowledgeably and purposefully in the world'. This signifies that knowledge as an economic resource means capacity for organizational action. Valuable knowledge is 'knowledge-in-action' or knowledge that works, and productivity means the capacity for value creation through organizational action. The knowledge praxis means that what is known is demonstrated in knowledgeable activity.

Contextually, philosophical and scientific knowledge were produced and disseminated during the Middle Ages in various traditional knowledge institutions, where churches, monasteries or universities are among the most important of those institutions. Today, knowledge is created, leveraged and applied in the context of business organizations.

Knowledge is socially constructed and essentially, the most important way to manage knowledge is to create contexts where knowledge can grow and flourish.

Second, there is a concept within the KE arena of 'increasing returns' (Arthur, 1996) – a fundamental feature of the 'new economy' – that challenges the traditional economical notion of 'diminishing returns'. Knowledge as resource causes great confusion for economists, as it is the only resource that increases with use rather than diminishes. Unlike physical goods that are consumed as they are used, providing decreasing returns over time, knowledge provides increasing returns as it is used. The more it is used, the more valuable it becomes, creating a self-reinforcing cycle (Clarke, 2001) where 'ideas breed new ideas, and shared knowledge stays with the giver while it enriches the receiver' (Davenport and Prusak, 1998:17). The knowledge one learns from another enriches both elements of the teaching dyad. Indeed, the value of knowledge to an economy comes from sharing with others.

Third, knowledge is subject to economies of scale and scope. While it may be expensive to generate, its subsequent replication is generally of little cost. Once created, it can spill over easily into the hands of others, at zero marginal cost.

These economics of knowledge explain much about the increased quality of life and wealth creation of recent decades and they imply the almost unlimited potential for economic growth that new innovations and knowledge-based products make possible.

1.2.4 Epistemological assumptions

As knowledge becomes more and more important in our society, companies need to 'know what they know' and the ability to manage knowledge is a critical issue. As Leonard-Barton (1995: xii) wrote: 'in order to manage knowledge assets, we need not merely to identify them but to understand them – in depth – in all their complexity: where they exist, how they grow or atrophy, how managers' actions affect their viability'.

The epistemological assumptions of people in organizations have a substantial impact on how organizations deal with the practicalities of creating, managing and using knowledge, and how they create and extract value. Some authors (Marr *et al.* 2003; Roos, 2005) found evidence of a correlation between the organization's strategic options and the epistemological outlook of the senior management. The results emphasize the importance of epistemology when dealing with knowledge from a managerial perspective: strategic models differ fundamentally because they are partly based on different epistemological assumptions.

Knowledge can be defined from different perspectives and it can be equally interpreted as an input, an output or a process of transformation. Following the works developed by von Krogh and Roos (1995) and Venzin *et al.*, (1998), three major perspectives on the nature of knowledge have been identified: a cognitivist; a constructionist; and an autopoiesis view. The cognitivist view interprets knowledge as a reflection of the world we live. Knowledge is explicit and objective and can therefore be codified, stored and transferred between persons or organizations with relative ease.

Unlike the cognitivist view, the constructionist perspective sees knowledge not as an act of representation, but as an act of the subjective creation of reality by an individual person.

From the autopoietic viewpoint, knowledge is always private, and not totally transferable. The term 'autopoiesis' – coined by Maturana and Varela (1980) – derives from the Greek, *auto* (self) and *poiesis* (production) and refers to the self-reproduction of living systems. According to this perspective, organization is seen as a system simultaneously open (to data) and closed (to information and knowledge), controlled by its rules. It is assumed that knowledge cannot be transmitted easily, since it requires internal interpretation within the organizational system according to the individual's rules, norms and, sometimes, values. Because of the unique nature of knowledge, Nonaka and Takeuchi (1995:61) use the word 'conversion' instead of 'transfer' of knowledge. The term 'conversion' means that the creation of knowledge is a 'social process *between* individuals and not confined *within* an individual'.

1.3 The key features of the knowledge economy

The KE comprises key features that we would not expect to find – or at least not in such abundance – in the previous stages of an economy.

Andriessen and Tissen (2000) trace some of those distinctive features:

- Knowledge replaces capital as the key resource in production and intangible assets represent a substantial part of the value added of companies;
- Products and services are knowledge intensive;
- Ownership of resources has changed: the proprietor of the fundamental economic resource – knowledge – is the individual since knowledge resides in the head of employees;
- Production structures have changed and the management of intangible resources is different from tangible and financial resources.

The notion that knowledge has become the primary force of wealth creation and the source of sustainable competitive advantage is driven by a number of interrelated movements of the new economy. The rise in knowledge intensity of economic activities, the increasing globalization of economic affairs, and the Information and Communication Technology (ICT) revolution are all recognized as the main drivers of KE. As depicted in Figure 1.2, these three forces strictly intertwined involve 'feed forward' as well as feedback movements.

1.3.1 Knowledge intensity of economic activities

Knowledge – embodied in individuals, technologies, systems and R&D programmes – has become vitally important to the performance of a nation or an organization. In more practical terms, the increasing knowledge-intensity of economic activities assumes two primary forms. First, the rising educational level of the workforce (subjective knowledge). Secondly, the growing scientific and technical knowledge materialized as an integral part of the development of new products and services (explicit knowledge).

Literature provides evidence that output, employment, and investment are expanding fastest in high-technology industries, and knowledge-intensive service sectors, such as education, communications and information, are growing even faster. Equally important are more intangible investments in research and development (R&D), the training of the labour force, computer software and technical expertise. It is estimated that more than 50 per cent of GDP in major OECD economies is now knowledge-based (OECD, 1996). Here, productivity and growth are largely determined by the rate of technical progress and the accumulation of knowledge. In this context, learning on the part of individuals

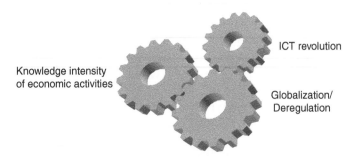

Knowledge intensity of economic activities

ICT revolution

Globalization/ Deregulation

Figure 1.2   The key features of the knowledge economy

and firms is crucial for realizing the productivity potential of new technologies and longer-term economic growth.

A large number of studies show that intellectual assets such as R&D, software and higher education – which measure the investment in knowledge – make a substantial contribution to economic growth, job creation and improved living standards.

Econometric studies suggest that R&D spending is associated with an increase in productivity. Recent research also reveals that there are differences across countries and that foreign R&D has a significant effect in countries with high levels of domestic business R&D. This is an indication that the size of knowledge *spillovers* depend on a country's ability to adopt foreign technologies.

Another point in international reports is that software has been the most dynamic component of ICT investment in OECD countries in recent years. Investment in software has generally contributed more to labour productivity than other ICT investments, such as communication and IT equipment.

Finally, the impact of higher education is largely evidenced in statistical documents. Human capital (measured as the improved composition of labour input) has been referred to as a key driver of growth, contributing between 15 per cent and 90 per cent to labour productivity growth in the G7 countries (OECD, 2006). In developed countries, both governments and enterprises are investing more and more heavily in training. On average a more highly trained labour force will be better equipped to meet the rapid change in technology, tastes and organizations that is characteristic of modern economies.

1.3.2   Information and Communication Technologies (ICT) revolution

The ICT revolution and the complex of ICT industries are profoundly interrelated in the move to a KE. Lundvall and Foray (1996:14) argue that

> even if we should not take the ICT revolution as synonymous with the advent of the knowledge-based economy, both phenomena are strongly interrelated ... the ICT system gives the knowledge-based economy a new and different technological base which radically changes the conditions for the production and distribution of knowledge as well as its coupling to the production system.

There is a growing belief that knowledge can lead to more than economic growth. It can also lead to structural change in the economy, and therefore society. New products and services resulting from technological revolution bring about profound changes in the way we can live, work and socially organize. For instance, this economic transition is characterized by the changing nature of work from low skilled to high skilled.

For most countries, the source of increase in investment in knowledge is the software component and this is the fastest-growing component of ICT investment.

However, the investment in ICT is only one side of the story. In innovative firms total quality management, lean management, flatter hierarchies, decentralized decision-making, and better communication channels are interrelated with skills and ICT. There is evidence in the literature that ICT investments are complementary to investment in human resources and skills. What really drives productivity are innovative business concepts and strategies, often underpinned by the use of new IT solutions. Mostly, IT investments, *per se*, do not provide competitive advantage and substantial productivity gains. Instead, it is the intelligent combination of technology processes and new strategies that drives organizational performance.

1.3.3   Globalization and deregulation

Another characteristic of the KE is the rapid globalization of economic activities. The pace and extent of the current globalization is without precedent as a consequence of the intertwined effects of both deregulation and developments in information technology, with the computing and communication revolution providing the basic infrastructure necessary for rapid integration of the world economy.

Two key aspects characterize the recent phase of globalization. First, foreign direct investment (FDI) and capital flows have grown more rapidly than trade flows, suggesting that the current phase of globalization is about capital movement rather than trade. Secondly, this process is so rapid and ubiquitous that it is not possible to understand it fully at the present time nor is it possible to have a clear view of the costs and benefits of such massive globalization (Sheehan, 1999).

A consequence of this globalization movement is that it is changing both the level and nature of competition, contributing to a transformation of the global economy where constant innovation is more and more critical to success. Globalization has accelerated industrial and occupational restructuring, leading to the decline of some industries and jobs, and the growth of others.

It is also recognized that the growing globalization of knowledge makes the long-term trend toward a knowledge-based economy an unceasing movement. It is now a competitive requirement that busi-nesses invest all over the globe to access markets, technology, and talent. FDI data are a clear indicator of the trend toward globalization. It includes corporate activities such as businesses building plants or sub-sidiaries in foreign countries, and buying controlling stakes or shares in foreign companies.

In this scenario, cost competitiveness is no longer a sufficient condi-tion for success. Innovation and knowledge are becoming central to creating and sustaining competitive advantage and, therefore, pressure on enterprises will increase in order to match global best practice and to undertake continuous innovation.

Equally, an important feature of the global KE has been the rapid proc-ess of international deregulation over the past decades. Deregulation combined with advances in communication technologies has strength-ened global competition, and the emergence of a new form of global competition. Consequently, there has been a shift in strategic manage-ment thinking toward studying how organizations not only react and adapt to markets, competition and industries, but also anticipate and lead their development (Prahalad and Hamel, 1994).

1.4   What is new in the knowledge economy?

What makes the emergence of the KE 'new' is that it is, in some sig-nificant aspects, different from the agrarian and industrial economies we have known in the past. First, in terms of factors of production, the role of knowledge in today's economy corresponds to that of land in the agrarian economy and that of capital in the industrial economy of the nineteenth and early twentieth centuries (Quinn, 1992; Burton-Jones, 2000). Given the economic nature of knowledge, the wealth equation is changing. Value creation is now directly linked to the intel-ligence, speed, and agility that come from a host of intangibles. The cor-responding 'powers of knowledge', described by Davenport and Prusak (1998) – such as complexity, speed, and flexibility – are precisely those needed in the rapidly changing and competitive context of a global economy.

Second, KE is focused on intangibles rather than tangibles. The ascend-ance of intangibles over tangibles is reflected in firms' valuation ratios. This trend represents not only a revolutionary change in the process of economic value creation, but also a sharp decline in the value relevance of traditional financial measures. The lack of agreed methods for valu-ing intangible assets has been a major deficiency in current accounting systems. This deficiency undoubtedly has serious economic effects, for example in capital markets and in valuation of knowledge.

Third, the KE is a hierarchy of networks driven by the acceleration of the rate of change and the rate of learning, where innovation is the result of numerous interactions between actors and institutions, which together form an innovation system. These innovation systems consist of the flows and relationships that exist amongst industry, government and academia in the development of science and technology. The interactions within these systems influence the innovative performance of firms and ultimately the economy. In this context, the advantage provided by a given amount of innovation may be decreasing with the increased diffusion of intellectual capital. Not only has globalization increased the mobility of goods and the transfer of risk capital, it is also responsible for the increased rate at which ideas become widespread. The speedy dissemination of knowledge, practices and methods enables lower wage countries to produce goods at higher productivity levels. In general, for innovator countries to sustain their competitive advantage, they have to innovate more quickly than the increasingly rapid global diffusion of ideas and technology.

Fourth, the KE is increasingly digital and commoditized. Whilst digitalization of information has had a huge impact on the capacity for transferring, storing, and processing information, the IT revolution has intensified the move toward knowledge codification, and increased the share of codified knowledge in the knowledge stock of advanced economies. All knowledge that can be codified and reduced to information can now be transmitted around the world at relatively little cost. Hence, knowledge is acquiring more of the properties of a commodity. Market transactions are facilitated by codification, and the diffusion of knowledge is accelerated.

1.5   Knowledge-based view of the firm

Along with developments in the macroeconomic context, a novel theoretical approach to organizations has emerged. If knowledge is indeed the main resource for the production of value, it is imperative to approach organizations themselves through the lens of knowledge. The increasing interest in a knowledge-based view of the firm (KBV) (Grant, 1996; Spender, 1996a; 1996b) has been closely linked to the recognition of the fundamental economic changes resulting from the KE. However, the 'emerging knowledge-based view is not, as yet, a theory of the firm in any formal sense' (Grant, 1996:110). It is more a set of ideas and perceptions about the existence and nature of the firm that deepens the more relevant role that knowledge must play in organizations and society (e.g. Quinn, 1992; Drucker, 1993).

A number of fundamental assumptions arise concerning the nature of knowledge and its role in organizations:

- The primary rationale for the firm is the creation and application of knowledge;
- Performance differences between firms derive from distinct stocks of knowledge and capabilities in using, combining, and developing knowledge (Nonaka and Takeuchi, 1995; Spender and Grant, 1996);
- Explicit and tacit knowledge vary in their transferability, which also depends upon the capacity of the recipient to accumulate knowledge;
- Tacit knowledge rests inside individuals who have a certain learning capacity;
- Most knowledge, especially explicit knowledge, when developed for a certain application, ought to be made available to additional applications, for reasons of economy of scale.

A firm is then seen as a knowledge stock that consists basically of codified and applicable knowledge as well as knowledge related to the coordination of actions in organizations. What will determine the firm's success is its efficiency in the transformation of knowledge and ideas into knowledge that can be applied, in comparison with the efficiency of other companies in this process (Kogut and Zander, 1993).

The KBV postulates that knowledge is the only resource that provides sustainable competitive advantage and therefore the firm's attention and decision making should focus primarily on knowledge and the competitive capabilities derived from it (Leonard-Barton, 1995). Moreover, a perspective based on the knowledge of the firm suggests that firms exist because they can better protect knowledge from expropriation or imitation than can markets (Liebeskind, 1996).

A central question in the literature is whether knowledge is an individual or collective possession. The KBV is based on the constructionist view of knowledge, which assumes that 'knowledge is a product and vehicle of human activity, bounded by the limitations of human cognitive and other psychological capacities, by the social and cultural environment of activity' (Pöyhönen and Blomqvist, 2006:426). The socio-historical context sets the environment for individual understanding and behaviour, while at the same time individuals modify the context by by their actions in the environment. The knowledge of the firm is the result of specific interactions occurring between individuals in an organization, and is therefore a socially constructed asset. Close to the autopoietic epistemology, Nonaka (1994:17) states that 'at a fundamental level, knowledge is created by individuals. An organization cannot create knowledge without individuals'. The company's role is to organizationally amplify the knowledge created by individuals, integrating and crystallizing it in the knowledge base of the company. Sveiby (1997) defines knowledge as a 'capacity-to-act' (which may be conscious or not). The focus of the definition is on the action (*praxis*) element: a capacity to act is only shown in action. Knowledge assumed as a 'capacity-to act' is dynamic, personal and distinctly different from data and information, which makes it a fair synonym for 'individual competence' (Sveiby, 2001).

Collective knowledge is developed in interactions between individuals that belong to groups within and between companies, and is therefore created and revealed in practices, and shared in work groups. Because of this, each firm develops idiosyncratic collective knowledge, sustained by common language and shared values, through unique interactions in a specific context. Collective knowledge that is tacit and embedded in work practices can be highly inimitable. When it also helps an organization to create value, it will be the basis for the firm's core competencies.

1.6   The drivers for the future wealth of individuals, organizations, regions and nations

The pace of change is more likely to accelerate than decelerate (OECD, 2006), given the relentless pace at which competition is becoming global. D'Avini (1994) has used the term 'hypercompetition' to describe the increasing intensity and pace of competition in the modern business landscape. The ongoing process of globalization has shifted the basis of industrial competitiveness from static price competition toward dynamic improvement, putting a premium on those individuals/ organizations/ regions or nations that are more efficient and effective at learning and more able to innovate systematically than their competitors (Maskell and Malmberg, 1999).

The shift toward a KE is widely considered to be a shift from 'intellectual-industrial' workers to 'creative-conceptual' workers (Rijn and Tissen, 2007). Such a transformation, from a resource-based to a knowledge-based economy, involves substantial structural adjustments and requires explicit transition strategies. Knowledge systems do not just involve the firm and its activities, but schools, research centres and universities, municipal institutions, governments, and organizations providing cultural and other leisure activities. The firm that is producing the value added is connected locally, as that is where its people live, but it is also connected globally to other firms involved with the same kind of knowledge.

A knowledge-based economy thus requires:

- An economic and institutional regime that provides incentives for the efficient use of existing knowledge, for the creation of new knowledge, and for the dissemination of knowledge;
- An educated and entrepreneurial population that can both create and use knowledge;
- A dynamic information infrastructures that can facilitate the communication, dissemination and processing of information;
- An efficient innovation system comprising firms, universities, research centres, think tanks, consultants and other organizations that can interact and apply the growing stock of global knowledge, and use it to create new knowledge and technology.

Indeed, the rising knowledge intensity of the world economy and our increasing ability to distribute that knowledge has increased its value to all participants in the economic system. The implications of this are profound, not only for the strategies of the firms but also for individuals, regions and nations. More and more the drivers for future wealth creation will rest on intangibles and values such as honesty, integrity, trustworthiness, and commitment.

1.6.1   Individuals

KE is giving rise to new organizational forms within and between companies and a radical shake-up in employment relationships as more and more 'knowledge work' is seen as imperative to business success. Knowledge work can be said to be of an intellectual nature and with knowledge work increasing, intellectual capital is a firm's only appreciable asset.

Within the context of the KE, individuals increasingly control their own developments, careers and destinies, rather than the organizations that employ them. The partial replacement of traditional resources by knowledge gives rise to new work forms with implications for the nature of relationships between individuals and organizations (Drucker, 1969; Gratton and Goshal, 2003; Viedma and Enache, 2007).

Such changes have led to a gradual transition from an era in which employees' responsibilities were those of loyalty, attendance, satisfactory performance and compliance with authority, to a time in which people are exhorted to be entrepreneurs, innovators, enactors of change and excellent performers (Schalk and Rousseau, 2001). In the face of increasing competitive pressures and the need for greater flexibility and skills requirements, companies can no longer promise lifelong employment and, consequently, the traditional career model with its assumption of predictability tends to become a mirage of the past (Cappelli, 1999). Replacing this model is now an emerging portfolio of diverse careers that are unpredictable, disorderly, and primarily involve horizontal mobility. These changes are leading to, among other things, the emergence of self-organizing 'knowledge nomads' (Edvinsson, 2000), likened to an independent or contractual worker on special assignment.

The more knowledgeable the worker is, the more likely he (she) is to be employable. The 'knowledge worker', a term coined by Drucker in 1959, describes individuals who carry knowledge as a powerful resource which they, rather than organizations, own. Vogt (1995) defines knowledge worker as a person with the motivation and capacity to co-create new insights and the capability to communicate, coach and facilitate the implementation of new ideas. If the definition of knowledge economy is challenging, so is that of the knowledge worker. At the heart of all the suggested definitions lies the idea that knowledge workers are participating in the utilization and creation of knowledge. Handy (2001) uses a metaphor and compares 'knowledge workers' to 'the fleas [that] sit on the backs of the elephants'. The elephants are the large corporations that increasingly dominate our economies, whilst the fleas are the small ventures, subcontractors and start-ups, as well as the self-employed specialists, consultants, entrepreneurs and small family business. The author suggests that the life of a flea has many attractions but security is certainly not one of them. Individuals are responsible for developing their own careers and for actively managing their personal human capital.

The term human capital refers to employees' productive resources which create value for themselves and for the organization to which they belong. Graton and Ghoshal (2003) define human capital as the composite of an individual's intellectual, social and emotional capital.

Intellectual capital refers to fundamental individual attributes such as cognitive capability, complexity, and learning capacity, together with the tacit and explicit knowledge, skills and expertise an individual builds over time. It is an essential element of human capital but two others complement the individual's human capital. The social capital is about *who* one knows, and *how well* one knows them. Sociability and trustworthiness provide the anchors for nurturing a network of relationships. Emotional capital refers to getting things done and moving into action. Self-awareness, self-esteem, personal integrity, courage, ambition and resilience are fundamental attributes to convert individual knowledge and relationships into action.

Based on these concepts, Viedma and Enache (2007) designed a practical methodology for managing personal human capital (the PHCN – Personal Human Capital Navigator). These authors demonstrate how individuals may develop a professional business formula by defining their personal strategic vision, taking into consideration the intellectual, social and emotional dimensions. The successful development of the business formula involves incorporating both professional and personal objectives into a meaningful whole.

1.6.2 Organizations

As we move into the third millennium, we are witnessing one of the most critical times in the history of organizations. Since developed economies have become knowledge-based and technology-intensive, our view of the firm has significantly changed and new (intangible) elements have become the fundamental determinants of value. Facing the challenges posed by the KE, firms have been forced to rethink their business models and increasingly pressured to adopt global strategies to deal with the new reality.

Pressures to innovate (continuously and quickly) and to seek out new sources of differential advantage will remain the essence of strategy. Because continuous innovation will be seen as the source of sustainable competitive advantage, 'every organization of today has to build into its very structure the management of change' (Drucker, 1993:53). As markets become more fragmented and sparse and product life cycles get shorter, the key to economic viability is not innovation *per se*, but systematic, repeated innovation, within ever shorter spans of time. 'Time to market' and 'time to decide' become the most critical cycle time metrics in businesses these days.

As the emphasis is not simply on applying existing knowledge but creating new knowledge that is transformative and oriented to combinations and interactions, all businesses need to be increasingly flexible, adaptable and fluid in their structures. Firms need strategies that can react to, and even predict, the changes occurring. Agility, that is, a systematic organizational value and a strategy driven by leadership (Pérez-Bustamante, 1999;

Crocitto and Youssef, 2003), will be a requisite for dealing with turbulent environments.

Managers and organizations are invited to develop certain characteristics critically important for innovation, creating an atmosphere where people feel absolutely free to come up with ideas and aspirations (as a source of energy and enthusiasm). Hence, the role of the manager in the KE will be to manage the environment or context in which the work is done, serving as coach and facilitator.

Johannessen *et al.* (1999) show a model that emphasizes the characteristics of an innovation-led company. These authors recommend focusing on both the management level (that is, the abilities and attributes of world-class performers) and the level of organizing (that is, organizing the work in process teams).

1.6.3 Regions

The relevance of regions as the key basis for economic organization and growth has been emerging in the literature in the last decade (Sotorauta, 2003; Cooke *et al.*, 1997; Ketels and Memedovic, 2008). The global KE highlights the role of regions as the appropriate 'strategy sites of intervention' (Langendijk, 2000:184) of every nation's economic growth, prosperity and competitiveness. Recent literature on the creative economy and knowledge-based urban development emphasizes the role of regions and cities in becoming basic 'building blocks' for economic growth (Yigitcanlar, 2009).

Networks and geographical clusters of firms are a particularly important feature of the KE, because it is the only effective way to share understanding. Skills and life-style are then becoming increasingly important location factors. As mentioned by DeVol (1999:9):

> As we enter the age of human capital, where firms merely lease knowledge-assets, firm's location decisions will be increasingly based upon quality-of-life factors that are important to attracting and retaining this most vital economic asset. In high-tech services, strict business-cost measures will be less important to growing and sustaining technology clusters ... Locations that are attractive to knowledge assets will play a vital role in determining the economic success of regions.

Systematic innovation and competence-building are seen as key drivers of nations' prosperity. Systematic innovation, supported by interactive learning and collective entrepreneurship, expands the regional knowledge base (Lundvall and Johnson, 1994). From a development perspective, the driving forces behind economic growth are those able to enhance reciprocal understanding and mutual trust and enable tacit knowledge transmission amongst the agents of the regional economy (for example, a set of habits, routines, norms and laws by which people shape their beliefs, values, behaviours and attitudes) (Martins and Viedma, 2006b).

This emphasizes the importance of the science and technology system (universities, research organizations, firms' in-house R&D and so on) and the region's organizational, institutional and policy-learning capabilities.

The role of regions and their potential for competence building

Competence building refers to the use of knowledge and thus how resources are deployed to achieve objectives. In a context in which competition is based on the creation and use of knowledge, regions appear as focal points for learning and knowledge development. As seen by some authors, the increasing role of the region and its potential for economic development is anchored in 'untraded interdependencies' (Scott and Storper, 2003), that take the form of conventions and informal rules and habits that aggregate and coordinate economic actors. Under conditions of uncertainty, such connections foster and shape entrepreneurial, productive and innovative activities. These untraded interdependencies are region-specific and together constitute the region's relational assets and the source of competitive advantages.

Regional institutions represent the cradle of a set of habits, routines, norms and laws under which its people shape their beliefs, values, behaviours and attitudes. Institutions – because they are the norms and principles that shape people's values, attitudes and behaviours – can greatly enhance an economy's capacity to continuously reconfigure itself by systematically assessing its learning capabilities and the wider innovation system.

The ability to achieve and maintain a high growth rate in the KE is determined by actors' ability to innovate and diversify into new technologies, products and industries and, in turn, this ability is a function of a set of factors, such as the level of technology and the extent to which it is used, the geographic location, the institutional framework, the strategies of economic actors, and the individual and collective competencies, values and attitudes of the region's human capital base. This approach recognizes that the nature and structure of the knowledge base upon which a region 'crafts' its competitive capacity includes a whole range of non-scientific and non-technical aspects (e.g. Sotorauta, 2003; Scott and Storper, 2003). It also depends upon a plethora of social, economic, political and cultural issues, including: learning and technology upgrading; financial capacity; collaboration between industry, science and government; macroeconomic stability; security; governance and regional stakeholders' values and commitment. They also encompass different perspectives: economic, sociological, psychological and managerial.

If 'in the flowing world to be competitive is to be attractive' (Sotorauta, 2003:3), seducing the talented workforce is a primary task that involves both physical (tangible) and emotional (intangible) elements. This means that a competitive regional structure can be created where decisions lie with the region's social, economic and political actors, and will depend greatly on their skills, competencies and willingness. This poses a question: 'How can one assess these new development paths and ascertain their real effects on regional economies?' A comprehensive framework is called for including an in-depth diagnosis of the region's economic, technical and institutional foundations, and a very strong commitment to a long-term vision, as well as a systematic and critical evaluation of the whole.

Martins and Viedma (2006b) have developed a learning strategy tool for regions, the Region's Intellectual Capital Benchmarking System (RICBS), designed to help regions and the microclusters within them to assess their capacity to create and exploit new opportunities and make the transition to more competitive knowledge economies. It is believed that effective economic growth occurs in microclusters, meaning that firms' strategies, and the subsequent behaviours and actions embodying them, are the ultimate drivers of a region's growth or decline.

The RICBS analytical tool consists of two main interrelated systems that determine two complementary aspects of a region's competitive capacity: (i) the region's overall competitive capacity to create the foundations that will sustain growth and support the activities of microclusters; and (ii), the region's capacity to create wealth through the microclusters. The former is the Region's Competitiveness Intellectual Capital Platform (RCICP) which represents the bundle of core resources and competencies bound together by core activities. The latter is the region's Microclusters' Competitiveness Intellectual Capital Framework (MCICF) and considers the microeconomic environment and capacity for innovation in each of the region's core microclusters. The RICBS is built on a broad concept of human capital: the overall pool of competencies (Man *et al.*, 2002), values and attitudes available in an economy at a certain moment, from which firms and other public and private institutions can fulfil their human-based demands. The system pays special attention to the quality and content of the first years of schooling, as they represent the pillars upon which a region's human capital is further developed.

Other cluster-based economic development models have emerged for providing the foundations for sustainable regional economic growth in the context of KE. For example, Smedlund and Pöyhönen (2005), using the networks approach, have modelled the intellectual capital creation for a wood-processing cluster in Eastern Finland and demonstrate how innovativeness and efficiency may be combined, improving the competitive advantage of a region. Viedma (2005) puts forward a model for measuring and managing the Cities' Intellectual Capital Benchmarking System (CICBS). To develop a set of different economic activities, intellectual assets are assembled into microclusters according to certain criteria of homogeneity. It is basically about managing the creation and development of a common and general knowledge – an intellectual capital platform – that strengthens the existing microclusters of a city and nurtures the building of new ones. Other works (Bounfour and Edvinsson, 2005) developing regional projects have demonstrated how European regions may play their part in achieving a KE. Building on their qualities, experience, and commitment, regional economies will be increasingly present in nations' efforts to achieve growth and competitiveness.

1.6.4   Nations

Economic growth is fundamentally a process of structural change, meaning it depends greatly on the capacity of the economy's organizations and institutions to reconfigure continually themselves and thus the landscape they occupy. The ability to achieve and maintain a high growth rate in the KE will increasingly depend upon the actors' (that is, individuals, organizations, institutions) ability to use and apply what they know to new processes, products and services. A country's capacity to take advantage of the KE depends on how quickly it can become a 'learning economy'. Learning means not only using new technologies to access global knowledge, it also means using them to communicate with other people about innovation.

Governments, in turn, should include in their country's competitive potential assessment far more than the traditional macroeconomic indicators. Financial and economic stability are a precondition of any policy aimed at promoting economic growth but are by no means sufficient to fulfil the KE's demand for innovation. Also, isolated investment policies are not sufficient to promote the positive effects that lead to economic growth, even if they involve technology upgrades. A set of tangible and intangible elements other than economic and financial aspects must be considered. Sustainable growth depends on credible and efficient institutions, high-quality education and research centres, new information and communication technologies, a wide and dynamic human capital base, and a set of values and attitudes that encourage creativity, aspirations, collaboration, flexibility, continuous learning and trustworthiness.

A high and rising standard of life is the main goal for any nation in the KE. Realizing this depends upon creating a high quality business environment that fosters innovation and rising productivity. The high quality business environment is based on the prosperity of a nation, which depends on the productivity of all its industries; and productivity does not rely on what industries a nation competes in, but on how it competes. In a global market, nations compete against each other and try to attract important flows (for example, capital, competent people, competitive industries, technologies) to themselves. Hence, nations should detect and reward individuals, organizations and sectors which are the main value generators, so that they and their businesses remain in the nation and contribute to national wealth creation and social well-being in the future. This, in turn, will lead to increased attractiveness for investors, partners, companies and human capital.

Although investment in human capital development, that is, education, provides an important foundation for productivity growth and the expansion of the KE, it is only one side of the story. As the transition to knowledge-based societies has accelerated, the need for greater competencies for all has strengthened. Sustainable development and social cohesion depend critically on the collective skills of the entire population, in addition to high levels of education. Most importantly, competencies should embrace a broader view, covering knowledge, skills, attitudes and values – to include the needs of a knowledge society and not just those of a knowledge economy.

It is an urgent task to reinvent the curriculum at all levels of education. Doing so, nations will improve the cultural life, intellectual life, economic life and social life of their population. Social partners may play an important role in ensuring an equitable distribution of training opportunities, but governments will almost certainly also have to play a role, particularly to ensure adequate learning opportunities for those excluded from the opportunities provided through work. So, investment in education and training and other learning opportunities – involving everybody in this goal: governments; non-government organizations; trade unions; employers and companies – is an investment in the future of our countries and our peoples (Hearn and Rooney, 2002).

ICT is playing the role of an enabler for knowledge work for nations as it does for companies. New technologies continue to emerge including broadband infrastructure, speech recognition and expert systems. These technologies evolve together into new user-consumer systems. Concurrently, new production regimes are generated through quantum computing, nanotechnology, biotechnology and bio-informatics.

The national R&D effort, a country's science and technology policy, is perceived by economists today as another major driver of economic growth and the wealth of nations. An important characteristic of twenty-first century science is that it becomes more humanistic and social than technical and introverted (Hearn and Rooney, 2002). The measure of science will not be technical and commercial prowess but how well it has served social and environmental needs.

So, today's knowledge-based global economy means that nations are facing challenges that are more and more like those that confront companies. They have to create better structural capital that better connects their different institutions as value creating constellations, as do companies, universities and other organisms. They must examine policies for strengthening the connections between educational institutions and their communities, and enhance the ways in which they work together to promote social values and citizenship. Nations have to explore how government, educational institutions, local communities and others can collaborate more effectively in the creation, sharing and use of knowledge and innovation to promote professional practice in teaching and management.

Finally, nations have to create national brands – an attractiveness that allows them to draw the most talented people, organizations and institutional investors to their countries.

1.7   Conclusions

Globalization, deregulation and incredible technological advances, particularly in the areas of information and communications technology, have created a new era that has reshaped the global socio-economic environment. These trends are changing the competitive structure of markets. A 'New Paradigm' economy has emerged in which knowledge is seen as the critical factor of production, the vehicle of economic benefits, and the source of the nation's prosperity and sustainable competitive advantage. In response, new models of business are emerging where the value chain has its nucleus in the creation, dissemination, application and leverage of intellectual resources.

Probably the most enduring aspects of KE issues relate to the notion that long-term economic growth is ultimately both constrained and driven by knowledge creation. This means that to an ever greater extent, individuals, organizations, regions and nations will differentiate them-selves not only on the basis of what they know, but also on what they do with what they know. As knowledge increasingly becomes the key strategic resource of the future our need to develop comprehensive understanding of knowledge processes for the creation, transfer and deployment of this unique resource are becoming all the more criti-cal. Knowledge industries add value by the reiterated use of knowledge and the re-configuration of knowledge with other forms of knowledge to solve problems or to meet a need. Hence, knowledge efficiency and knowledge productivity will become the economic challenge of the KE.

With knowledge being the major driver behind economic growth, we can expect that an emphasis on knowledge creation, development, organization, and leveraging will continue to be a prime focus for a long time. Continually improved and well applied knowledge will be the fuel to improve the quality of life for all the citizens of the world.

2
Entrepreneurial Excellence in the Knowledge Economy Context: The Theoretical Foundations

2.1 Introduction

Achieving entrepreneurial excellence has always been the fundamental aim of any organization. One of the most widely discussed contributions to the determinants of business excellence is that made by Peters and Waterman (1982) in their book, *In Search of Excellence*. Since then, the attributes of the concept have been reshaped in line with dramatic changes in economic, social and demographic conditions. New economic laws and social trends have arisen, and many other drivers have started to transform markets.

In fact, we are witnessing a burgeoning public consciousness of the role of business in helping to cultivate and maintain highly ethical practices in society and particularly in the natural environment. Notably, a differentiated feature in the context of KE is that not only do economic laws drive excellence, but corporate social responsibility and ethics will also shape it in the future. That is, to achieve excellence in the KE, organizations have to deal with the dual challenge facing management businesses: to earn a higher rate of profit than the industry average, while integrating corporate social responsibility and ethics into their business management models.

An excellent business is one that achieves growth and extraordinary profits over a long period of time due to the fact that it has sustainable competitive advantages. In the KE, sustainable competitive advantages are usually based on intangibles or intellectual capital (IC), and have to be achieved within an ethically and socially responsible business model.

As a unifying theme that gives coherence and direction to the actions and decisions of an individual or organization, strategy is the crucial management perspective for achieving excellence in the context of KE. While there are several perspectives in the management field, there is one that is vital for organizational success. That is the strategic perspective. As Drucker (1954:352–3) says:

> The important decision [or those] decisions that really matter, are strategic. They involve either finding out what the situation is, or changing it, either finding out what the resources are or what they should be ... Anyone who is a manager has to make such strategic decisions, and the higher his level in the management hierarchy, the more of them he must make.
>
> Among these are all decisions on business objectives and on the means to achieve them ... The important and difficult job is never to find the right answer, it is to find the right question.

Formulating the right questions requires organizations to understand which resources, capabilities and competencies they need in order to gain and sustain the competitive advantage. At the same time, to be successful or to be excellent, organizations need to know what their competitive advantage is.

More precisely, for achieving excellence in the KE, organizations have to focus on the strategic perspective. As illustrated in Figure 2.1,

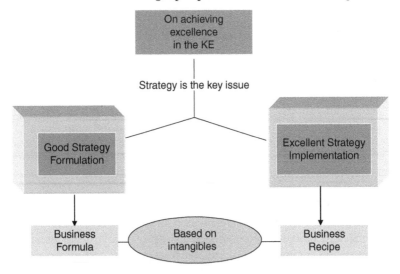

Figure 2.1   On achieving excellence in the KE

a good strategy formulation (business formula) and an excellent strategy implementation (business recipe) based on intangibles are the key to success and excellence in this new context.

In this chapter, we analyse the concept of entrepreneurial excellence and its attributes in the context of the KE. Today, economic activity is increasingly intangible and entrepreneurial excellence is challenged to do business in both profitable and socially responsible ways. We argue that, in the fast-changing business environment, entrepreneurial excellence depends on a soundly formulated strategy (business formula) and an effectively implemented strategy (business recipe), based on core competencies, core capabilities and IC, and we examine both business formulas and business recipes below. Intangibles, core competencies or IC are the key ingredients of a sound business formula, which when properly combined can develop a range of unique products and services generating an excellent business recipe. Formulating good strategies and making them happen are like two sides of the same coin.

The concept of IC and its definitions are analysed within the 'intellectual capital standard theory', which we consider to be the prevailing IC paradigm. This chapter also examines the foundations and principles on which the new alternative theory, referred to as the 'new paradigm', is based. Finally, we synthesize both these theoretical approaches with other new views and contributions, seeking to develop the basis for a first 'general theory of intellectual capital'.

2.2 Entrepreneurial excellence in the knowledge economy context

In the context of the global economy, entrepreneurial excellence is related to the ability to achieve and sustain competitive advantages in our organizations by building long-term value from IC. Management literature explores this theme extensively, linking entrepreneurial characteristics and strategy to the firm's success. Intelligent enterprise is here presented as a new paradigm for a 'new era' to build sustainable competitive advantages.

2.2.1 Entrepreneurial phenomenon

The literature describes the entrepreneurial process as a multi-dimensional and complex phenomenon (Murphy, 2009). Most conceptual frameworks focus on the individual entrepreneur and his or her characteristics and actions. Some authors (Venkataraman, 1997; Shane and Venkataraman, 2001), advocating an opportunity-based framework, argue that entrepreneurship is a function of the individual and the opportunity. They consider the individual and the opportunity to be the essential elements of the entrepreneurial equation:

Entrepreneurship = f (individual, opportunity)

According to these authors, the key aspects of entrepreneurship are:

- the sources of opportunities;
- the process of discovery, evaluation and exploitation of opportunities; and
- the set of individuals who discover, evaluate and exploit them.

An important but problematic issue shaping this discussion is the ontological assumption about whether opportunity is an endogenous or exogenous phenomenon. The Austrian school of economics (for example, Kirzner, 1973) considers opportunity to be exogenous. Although the discovery process depends on the individual and the opportunity, the domain of entrepreneurship is quite narrow because opportunity is a specific possibility, situation, venture or chance, which is not created by the entrepreneur. Kirzner (1997:72) notes that 'an entrepreneurial attitude is one which is always ready to be surprised, always ready to take the steps needed to profit by such motives'. Therefore, the key to entrepreneurial success is a disposition to be alert to new opportunities and the ability to act quickly when an opportunity is revealed (Alvarez and Barney, 2007).

In contrast to this, other scholars view the concept of opportunity as depending on endogenous factors (for example, Rindova and Fombrun, 2001; Gartner and Carter, 2003). They believe that opportunities are a product of individual entrepreneurial actions or, perhaps more important, a product of collective action. Their basic assumption is that entrepreneurs can shape their market and the institutional environments, that they can create opportune changes in them and, in so doing, can construct their own context.

More recently, Ihrig *et al.* (2006) have developed a knowledge-based perspective on entrepreneurship, suggesting that entrepreneurship can be thought of as a function of knowledge and attitude. Knowledge drives the process of discovery and, in this sense, it is the enabling force of the entrepreneurial process. However, there are people who have the knowledge to start a new venture but never do so. Basically, what the potential entrepreneur needs in order finally to start a new venture is the critical attitude. The concept of a critical attitude should not only consist of the 'perceived desirability and the perceived feasibility' but also of the 'emotional, intellectual, and physical energy to see a venture through to fruition' (Erikson, 2002:282). Then, the mathematical formula changes to this one:

Entrepreneurship = f (knowledge, attitude)

A perspective of entrepreneurship based on knowledge proposes that there is one single dominant factor upon which the opportunity, the individual and the whole entrepreneurial process is based. This factor is knowledge, as a property of individuals or organizations which are intelligent agents in their own right (Quinn, 1992), and which are challenged to have a critical attitude in order to execute the entrepreneurial process.

2.2.2   Entrepreneurial excellence

Global competition and the technological revolution have created a 'new era', and a new paradigm economy has emerged in which intangibles are seen as the critical factor for production and the source of prosperity and sustainable competitive advantage. Today, economic activity is increasingly intangible and entrepreneurial excellence must meet a dual challenge to:

- earn a higher rate of profit than that of general industry; and
- respond to business' economic, social and environmental issues with social responsibility and ethics.

Excellent enterprise is thus involved in doing business in both profitable and socially responsible ways. These two purposes accommodate the sustainability development paradigm.

Essentially, corporate social responsibility is about a modern approach to business that emphasizes the leveraging of social, environmental and economic objectives in business activities. The idea has become very popular through Elkington's 'Triple P' concept, which labels these objectives as people, planet, and profit (Elkington, 1997). In practice, and in business literature, various terms are used to describe corporate social responsibility, including sustainability, corporate citizenship, corporate accountability and business ethics.

The modern era of management thought provides the paradigm for the competitive or excellent company in the context of global markets.

One of the pioneering efforts to establish the business tools for long-term dominance through intangibles was made by James Brian Quinn in his influential book, *The Intelligent Enterprise*. Such business dominance through intangibles is not just about modern technological industries. Rather, it applies to all industries, manufacturing and services, high-tech and low-tech, retailing and agriculture, as advanced by Quinn (1992:53–6):

> Intellectual and service activities now occupy the critical spots in most companies' value chains, regardless of whether the company is in the services or the manufacturing sector.

Adding that:

> If one is not 'best in the world' at a critical activity, the company is sacrificing competitive advantage by performing that activity internally or with its existing technique. This dictates that managers consider each activity in their value chain on a 'make or buy' basis.

In this sense:

> Each company should focus its strategy investments and management attention on those core competencies – usually intellectual or service activities – where it can achieve and maintain 'best in the world' status, i.e. a significant long-term competitive advantage.

From the excerpts above, we contend that in seeking sustainable competitive advantages, intelligent enterprise (presented as a new paradigm for a new era (see Figure 2.2), concentrates on building and exploring core activities and core competencies, while relying on the capabilities of external suppliers for non-strategic and non-core activities.

Intelligent enterprise continuously aims to excel in business. We define business excellence as a long-term sustainable competitive advantage based on intangibles. A way to measure business excellence is to examine the long-term financial results within a framework of ethics and corporate social responsibility.

The root to achieving excellence in strategy, whatever we do, is to be clear about what our strategy is and consistently communicate it to our employees, customers, and other stakeholders. Staying clear on strategy means that organizations should decide where they want their business to go, and decide how to go there. As noted in Figure 2.3, in the

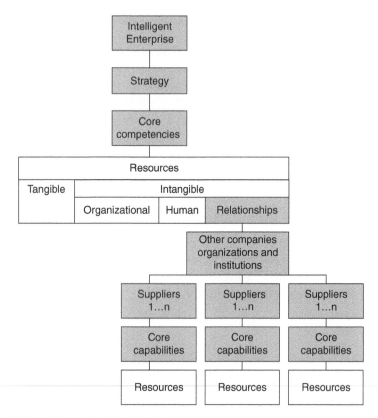

Figure 2.2   Intelligent enterprise network
Source: Viedma (2004b).

fast-changing business environment entrepreneurial excellence will depend on soundly formulated strategy (business formula) and effectively implemented strategy (business recipe), based on core competencies, core capabilities or IC.

2.3   The prevailing strategic perspective on achieving entrepreneurial excellence: good strategy formulation (business formula) and excellent strategy implementation (business recipe)

According to Grant (1998), a key common element in all business success stories is the presence of a soundly formulated and effectively implemented

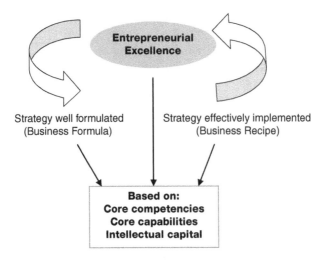

Figure 2.3 Entrepreneurial excellence in the knowledge economy

strategy. Notions of what constitutes a sound strategy have consumed researchers and senior managers' time since Alfred Chandler's (1962) work. In an interesting review on strategic thinking, Kay (1993) addresses the problem of how to achieve this elusive 'perfect strategy'. His study covers rationalist, emergent and organizational behaviourist perspectives.

Whilst the rationalist approach to strategy states that a study of the company's environment, its competitors, clients and its own resources will enable the formulation of a strategy that achieves success, the emergent theory assumes that strategy is the result of a reactive solution to existing problems. Finally, the organizational behaviourist perspective is based on the contingency or resource-based approach. This view of strategic management states that organizations are open systems and there is no 'one best way' to manage firm performance. Those strategies that are effective in one specific situation may not necessarily be efficient in another. The essence of a contingency perspective is that performance is contingent not only on various firm behaviours and resources (internal conditions), but on situational and environmental factors (external factors).

This raises interesting questions about which business structures and strategic choices are best suited to take advantage of constant emerging trends. Given an uncertain environment, strategies must be both focused and flexible. That is, strategy should provide a clear statement of where, how, and when to compete, and, at the same time, it should be able to perform well in a variety of possible future environments. As well explained by Kay (1993), the key challenge is to be both a competitor and an evolver. This means excelling at seeking sustainable competitive advantage, whilst innovating systematically. The move toward this approach implies that strategy is not merely a process, but it is also an outcome of a process which is shaped by human creativity.

2.3.1   Strategy is about the direction of organizations

The term strategy has its historical roots in the time of the ancient Greeks. The word 'strategy' comes from the Greek *strategos,* 'a general', and the verb *stratego* means 'to plan the destruction of one's enemies through effective use of resources' (Bracker, 1980:219). After the Second World War, as business entered a more complex and dynamic context, the need for a concept of strategy related to business became a crucial issue.

Rumelt *et al.* (1994), in their *Fundamental Issues in Strategy,* explain that the foundation of strategic management as a field may be traced to three works of the 1960s:

- Alfred Chandler's seminal book *Strategy and Structure* (1962);
- Igor Ansoff's *Corporate Strategy* (1965); and
- the text published by Kenneth Andrews in *Business Policy: Text and Cases* (Learned *et al.,* 1965).

For Chandler (1962:15–16), strategy can be defined as the determination of the basic long-term goals and objectives of an enterprise, and the adoption of courses of action and the allocation of resources necessary for carrying out these goals.

Ansoff (1965) viewed strategy as a combination of five component choices:

1. product/market scope (the products and markets the firm was in);
2. growth vector (the changes the firm planned to make in its product/ market scope);
3. competitive advantage (those particular properties of an individual product/market that gave the firm a strong competitive position);
4. synergy (a measure of joint effects) internally generated by a combination of capabilities and competencies; and
5. 'make or buy' decisions (to produce or to outsource).

Finally, Andrews added to the strategy concept the notion of an uncertain environment to which firms had to adapt. According to Andrews, the changes in environment give rise to opportunities and threats and the firm's strengths and weaknesses are adapted to avoiding the threats and taking advantage of the opportunities. In the view of Rumelt *et al.* (1994:17) 'these twin appraisals were the foundation for strategy formulation, a process analytically (if not practically) distinct from strategy implementation'.

According to those approaches, organizations tried to cope with the new and rapidly changing technological, economic and organizational developments through a form of long-range planning. Firms started by defining the objectives, then established the plans to achieve those objectives and, finally, they allocated resources according to the plans. The main goal of this process was to reduce the gap between a firm's aspirations and plans (Fox, 1975), where planning was seen to be simply a matter of projecting forward trends. In such a scenario, mathematical modelling was the favoured solution.

However, in a highly uncertain context, the use of long-range plans for formulating strategy became restricted. As a consequence, long-range planning has been replaced by strategic management, which incorporates the possibility that changes in trends can and do take place, and recognizes that both industry and firm effects are important in shaping profitability.

During the 1980s, the developments in strategy analysis focused on the link between strategy and external environment. Examples of this focus are Porter's (1985) analysis of industry structure and competitive positioning. Companies should search for a favourable competitive position in an industry and the strategy should seek to establish a profitable and sustainable position against the competing forces in such an industry.

This industrial organization (IO) economic approach dominated thinking in the strategic management field from the 1960s to 1980s. New approaches to strategy emerged proposing to address multiple questions derived from the rapid pace of technological change, the rise of global markets and global companies, intensification of competition, and deregulation. Studies in the field evolved thereafter with numerous schools of thought emerging in the practice of management. Probably the most popular framework is that studied by Mintzberg *et al.* (1998) over viewing ten schools of strategic management, as those mentioned in Figure 2.4.

Based on the different world views of organizations, Mintzberg divided the ten schools of strategic thought into two groups. The first group comprised those schools based on rational planning, guided by

Schools of thought	Strategy process
1) Design Strategy formation as a process of *conception*	Strategy process is the result of a fit between internal capabilities and external environment.
2) Planning Strategy formation as a *formal* process	Strategy is seen as an elaborated sequence of steps.
3) Positioning Strategy formation as an *analytical* process	Analyses business in the context of its industry looking at how organization can improve its strategic positioning within that industry.
4) Entrepreneurial Strategy formation as a *visionary* process	The insights, vision and wisdom of a single leader guide the strategy formation.
5) Cognitive Strategy formation as a *mental* process	Strategy formation is a cognitive process that takes place in the mind of the strategist.
6) Learning Strategy formation as an *emergent* process	Strategy emerges in small steps, as people come to learn about a situation as well as organizations adapt or learn.
7) Power Strategy formation as a process of *negotiation*	Strategy formation is a process of influence, emphasizing the use of power and politics to negotiate strategies.
8) Cultural Strategy formation as a *collective* process	Strategy formation is based on social interaction, i.e. values and beliefs shared by the organization's members.
9) Environmental Strategy formation as a *reactive* process	Strategy is a response to the challenges imposed by the environment.
10) Configuration Strategy formation as a process of *transformation*	Strategy arises from periods when an organization adopts a structure to match to a particular context, giving rise to certain behaviours.

Figure 2.4   Schools of thought in the strategy process
Source: Adapted from Mintzberg *et al.* (1998).

economic and normative considerations. Strategy is then associated with the entrepreneur, who is able to analyse, in a rational way, the environment and the resources. Belonging to this group are the design, planning and positioning schools of thought. The second group comprises those schools focused on the decision-making processes. Belonging to this group are the other schools of thought.

Balancing these different perspectives, a number of authors argue that successful strategy is not a preconceived and detailed set of steps for achieving defined goals within a given period of time. Neither is it a rational process shaped by mathematical models. Rather, it is the outcome of a process of decision-making and resource allocation that should be directed by a vision (the intent) and pursued with determination (Burnes, 1992). Theories that draw analogies between biological evolution and economics or business, suggest that strategies based on flexibility, experimentation, and continuous change and learning can be even more important than rigorous analysis and planning.

Strategic management is then about managing change at its most fundamental level. Both organization and competition are clearly important in shaping strategy and performance. Reciprocal interactions at multiple levels of analysis between the environment and the organization shape business strategy and performance, while interactions between strategy and performance, in turn, shape both organizational capabilities and competitive environments and become exogenous events in the environments of other organizations.

As with many other concepts in the field of management, there is no agreed definition of the term 'strategy'. The difficulty with defining strategy is that it has different meanings for different people and organizations, which makes it an abstract and elusive concept. Because it deals with the unpredictable and the unknowable, strategy implies thinking, planning, directing, coordinating, and executing. Fundamentally, it is a systematic way of thinking and acting.

Although the development of a comprehensive definition of strategy is beyond the scope of this book, the revision of strategy definitions shown in Table 2.1 emphasizes some key characteristics.

Johnson and Scholes (2002:10) define strategy as: 'the direction and scope of an organization over the long term, which achieves advantage for the organization through its configuration of resources within a changing environment and to fulfill stakeholder expectations'. It follows that strategy is basically about taking strategic decisions that answer the questions posed in Figure 2.5.

Table 2.1   Strategy definitions

Source	Definition
Drucker (1954:17)	Strategy is analysing the present situation and changing it if necessary. Incorporated in this is finding out what one's resources are or what they should be.
Ansoff (1965:118–121)	Strategy is a rule for making decisions determined by product/market scope, growth vector, competitive advantage and synergy.
Cannon (1968:9)	Strategies are the directional action decisions that are required competitively to achieve the company's purpose.
Mintzberg (1979:25)	Strategy is a mediating force between the organization and its environment: consistent patterns in streams of organizational decisions to deal with the environment.
Schendel and Hofer (1979:516)	Strategy provides directional cues to the organization that permit it to achieve its objectives, while responding to the opportunities and threats in its environment.
Grant (1991:114)	Strategy can be defined as the match an organization makes between its internal resources and skills ... and the opportunities and risks created by its external environment.
Rumelt *et al.* (1994:426)	Strategy is the act of aligning a company and its environment. That environment is subject to change, as are the firm's own capabilities. Thus, the task of strategy is to maintain a dynamic, not static, balance.

It is the systematic answer to the questions above and the integration amongst those choices that makes the strategy a system that gives coherence to the growth and success of organizations (Enders *et al.*, 2009). In practice, a thorough strategic management process includes strategic thinking, strategic analysis, strategy formulation and strategy implementation, each phase generating respective outcomes, as examined in Figure 2.6.

Strategic thinking is about how strategic decision-makers actually think. The literature suggests three key elements that are relevant to strategic thinking, namely, systems thinking, creativity and vision. Systems thinking involves thinking in terms of processes and requires

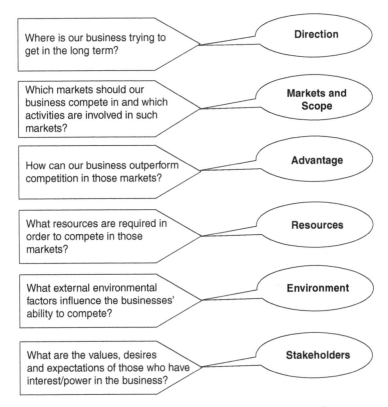

Figure 2.5 Strategy is about taking strategic decisions that answer to the questions
Source: Adapted from Johnson and Scholes (2002).

a thorough understanding of the internal and external dynamics of organizational life. Creativity thinking refers to how people approach problems and their ability and agility in generating alternative solutions. Finally, a common vision helps to provide meaning and gives a sense of direction in the decision-making process (Holloway, 2009).

Strategy analysis is about analysing the strength of businesses' position and understanding the important external factors that may influence that position.

Strategy formulation involves understanding the nature of stakeholder expectation, identifying strategic options, and then evaluating and selecting strategic options – ranging from the overall business (corporate strategy) to business units and functional levels.

Phases of strategic management ⟶ **Outcomes**

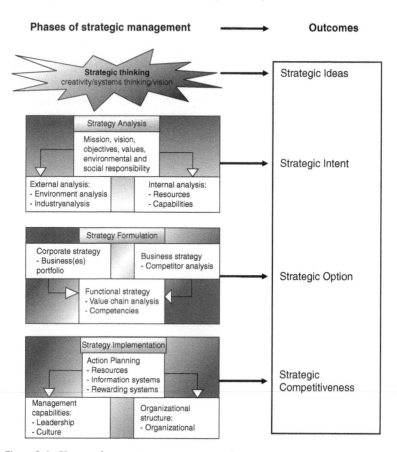

Figure 2.6   Phases of strategic management and outcomes

Strategy implementation is the third phase of strategic management. Once a strategy is selected, the task is to translate it into organizational action. This means that, for an organization to be successful, it must structure its internal operations in order to promote the achievement of the vision and ensure that its culture reinforces this direction. The organization is then looking for strategic competitiveness focusing on activities that allow higher performance returns and innovation.

Each of the strategic management phases, though they are interrelated, has its own distinct strategic concerns and each can draw on different strategic tools to aid them. Our work focuses on the strategy formulation phase as an activity that draws heavily on the creativity of the human mind, and the formula for success of which is based on the way the firm understands and combines its valuable resources, capabilities and competencies and matches its activities to the environment in which it operates.

2.3.2 Strategy is about a systematic way of thinking and acting

Several studies note that strategic thinking represents an important antecedent to strategic decision-making. But strategy is not so much a matter of intellect, it is much more a 'whole range of possibilities in between, where thought and action respond to each other' (Mintzberg *et al.*, 1998:42). In this ability to 'act thinkingly' (Weick, 1995:225), managers can take actions informed by a framework of previous thinking and, at the same time, inform future thinking (Bonn, 2005). It represents an integrated perspective or a systematic way of thinking and acting.

Senior managers need to convert their understanding into action, otherwise, as the Japanese proverb says:

Vision without action is a daydream
Action without vision is a nightmare

Vision is the starting point of any organizational transformation process and should underpin business strategy (Kantabutra and Avery, 2010). A vision of the organization's future – strategic intent – is created which should then be pursued by the organization. Strategy then emerges from the decisions that are taken regarding resource allocation, organization structure and other operational areas. As described by Mintzberg (1987) in his metaphor of strategy as 'craft', managers, like the potter, establish objectives for the organization (i.e. create a vision of a desired future) and through a combination of experience and resources they pursue their objectives. Crafting strategy is a continuous and adaptive process, with formulation and implementation inextricably interwoven.

There is a consensus in literature that one of the most important formative steps in the strategic decision process is generating strategic ideas, which evolve from strategic thinking. Strategic ideas are viewed as the outcome of the strategic thinking process or the 'dominant images we hold in our minds' (Sworder, 1995:72). Strategic ideas evolve amongst strategic thinkers or the 'innovative entrepreneurs' (Mintzberg, 1995) who are able to think creatively. In a dynamic context, strategic ideas stem from the complex interaction of individual, group and organizational characteristics and behaviours.

Organizational culture is then, an important issue for generating successful strategic ideas. Barney (1986) proposes that a particular cultural context presents a source of competitive advantage in developing strategic ideas, while Schwarz and Nandhakumar (1999) contend that combining the existing intellectual, social and cultural resources is crucial for the development of successful strategies by a company. The quality of strategic thinking is largely influenced by cultural aspects such as attitudes, traditions, habits, beliefs and emotional commitments. Senior managers are faced with a high level of uncertainty, unpredictability and incomplete information. Change can only succeed in an environment that allows individuals to try new skills and habits and even fail repeatedly. Senior managers need to have a thorough understanding of the internal and external dynamics of organizational life – in particular how organizations interact with complex systems such as markets, industries, nations and economic blocks, and how they are influenced by the dynamics of such systems.

That is, for an organization to follow a successful path, senior managers have to create a vision of its desired future – its intent – and formulate a strategy (business formula) that gathers and allocates the organization's resources into a unique, viable and winning posture based on its internal resources, competencies and capacities, which anticipates changes in the environment, and is contingent upon the moves made by its competitors.

2.3.3 Strategy formulation (business formula)

The starting point for the formulation of strategy must be some statement of the firm's identity and purpose (Grant, 1998). This generally takes the form of a mission statement that answers the question: 'What is our business?' Traditionally, firms have defined their business in terms of the market they serve: 'Who are our customers?' and 'Which of their needs are we seeking to serve?' Nevertheless, in a world where customer preferences are volatile and the identity of customers and the technologies for serving them are changing, a market-focused strategy may not provide the stability and constancy of direction needed as a foundation for long-term strategy. That is, when change becomes the standard, as is the case today, organizations cannot find stability in their products and customers. When the external environment is in a state of flux, the firm itself, in terms of its bundle of resources and capabilities, may be a much more stable basis on which to define its identity. Hence, a definition of the firm in terms of what it is capable of doing may offer a more durable basis for strategy than a definition based upon the needs the business seeks to satisfy (Quinn, 1992).

Since strategy determines the whole direction and action focus of the organization, its formulation cannot be regarded as the mere generation and alignment of programmes to meet predetermined goals. The *Oxford English Dictionary* (2004) defines strategy, as used in business administration, as a plan for successful action based on the rationality and interdependence of the moves of the opposing participants. This definition, like most strategy definitions, highlights the perspective of movements of the opposing parties (that is, competitors) in the process of strategy formulation. Hence, the essence of strategy formulation is to deal with the markets and competitors.

Strategy can be formulated at several levels (Hofer and Schendel, 1978; Johnson and Scholes, 2002). One way of categorizing these is to recognize that there are three levels of strategic decision-making in organizations: corporate; business; and functional, as illustrated in Figure 2.7.

Corporate strategy seeks to exploit actions to be taken in order to gain a competitive advantage. It is fundamentally concerned with the selection of the various businesses in which the company should compete and with the development and coordination of the portfolio of Strategic Business Units (SBUs).

Business unit strategy is concerned with how a business competes successfully in a particular market. At this level, organizations make strategic decisions about the choice of products, meeting the needs of customers, anticipating changes in demand and technologies and adjusting the strategy to accommodate them, exploiting or creating new opportunities, influencing the nature of competition, sometimes at a political level.

Functional strategy is concerned more with how each part of the business is organized to deliver the corporate and business-unit level

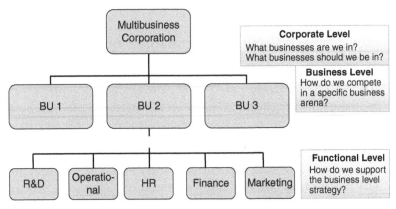

Figure 2.7   Levels of strategy formulation and management decision

strategic direction. At this level, organizations focus on how the component parts of the organization in terms of resources, processes, people, and their skills are pulled together to put strategy into effect.

A prerequisite of an organization's success is that all levels of strategies fit together to form a coherent and consistent whole. For the purpose of this book, we will focus on the strategy formulation at the business unit level. That is, strategy formulation that attempts to answer questions about

- How advantage over competitors can be achieved?
- What resources and competencies are required in order to compete?
- What external environmental factors affect the businesses' ability to compete?

In practice, strategy formulation crystallizes around a business formula, which in most cases, is not explicit. Because of this, the business formula may be deduced from what the company does. When a firm implements its business formula, this is converted into business recipe.

2.3.4 Strategy implementation (business recipe)

To ensure that a firm knows where it is going, senior managers must make strategy that is operative, map the actions that will deliver it, and put into place the measures that monitor real-time progress. A major point to note is that organizations must adopt appropriate structures, practices and cultures.

Moving from thinking to action – translating strategy into action – requires more than just a long-range blueprint. Unfortunately, many organizations come off the strategy execution track. Kaplan and Norton (1996a; 1996b) demonstrate that there are primarily four barriers that must be overcome before strategy can be effectively implemented. According to the authors, only 5% of the workforce understands the strategy (vision barrier); only 25% of managers have incentives linked to strategy (people barrier); 85% of executive teams spend less than one hour per month discussing strategy (management barrier), and; 60% of organizations don't link budgets to strategy (resource barrier).

The complex, embedded and dynamic nature of modern organizations requires a systemic approach to strategic management. The strategy may be seen as an on-going and dynamic process (Figure 2.8) of driving organization towards vision, by finding and maintaining a defensible space and trajectory in a given business environment.

An organization's performance depends on the quality and sustainability of its strategies. The best strategy ever formulated (business formula) is still only a hypothesis developed by its creators. It represents their best guess as to an appropriate course of action, given their knowledge of information concerning the environment, competencies, capabilities and resources. When a company implements its business formula, we have the business recipe, as depicted in Figure 2.9.

In order to create value, the *ingredients* in the business formula must be transformed into products or services that deliver value. The business

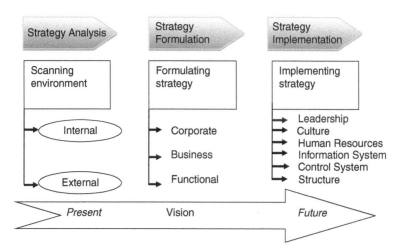

Figure 2.8 Systemic approach to the strategy

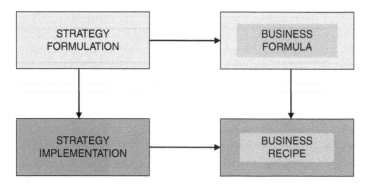

Figure 2.9 The concepts of business formula and business recipe

formula only converts into a business recipe when the business formula is implemented. In other words, the business formula is the result of strategy formulation, whereas the business recipe is the result that comes from strategy implementation.

2.3.5   Sustainable competitive advantage and performance

The purpose of strategy is to ensure the achievement of competitive advantage by defining the direction and scope of an organization. Because achieving, developing and sustaining the competitive advantage enables firms to earn superior profit, competitive advantage is the firm's ability to outperform its industry, that is, to earn a higher rate of profit than that of the industry.

Attempts to understand and test the connection between performance and sustainable competitive advantage began in the 1970s and have become a central matter in the strategic management field. In a context of global competition, the concept of sustainable competitive advantage has evolved as a response to an increasingly turbulent environment and shifting competitive behaviour.

Porter's (1985) work has encouraged managers to seek out market-based competitive advantage through differentiation or cost reduction. Hamel and Prahalad (1994) emphasize a competence approach, where managers seek to find advantage through an internal analysis of key resources that the organization owns. Barney (1991) states that a firm is said to have a competitive advantage when it implements a strategy not simultaneously implemented by any current or potential competitor, while Mahoney and Pandian (1992) claim that competitive advantage is a function of industry analysis, organizational governance and firm effects in the form of resource advantages and strategies.

From the above, we may conclude that the concept of sustainable competitive advantage remains unclear. Further, competitive advantage is often used interchangeably with concepts like distinctive competence (Day and Wensley, 1988). Understanding competitive advantage requires an analysis of its components. Advantage is a relative concept that highlights a comparison with another entity or a set of entities (Hu, 1995). Hence, a competitive advantage is an advantage one firm has over a competitor or group of competitors in a given market, strategic group or industry (Kay, 1993). A firm may have many advantages over a competitor or a group of competitors, such as a lower cost of production, an easier access to scarce resources, a strong brand, an agile structure, a lean supply chain, a more efficient distribution channel, a technological advance, or a superior client delivery service, but the important advantages are those in which customers place some level of value (Coyne, 1986).

Another component of the sustainable competitive advantage refers to its sustainability. When is a competitive advantage sustainable? Sustainability does not refer to a specific period of time, much less confidence that it will persist indefinitely. Rather it depends on the possibility of replication by the firm's competitors. The harder it is to imitate such advantage the more sustainable it will in the future.

Summarizing, Coyne (1986) argues that for a sustainable competitive advantage to exist, three conditions must apply:

• customers must understand or perceive a consistent difference in important attributes of the firm's products or services when compared to the attributes of those offered by competitors;
• this difference must be the direct consequence of a capability gap between the firm and its competitors; and
• both the difference in important attributes and the capability gap can be expected to endure over time.

Coyne's argument is based on the assumption that the attributes recognized by the customer as superior are the direct consequence of a firm's capabilities, identified as bundles of skills, knowledge (namely, tacit knowledge) and technologies. According to Hofer and Schendel (1978), competitive advantage can be based on superior skills, resources or position in a market. More recently, strategic management literature puts the emphasis on intangibles as a source of competitive advantage (Itami, 1987; Teece *et al.*, 1997; Nahapiet and Ghoshal, 1998), because they are less visible and subsequently more difficult to understand and imitate than tangible resources. Firms hold heterogeneous or idiosyncratic resources on which their individual strategies are based.

Figure 2.10 illustrates the nature of competitive advantage in the context of the KE which is based on the identification of core intangibles, which must be embedded in the business formula, and can be sustained through the deliberate, purposeful and systematic transformation of those core intangibles into market-valued products and services, realized in the business recipe.

2.4 The fundamental role of intangibles and intellectual capital on creating successful business formulas and building sound business recipes

Far from being new topics, knowledge and intangibles have been recognized as important throughout history. The difference is that today

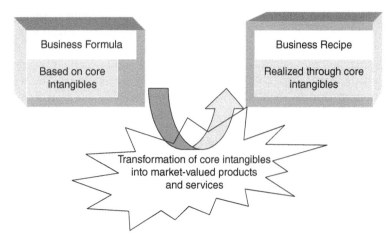

Figure 2.10   Competitive advantage in the context of the knowledge economy

a firm's intangible assets are often the key element to be considered in its growth and competitiveness. In the past, competitive advantage was derived from the successful exploitation of scale economies, underpinned by a unique technology or dominance of a geographic market or supply-chain. Today, the consensus is that winning strategies are more grounded in the development and creative application of intangibles. Over the past two decades, intangibles have become a major concern not only for academics but for business managers, investors, analysts, a large number of stakeholders, and policy makers, as well.

2.4.1   The role of intangibles

We have seen increasing attention directed to the study of the value of intangibles in the process of value creation in organizations. The ratio of intangible to tangible assets has grown in recent years, suggesting that the earlier style of business management, based on tangible assets, is undergoing a major transformation (Adams and Oleksak, 2010). Top executives all over the world view intangible resources as being critical for a firm's success. Hope and Hope (1998) discuss the growing importance of the role of intangibles in the organization's value creation.

The authors provide evidence that between 50–10 per cent of value created in organizations comes from the management of tangible assets while the remaining 50–90 per cent of value created results from the management of intangibles, as shown in Figure 2.11.

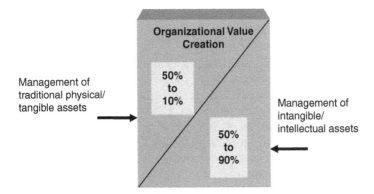

Figure 2.11   Importance of intangibles in value creation
Source: Adapted from Hope and Hope (1998).

These developments are theoretically driving a shift in the basis of business management from tangible to intangibles, or IC. Many international initiatives have been carried out to create management tools to assess, report, and develop the IC in organizations.

The first attempt to measure IC, in the early 1990s, can be traced back to the initiatives of the Organization for Economic Cooperation and Development (OECD). It was noticed that intangible investments such as training, R&D, patents and software appeared to increase more rapidly than tangible investments (OECD, 1996), whilst with respect to the measurement difficulties the OECD clearly stated that 'a major reason for underinvestment in intangible assets, such as technology and human resources, was their lack of visibility' (OECD, 1998:294). Ever since, the OECD has been encouraging research in this field and emphasizing the need to develop a set of indicators of intangibles within firms and a reporting structure that facilitates comparability, which would be of use to managers, stakeholders and policy makers. OECD initiatives were founded on the basis that intangibles were an increasingly important determinant of enterprise growth, productivity gains, profitability, and the creation of wealth.

From November 1998 over a 30 month period, a project called MERITUM (MEasuRing Intangibles to Understand and improve innovation Management, 2002), funded by the TSER (Target Socio-Economic Research) Programme of the European Union, was launched with the aim of producing a set of guidelines to measure and disclose information on intangibles in order to improve the decision-making process of managers and stakeholders. This research project – later followed up by a new project, E*Know-Net – produced an operational conceptualization of intangibles, and contributed to three areas: classification of intangibles; management control of intangibles; and capital market deficiencies related to intangibles.

At the same time, the European Commission (EC) encouraged the creation of a 'learning society', promoting training and education in member countries and making learning a lifelong endeavour. The European Commission published a White Paper titled *Teaching and Learning – Towards the Learning Society* (1995) proposing a Human Resource Accounting approach that treated training investment in the same way as other capital investment on the balance sheet. There are, however, differing approaches.

A number of other initiatives also took place in the United States. At the end of the 1990s, the Brookings Institution in Washington published a report, *Unseen Wealth* (Blair and Wallman, 2001), which supported the OECD's and EC's argument that intangibles constitute a potential resource for the generation of wealth. Also the Securities and Exchange Commission (SEC) published a report *Strengthening Financial Markets: Do Investors Have the Information They Need?* (SECITF, 2001) and two recommendations were made to improve supplemental disclosures: a) SEC's initiatives to pull together the efforts on improving reporting and facilitate the creation of a framework for the voluntary supplemental reporting of intellectual assets, operating performance measures and forward-looking information; and b) government initiatives to create an environment that encourages firms to disclose more information.

In the same line, government initiatives in The Netherlands, Denmark, and Norway have provided incentives for investigation and experimentation with intellectual capital. The Danish Agency for Trade and Industry (DATI, 1998) sponsored the preparation of a report on various attempts, at the company level, to prepare 'intellectual capital accounts', based on the experience of ten Nordic companies. Further initiatives were taken by the Danish, Finland and Norway governments. At the same time, empirical research into intellectual capital management and reporting practices was conducted in The Netherlands, Denmark, Sweden, Canada, Spain, Australia and Ireland.

In 2008 a group of five countries became involved in a collective research project, the 'Intellectual Capital Statement – Made in Europe' (InCaS-Made in Europe), seeking to implement Intellectual Capital Statements (ICS) in over 1,000 European small and medium sized enterprises (SMEs), based on an EU-wide consolidated Intellectual Capital Statement (ICS) methodology.

Although many agree that intangibles are the key drivers of a firm's success and the competitiveness of countries, there is still a lack of consensus on a precise definition of the term *intangibles* (Marr and Chatzkel, 2004). It is a word that applies to different concepts, such as assets, activities and resources. Nevertheless, the wide range of definitions of intangibles that can be found in the literature has some attributes in common. Intangibles can be considered as the source of probable future economic profits lacking physical substance, which are controlled, or at least influenced, by a firm as a result of previous events and transactions (self-production, purchase or any other type of acquisition) and may or may not be sold separately from other corporate assets. This classification of intangibles raises important issues in the scope of the intangible economy.

International Accounting Standard (IAS) 38 (1998) prescribes the classification of intangible assets in terms of expending resources or incurring liabilities on the acquisition, development, or enhancement of intangible assets such as: scientific or technical knowledge; design and implementation of new processes or systems; licences; intellectual property; market knowledge; and trademarks. This classification of intangible assets is still very narrow, failing to include assets generated internally, such as: employee satisfaction; human resources; customer loyalty; and company reputation. Despite not adhering to the generally accepted accounting practice (GAAP), companies feel that if properly managed, those intangibles have huge potential for creating value, and so they can no longer be ignored.

Although intangible assets cannot be touched, they can be identified and reasonably classified. One such simple classification is that presented by Sveiby (1997) and depicted in Table 2.2.

Table 2.2 Classification of intangibles according to Sveiby

Intangible Assets		
External structure	**Internal structure**	**Individual competence**
(Relationships: brands, customer and supplier Relations, trademarks, reputation, image)	(Organization: management, legal structure, manual systems, attitudes, patents R&D, software)	(People: skills, education, experience, values, social skills)

Source: Adapted from Sveiby (1997).

Assets of external structure

This term refers to the company's portfolio of customers and its relationships with suppliers, banks, shareholders, and other stakeholders, its cooperation agreements and alliances (strategic, technological, production, and marketing), its commercial brands, and its image. These assets are owned by the company and some can be legally protected (e.g. commercial brands). There are other frameworks that identify such assets as 'relational capital'.

Assets of internal structure

This term relates to the company's formal and informal organizational structure, work methods and procedures, software, databases, R&D systems, management systems, and culture. These assets are owned by the company and some can be legally protected (patents, intellectual property, and so on).There are other frameworks that name them as 'structural capital'.

Assets of individual competence

This term alludes to assets such as the employees' education, experience, know-how, knowledge, skills, and values and attitudes. These assets are not owned by the company, but their use and application is accessed by the company's hiring of employees. This type of asset is also known as 'human capital'.

A number of other classifications of intangibles have been proposed in the literature. Based on 'the properties of ownership', Hall (1992:136) classifies intangible assets into two categories:

- those assets for which the company has property rights, with legal context (intellectual property) and without legal context (reputation); and
- those assets for which the company has no property rights (competencies and skills).

Adopting a similar approach, Eustace (2000) developed a scheme for the categorization of intangibles, dividing them into:

- intangible goods (e.g. licences, copyrights, contractual rights, trademarks); and
- intangible competencies (innovation competencies, market competencies, human resources).

Intangible goods are those that can be bought, sold, stocked, leased and otherwise traded. Intangible competencies are valued by successful companies as vitally important in differentiating their market offer from those of their competitors. Although the assets involved are generally bundled together and interdependent to such an extent that they are difficult (but not impossible) to isolate and value, they are now widely deployed as key factors of 'non-price competition'.

On the other hand, Hussi and Ahonen (2002) classify intangibles into generative and commercially exploitable, emphasizing the synergic nature of intangibles. Although a company's current performance is based on its existing commercially exploitable intangibles (e.g. expanding markets, management trust, cost-efficiency), the company has to rely on its generative intangibles (human capital, internal and external structures) to maintain profitability in the future and also to make sure that its commercially generative intangibles are continuously renewed.

Further, the MERITUM (2002) Project states that intangibles may be defined in static (that is, resources) and dynamic (that is, activities) terms. Static intangible resources are the stock or current value of a given intangible at a certain moment in time. In this category are worker competencies, intellectual property rights or customer satisfaction. Dynamic intangible activities are those which imply an allocation of resources aimed at developing them internally or acquiring new intangible resources, increasing the value of existing ones, or evaluating and monitoring the results of the former two activities. Examples are training activities (to improve employee skills), specific marketing activities (to attract loyal customers), R&D (to improve technological capabilities), or a survey to assess employee or customer satisfaction (to monitor the effectiveness of improvement activities).

The key questions about intangibles are whether or not they are relevant and why and for what they are relevant (Marr *et al.*, 2003). Several studies provide evidence that intangibles are crucial sources of competitive advantages that must be identified measured and controlled in order to maximize the individual and organizational knowledge's value.

However, given their often socially complex nature, it is difficult to understand how they are created and why they are valuable. This is due to the fact that the value of intangibles depends greatly on the owning company's context, that is their value can only be calculated based on the use of intangibles in the owning company's context. Intangibles may then have a highly variable value from context to context (Ortiz, 2009). This represents a central element of the current dilemma of reporting on the value of intangibles. The critical issue is that intangibles are fundamentally different from tangibles

- Intangibles may be deployed simultaneously for multiple uses
- Although unique in many cases, intangibles can be used by multiple people
- Intangibles have strong network effects in the sense that intangibles often form the nucleus of important networks
- Intangibles are future-oriented because they create future value; and
- The value of intangibles is very dependent upon specific use and context.

Given these characteristics, the relationship between intangibles and firm performance is often causally ambiguous (Coff, 1997). As stated by Lev (2001:7),

> intangibles are frequently embedded in physical assets (e.g. knowledge contained in technology) and in labour (e.g. tacit knowledge), leading to considerable interactions between tangible and intangible assets in the creation of value ... when such interactions are intense, the valuation of intangibles on a standalone basis become impossible.

For example, it is difficult, or even impossible, to imitate a corporate culture because of its path-dependent nature and its social complexity (for example, it involves many human interactions and a large set of embedded routines). This suggests that the firm's intangible assets should be one of the central issues in formulating strategy and one of the most important features upon which a firm can establish its identity and frame its strategy (Grant, 1991).

2.4.2   Defining intellectual capital

The term 'intellectual capital' is often treated as synonymous with 'intangibles'. The literature offers a multitude of different definitions for IC, though there still exists little consensus about what constitutes a good definition of it (Abeysekera, 2006). A reason for this may be the fact that too much of the nature of IC is still unknown and hard to capture in explicit terms. As suggested by Marr (2005), this invites different people to talk about IC from different perspectives or disciplines, using the same language to describe different things or phenomena. Differences in national cultures may be another reason for the fuzziness of IC as a construct, since culture alters assumptions about knowledge, its creation and its implementation (Chaminade and Johanson, 2003). While Table 2.3 summarizes some definitions of IC, we recommend reading the *Journal of Intellectual Capital* (2006), Volume 7, Number 1, which offers an important contribution to the field of IC theory, providing a common platform for dialogue and cross-disciplinary learning on definitions and diverse frameworks.

Although still requiring a universal definition, it is noticeable that in most cases definitions have some common elements, namely:

- intellectual capital has an intangible nature;
- it refers to knowledge that creates value;
- it is the effect of collective practice; and
- its benefits are not necessarily immediately identifiable, but rather are accrued over a long period of time.

Because IC is knowledge that creates value, all irrelevant intangibles that have no function in the firm's future potential are excluded. Since

Table 2.3 Definitions of intellectual capital

Author(s)	Definitions
Edvinsson and Sullivan (1996)	Knowledge that can be converted into value.
Brooking (1996)	Combined intangible assets of market, intellectual property, human-centred and infrastructure which enable the company to function.
Klein and Prusak (1994)	Intellectual material that has been formalized, captured, and leveraged to produce a higher value asset.
Andriessen (2001)	Unique bundle of intangible assets that are the basis of sustainable competitive advantage.
Lev (2001)	Sources of future benefits (value) that are generated by innovation, unique organizational designs, or human resource practices.
Edvinsson *et al.* (2005)	All factors critical to an organization's future success that are not shown in the traditional balance sheet, i.e. future earnings capabilities.
Marr and Moustaghfir (2005:1116)	Embraces any valuable intangible resource gained through experience and learning that can be used in the production of further wealth.

intellectual assets are often internally generated, interrelated and inter-dependent, their value is context-specific. Prominent amongst those assumptions is that the value companies place on their IC largely depends on the company's view of itself. It gives sense to the importance of management epistemological assumptions.

Roos *et al.* (1997) define the theoretical roots of IC and refer to two different perspectives: the strategic perspective and the measurement perspective. The strategic perspective focuses on the creation, dissemination and use of knowledge to enhance firm value, while the measurement perspective focuses on the need to develop a new information system, measuring and reporting intangibles. For Marr and Moustaghfir (2005), if we enter into a strategic perspective, the way to address IC is through strategy formulation and the identification of value drivers in firms. On the other hand, if we follow IC from a measurement perspective, our concern is external validation and the aim is to provide useful information for making decisions on the economic and financial position of a firm.

Another important point to stress is the variety of practical approaches that IC tends to be divided into. From Sullivan's (2000) perspective IC may be seen as creating value or about extracting value. Companies focusing on value creation usually concentrate their efforts on how knowledge is created and its transformation into organizational wealth. Those who focus on value extraction (profits) aim to create intellectual assets and intellectual property of intangible assets. For example, in the early 1990s the Dow Chemical Company focused on value extraction based on a corporate goal of creating intellectual assets and intellectual property from its intangible assets (a portfolio of over 29,000 patents). In 1993, the company introduced the Intellectual Assets Management (IAM) process to classify value and extract wealth from its Intellectual Assets Portfolio (IAP). On reviewing the patent portfolio, the company verified that from its 29,000 patents only 200 (less than one percent) were considered to be fundamental to Dow's businesses. With a more focused IAP, licensing revenues have increased substantially and savings in tax maintenance costs are significant. Most important, Dow Chemical is now able to have an accurate valuation of its patents.

Beyond the lack of consensus concerning IC definitions, the literature reports a number of other terms used interchangeably with IC, such as intangible assets, intellectual capital assets, intellectual assets and knowledge assets. However, according to Lev (2001), the terms knowledge assets, intangible assets, and IC, which are widely used (intangible assets in the accounting literature, knowledge assets by economists, and intellectual capital in the management and legal literature), refer to the same thing: a non-physical claim to future benefits.

The debate around the IC concept also includes its categorization and its dimensions. Managers' increasing awareness of IC as a key driver for sustainable competitive advantage, together with the limitations of the existing financial reporting system for capital markets and other stakeholders, have motivated a spirited dialogue on finding new ways to measure and report on a company's IC. As a result, a plethora of new measurement approaches for synthesizing financial and non-financial measures have emerged. Table 2.4 synthesizes some of best known intellectual capital classifications.

Despite the plethora of IC classifications presented in the literature there has been a steady convergence in its categorization and language into a single model. IC has been traditionally defined in a tripartite dimension (Bontis, 1998; Sveiby, 1997) covering the human aspects (for example, human capital, competencies), intra-organizational structures (for example, structural capital, internal structure) and external environment (client capital, structural capital, external structure), as depicted in Figure 2.12. Rothberg and Erickson (2002) expand the concept of IC, adding a fourth pillar: the competitive capital generated through activities in competitive intelligence systems.

Human capital

Human capital is the brain and soul of an organization, the foundation of IC. It is a primary element in the performance of IC functions because 'human interaction is the critical source of intangible value in the intellectual age' (O'Donnell *et al.*, 2003:82). It refers to such factors as employee's knowledge, skill, capability, and attitudes in relation to fostering performances which customers are willing to pay for and that the company's profit comes from.

A macroeconomic perspective recognizes human capital as the driver of national economic activity, competitiveness and prosperity (OECD, 1996). At the individual level, human capital is defined as a combination of four elements: *(i)* genetic inheritances; *(ii)* education; *(iii)* experience and; *(iv)* attitudes about life and business (Hudson, 1993). The organizational perspective refers to human capital as 'the source of innovation and strategic renewal' (Bontis, 1998). Gupta and Roos (2001) added that 'core intellectual capital' comprising competence, intellectual agility and attitude are potential synergies for value creation.

Table 2.4   Summary of intellectual capital classifications

Author	Classification of intellectual capital
Brooking (1996) UK	**Human-centred assets** Skills, abilities, expertise, problem solving abilities and leadership styles, the embodied knowledge of the workforce. **Infrastructure assets** All the technologies, processes, routines, organizational structures, internal information networks, management methodologies. **Market assets** Brands, customers, customer loyalty and distribution channels, relations and networks with stakeholders, and also wider social citizenship and environmental health investments. **Intellectual property** Patents, trademarks, copyright, designs, legal protection of confidential information.
Roos, Roos, Dragonetti and Edvinsson (1997) UK	**Human capital** Competence, attitude and intellectual agility. **Organizational capital** All organizational, innovation, processes, intellectual property and cultural assets. **Relational capital** Relationships that include internal and external stakeholders. **Renewal and development capital** New patents and training efforts.
Stewart (1997) USA	**Human capital** Employees are an organization's most important asset. **Structured capital** Knowledge embedded in information technology. **Customer capital** Market information used to capture and retain customers, all patents, plans and trademarks.
Edvinsson and Malone (1997) Sweden	**Human capital** Competence matrix, number of professionals, total staff, temps. **Process capital** Average throughput time of invoicing, average throughput of monthly reporting. **Customer capital** Service-based sales spread, percentage of key clients. **Innovation capital** Current innovation areas, staff deployable in these areas.

(Continued)

Table 2.4 (Continued)

Author	Classification of intellectual capital
Sveiby (1997) Australia	**Internal structure** Systems, databases, processes and routines that support an organization's operations and employees. **External structure** External relations and networks that support the organization's operations. **Competence** Individual experience, knowledge, competence, skills and ideas.
Bontis (1998) Canada	**Human capital** The individual level knowledge that each employee possesses. **Structured capital** Non-human assets or organizational capabilities used to meet market requirements **Relational capital** Customer capital is only one feature of the knowledge embedded in organizational relationships.
International Federation of Accountants – IFAC (1998)	**Human capital** Know-how, education, vocational qualification, work-related knowledge, occupational assessments, psychometric assessments, work-related competencies, entrepreneurial élan, innovativeness, proactive and reactive abilities, changeability. **Relational capital** Brands, customers, customer loyalty, company names, backlog orders, distribution channels, business collaborations, licensing agreements, favourable contracts, franchising agreements. **Organizational capital which comprises:** - Intellectual property: patents, copyrights, design rights, trade secrets, trade marks, service marks. - Infrastructure assets: management philosophy, corporate culture, management processes, information systems, financial relations.
Allee (2000) USA	**Human capital** Competence, individual capabilities, knowledge, skills, experience and problem solving abilities that reside in people. **Corporate identity** Value of one's vision, purpose, values, ethical stance and leadership.

(Continued)

Table 2.4   (Continued)

Author	Classification of intellectual capital
	External relationships Business relationships with customers, strategic partners, suppliers, investors, quality relationships enjoyed with larger society, relationship with earth and resources and contribution to health and sustainability of environment. **Internal structure** Systems and processes that leverage competitiveness, including ICT, databases, documents, IP.
Bounfour (2003) France	**Human Capital** All tacit knowledge and routines in the mind of employees. **Structural Capital** All intangible assets are separable from tacit knowledge. **Market Capital** The organization's endowments related to its relationship with the outside world. **Innovation Capital** The innovation capabilities of the organization.
New Guidelines (2003) Denmark	**Employees** Employees' skills, competencies, experience, education, motivation, commitment. **Processes** Knowledge embedded in stable procedures, innovation processes, quality procedures, management and control, mechanisms for handling information. **Customers** Customer mix, relations to customers and users, their satisfaction and loyalty, their referral of the company, insight into users' and customers' needs and the degree of co-operation with customers and users in product and process development. **Technologies** Technological support of the other three knowledge resources.
New Guidelines (2003) Germany	**Human capital** Employee skills, employees' conduct, etc. **Structured capital** IT, intellectual property, organizational culture, process, organization, etc. **Relational capital** Customer relations, relations with suppliers, relations with the public, etc.

(Continued)

Table 2.4   (Continued)

Author	Classification of intellectual capital
Huang and Wu (2010) Taiwan	**Human Capital** Knowledge, skills, and abilities residing within and utilized by individuals. **Organizational Capital** Organization's capabilities to meet its internal and external challenges, including infrastructures, information systems, routines, etc. **Social Capital** Enhances the quality of group work and richness of information exchange among team members.

Note: Only a few of the best known models are included.
Sources: Roos *et al.* (2006); Marr (2005); ICS – Made in Germany (2003); Andriessen (2004); Pike and Roos (2004); EC (2003:190); IFAC (1998); Martins (2006).

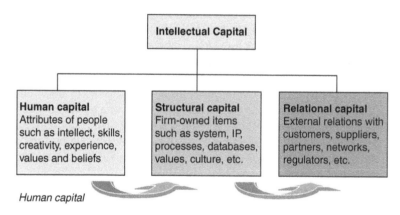

Figure 2.12   Intellectual capital components

Structural capital

Structural capital is what remains in the company when employees go home at night. It comprises internal processes, infrastructures, information systems, routines, organizational structure, databases, culture and everything that enables organizations to make their human capital more productive. Roos *et al.* (1997) classify IC into human and structural capital, 'thinking' and 'non-thinking' assets. Organizations are not rendered intelligent simply because they have some intelligent people.

Structural capital is the skeleton and the glue of an organization because it provides the tools (management philosophy, processes, culture) for retaining, packaging and moving knowledge. Organizations have to create systems and procedures that convert human intellectual capital into organizational intellectual capital allowing it to be used repeatedly. The role of organizations is to provide the necessary structure for individuals to collaborate in a way that leverages their talent and existing market opportunities in order to create economic value. The focus is on getting a higher leverage of the human capital through structural capital, producing a 'multiplier effect' (Edvinsson *et al.*, 2005).

Relational capital

Relational capital is the knowledge embedded in the relationships with any stakeholder that influences the organization's life. Relationships with stakeholders are the necessary conditions for building, maintaining and renewing resources, structures and processes over time, because through external relationships firms can access critical and complementary resources. Customers become a new source of competence for the organization because they renew the overall competence of the organization and rejuvenate the knowledge base, preventing it from becoming obsolete in a turbulent environment (Prahalad and Ramaswamy, 2000; Gibbert *et al.*, 2001).

The IC literature has concerned itself with the nexus between the three IC categories. Some calls have been made for a better understanding of the tangible and intangible assets of the firm as a highly interdependent bundle of resources. One of the most interesting images to explain how these three components of IC combine to create value is given by Edvinsson and Malone (1997) when describing the tree metaphor. The authors explain:

> If we imagine a firm as a living organism; for example a tree, one can say that organizational plans, annual and quarterly reports, firm brochures, and other documents are the trunk, branches and leaves. The wise investor will examine the tree whether he can harvest ripe fruit. But to assume that we have now seen the whole tree because we have seen the visible is a grave mistake. At least half the tree is below surface in the roots. And while the taste of the fruits and the colour of the leaves make a good presentation of the tree, it is much more effective to look at what goes on the roots if one wants to form an opinion about the health of the tree for the coming years. There may be rot below the surface, which as time goes may kill the tree

that looks healthy presently. This is what makes intellectual capital – investigation of roots of a firm's value, measurement of the dynamic factor, which are found below the visible surface of a firm's buildings and products – so important.

Although this metaphor does not yield a useful model, or even a description, of how value is created from the interaction between the knowledge of individuals and the internal structure and processes within an organization, it illustrates that intervention is necessary in order to make future earnings maximally efficient. The fruits represent financial results and, as evidenced by the story, it is in roots where the most crucial activities may take place for future fruition.

From the IC perspective, a firm is seen to consist of a bundle of tangible and intangible resources (Andriessen, 2001; Viedma, 2003a; 2004a). In describing how organizations create and leverage competitive advantage, we note that it depends upon what the firm has, but no less important is what the firm does with what it has. In strategy management, two relevant perspectives still coexist in understanding how firms deploy scarce resources to create superior value (Haanes and Fjeldstad, 2000). These two perspectives are an activity-based view (Porter, 1985, 1996) and the resource-based view. The two are complementary. The activity-based view focuses on what the firm *does*, whereas the resource-based view focuses on what the firm *has*. These two perspectives are described below.

2.4.3   Activity-based view

The activity-based view (ABV) sees firms as value chains that create value by transforming a set of inputs into a more refined output. More precisely, a firm is viewed as a collection of discrete but interrelated economic activities such as products being assembled or orders being processed. A firm is disaggregated into its strategically relevant activities (value chain) in which it is engaged to design, produce, support, deliver, and market its products and services. A company gains competitive advantage by performing these strategically relevant activities more cheaply and better than its competitors.

Porter's theory centres around activities and the basic unit of competitive advantage is the discrete activity. These discrete activities are part of an interdependent system in which the cost or effectiveness of one activity can be affected by the way others are performed. How each activity is performed will determine whether a firm is high or low cost relative to competitors and will also determine its contribution to buyer needs, differentiating it from the competitors. At the same time, sharing value activities (between two or more business units) may lead to a competitive advantage that comes from significant cost advantage and differentiation. In either case, it may be difficult for competitors to match these strategies. Comparing (benchmarking) the value chains of competitors, the company can identify the differences that comprise the competitive advantage.

This notion of value chain helps us to understand the increase of value along the chain of activities in bringing a final offering to customers. Value chain analysis is a systematic way of examining all the activities a firm performs and how they interact at each link in the chain to see where value is added and how it might be increased. It scrutinizes each of the activities of the firm (e.g. marketing, sales, distribution, operations) as a potential source of advantage. A clear sense of what a company does – how and why – helps to focus on maximizing value at minimum cost and allocating resources to those activities that generate the most value – thereby maximizing profitability.

To Porter (1996:64–77), strategy is about building the value chain across the firm, and,

> [the] essence of strategy is in its activities – choosing to perform activities differently or to perform different activities than rivals ... Deciding which target group of customers, varieties, and needs the company should serve is fundamental to developing a strategy. But so is deciding not to serve other customers or needs and not to offer certain features and services.

Given that competitive advantage is the outcome of a firm's ability to perform activities at a lower cost than rivals, or in unique ways that allow the firm to command a premium price, a firm's strategy directs the configuration of its activities and how they are built. The skills and market position that the firm has today are the result of past choices about how to configure activities and skills (learning). This means that a firm's history affects which activities it will be engaged with in the future and how well they will perform. This learning is a reflection of past strategy choices which have defined how present activities are configured.

Within the KE, a service activity strategy might be a key component of the firm's competitive advantage, because companies are becoming more and more dependent, within the value chain, on links consisting of services and intellectual activities (Quinn, 1992). A firm should focus its strategic investments and management attention on those core competencies – usually intellectual or service activities – where it can achieve and maintain 'best in world' status, that is, a sustainable competitive advantage. For that, the firm's strategy has to develop 'best in world' capabilities internally, within selected key activities, and also focus externally on those networks of suppliers that perform activities that must be subcontracted.

2.4.4 Resource-based view

The resource-based view (RBV) of the firm proposes that resources are the main determinant of the competitiveness of the firm, in opposition to the approach of industry analysis in which the main determinant of the firm's competitiveness is its industry position. The RBV provides the basis for taking an inward-looking approach to strategy development, rather than simply accepting the outside-looking approach. A central issue in the RBV is the classification of resources into either tangible or intangible and the notion that these resources provide the basis for capabilities.

Although attributed to Penrose (1959), the RBV gained popularity through the work of Wernerfelt (1984) and Prahalad and Hamel (1990) because it provided a satisfactory answer to an emerging problem: why was it that firms competing in the same industry and facing the same forces could produce different financial results? It seemed that taking a static snapshot of an industry using tools such as Porter's (1985) five forces was not enough. As dictated by Barney (1991), firms cannot 'purchase' sustained competitive advantage on open markets, rather, such advantages must be found in the rare, imperfectly imitable, and non-substitutable resources already controlled by a firm. Dierickx and Cool (1989:1510) also state that companies operate in markets with strategic assets that are 'non-tradable, non-imitable and non-substitutable'.

A firm is considered to be a unique bundle of resources, and its competitive position may be more a function of its resource portfolio than of its market position. Penrose (1959:24) notes that '[a firm] is a collection of productive resources the disposal of which between different users and over time is determined by administrative decisions'. She relates firm growth and diversification to 'inherited' resources, especially managerial capacities, that a firm possesses. Wernerfelt (1989) refers to the possibility of using resources to develop a competitive position more difficult for others to catch up with. Literature highlights examples and cases where firms with particular skills and capabilities were able to outperform their rivals (Coyne, 1986; Grant 1991; Hall, 1989). So, of interest to the RBV is the role of managers in the development and deployment of resources. The RBV suggests that firms use resources to build competencies upon which their strategies are based, or firms' strategies are derived from their resources.

One of the principal insights of the RBV is that resources are not usually productive in isolation. They become productive in collaboration in the context of a team dedicated to a specific purpose. Furthermore, not all resources are of equal importance or possess the potential to be a source of sustainable competitive advantage. Alternative classifications of barriers to resource duplication abound in the organizational literature. Table 2.5 enumerates some of them.

Perhaps a useful point in explaining barriers to duplication is the idea of transparency supported by Grant (1991). The author explains that the most basic problem a competitor might have is an information problem concerning the fact that the competitor is unable to identify what the reasons are behind a given firm's success. The concepts of causal ambiguity developed by Reed and DeFillippi (1990) or uncertain imitability (Lippman and Rumelt, 1982) essentially concern the connections between actions (*praxis*) and results. Reed and DeFillippi (1990) note that the ambiguity may be so great that not even managers within the firm understand the relationship between actions and outcomes.

Seeking to explain the causes of such ambiguity, Reed and DeFillipi (1990) suggest three characteristics of resources that can simultaneously be sources of ambiguity and advantage, namely, tacitness, complexity and specificity. Tacitness is a characteristic of skill-based activities (Polanyi, 1983) and relates to the inability to codify a pattern of activities. Skilled activities are based on learning by doing that is accumulated through experience, practices and routines over time. Complexity

Table 2.5 Barriers to resource duplication

Author	Barriers
Barney (1991)	Conditions of resources: value, rarity, inimitability, non-substitutability
Grant (1991)	Resource levels of: durability, transparency, transferability and replicability
Reed and DeFillippi, (1990)	Causal ambiguity (tacitness, complexity, and specificity)
Lippman and Rumelt, (1992)	Uncertain imitability

results from the interconnectedness of asset stocks (Dierickx and Cool, 1989), the social relationships (Barney, 1991) and from co-specialized assets (Teece, 1986) resulting from the use of assets in connection with one another. Specificity refers to the idea that transactions within the firm and with its external constituents are idiosyncratic to individual firms (Williamson, 1975). In short, the RBV places a premium on resources that are accumulated within the firm (Dierickx and Cool, 1989; Peteraf, 1993; Teece *et al.*, 1997) because such resources are likely to be inimitable or imperfectly imitable, meaning that their relationship with the advantage is difficult to understand.

The above discussion points to the fundamental role of resources, capabilities and competencies for the formulation of strategies in an environment of rapid change in technology and in the needs of customers and industry. The first point to consider is the variety of labels used to describe the firm's resource set. The literature discusses the notion of 'unique resources' under a variety of names, for example, distinctive competencies, core competencies, invisible assets, intellectual assets, core capabilities, core knowledge, core intangibles, corporate culture, and amongst others, unique combinations of business experience.

Generically, resources are inputs or factors available to a company through which it performs its operations or carries out its activities, and they can be tangible or intangible (Itami, 1987). Tangible resources are substantive, physical, and easy to identify and evaluate, whilst intangible resources are generally more difficult to measure, evaluate, and transfer. They include skills, knowledge, relationships, motivation, commitment, trust, culture and reputation.

To define the competitive base of a company's strategy, we must consider those resources that are strategically valuable. Black and Boal (1994) define them within the term 'system of resources', in order to show that they are valuable at the strategic level but their value results from a configured and complex network of factors. Such a 'complex network' is viewed as consisting of a set of direct and indirect connections, interactions, interdependencies amongst a number of factors, whose limits are difficult to establish and to assess.

Regarding the terms 'capabilities' and 'competencies', these are sometimes interchangeably used, and are also frequently preceded by the adjectives 'core' and 'distinctive'. Although some differences exist in terms of focus and interpretation, all have a common approach to strategic management. Capabilities and competencies represent the links between strategies and performance (Teece *et al.*, 1990). Focusing on strategy implementation is to leverage the distinctive capabilities and core competencies of the organization, as sustainable performance is based on the organization's ability to provide the necessary capabilities for individuals to take effective action.

Capabilities have been referred to as difficult to define and are often described as invisible assets (Itami, 1987). Capabilities are viewed as a collection of cross-functional elements – attributes, skills, and knowledge – that come together to create the potential for taking effective action (Saint-Onge and Wallace, 2003). Essentially, capabilities comprise the skills of individuals or groups as well as the organizational routines and interactions through which all the firm's resources are coordinated (Grant, 1991). In addition, capabilities represent what the firm is capable of doing with a combination of resources and it is these interrelationships between them that give the system its uniqueness.

Capabilities may be understood to be the way resources, talents and processes are combined and used (Teece *et al.*, 1997) or 'a set of business processes strategically understood' (Stalk *et al.*, 1993:26). Simply having resources and organizational routines does not guarantee the development of capabilities. To develop capabilities, a firm also needs coordination mechanisms to ensure that people not only know their own jobs but are also able to interpret and respond to information that flows into the organization (Nelson and Winter, 1982). Such coordination mechanisms, namely those from key professional people, would enable good quality services to be extracted from resources (Penrose, 1959).

It is useful then to think of capabilities on two levels (individual and organizational). Individual capabilities are the attributes, competencies, mindsets, and values of an individual within an organization. Organizational capabilities are the strategies, systems, structures, leadership, and culture that make up an organization. To be successful, an organization has to nurture and develop a strong link between individual and organizational capabilities.

As capabilities are interaction-based, they are even more difficult to duplicate due to causal ambiguity, and RBV has favoured capabilities as the most likely source of sustainable competitive advantage (Collis, 1994). Rather than single discrete skills and technologies, capabilities are bundles of constituent skills and technologies (Tovstiga and Birchall, 2002) that create superior value for the customer, differentiate its owner from competitors, and allow entrance to new markets (Hamel and Prahalad, 1994).

Much has been written about the concept of core capabilities. They are normally defined as those capabilities that give the firm its competitive advantage. They represent an accumulation of learning over time ('path-dependent') or they may be a unique ability in an important area of business. Hence, a capability can only be distinctive if it is derived from a characteristic that other firms do not have. Yet it is not enough for that characteristic to be distinctive. Rather, it is necessary for it to be sustainable and appropriable, and it is sustainable only if it persists over time.

A more dynamic perspective is introduced by Teece *et al.* (1997:516), focusing on how some organizations first develop firm-specific capabilities and how they renew competencies to respond to shifts in the business environment. The authors define dynamic capabilities as 'the firm's ability to integrate, build, and reconfigure internal and external competencies to address rapidly changing environments'. The term 'dynamic' refers to the renewal of competencies to address the constant changes in environment. As explained by Teece *et al.* (1997:510), dynamic capabilities can be seen as 'an emerging and potentially integrative approach to understanding the newer sources of competitive advantage'.

All of the above-mentioned tangible and intangible resources represent a basis for the creation of economic value, but competencies, in particular, have received special attention in the recent strategy literature as being a potential source of sustained competitive advantage. Despite all the attention this concept has received, its intangible impact on business performance is still elusive. This is because most managers are uncertain as to exactly what qualifies as a core competence (Coyne *et al.*, 1997).

Generically, competencies are the means by which a firm deploys resources in a characteristic manner in order to compete (Haanes and Fjeldstad, 2000). As a firm's competencies are based on its capabilities – organizational routines and ability to learn –one can hardly conceptualize a capability or competency without the people who comprise them or the system that maintains them. Professional competencies integrate professional skills and knowledge, and organizational competencies include a firm's knowledge, routines, and culture. The European Commission (2003) defines competence as an appropriate blend of knowledge, experience and motivational factors which enables a person or a team to perform a task correctly, efficiently and consistently to a high quality, under varying conditions. By the definition, it is clear that professional competencies and organizational competencies are interrelated.

Some authors, especially Prahalad and Hamel (1990), have distinguished particular competencies, which they call 'core competencies', as being fundamental to the firm's superior performance and successful strategy.

These authors consider the cumulative development of a firm's core competencies at the centre of business strategy. Essentially they argue that

- The sustainable competitive advantage of a firm lies not in its products, but in its core competencies. As mentioned by the authors: 'the real sources of advantage are to be found in management's ability to consolidate corporate-wide technologies and production skills into competencies that empower individual businesses to adapt quickly to changing opportunities' (1990:81)
- Core competencies feed into more than one product, which, in turn, feed into more than one business unit;
- Core competencies require focus. In fact, 'few companies are likely to build world leadership in more than five or six fundamental competencies. A company that compiles a list of 20 to 30 capabilities has not probably produced a list of core competencies' (1990:84). So, this suggests that competencies are a bundle of assets, knowledge and skills, and are much more than organizational strengths and weaknesses. They suggest three acid tests for competencies: it adds value to end products; applies to a range of different markets; and is difficult to develop and imitate.

Because successful core competencies are rare, a strategy led by core competencies requires that the company be the best (or at the very least, nearly the best) at its chosen competence. Coyne *et al.* (1997) help us to determine how a competence is likely to prove worthwhile. Managers should ask the four key questions presented in Table 2.6.

From the discussion above, it is clear that a number of organizational elements of a competence contribute to its sustainability. A core competence comprising only a few elements is much easier to understand and imitate than another one that relies on the alignment of myriad elements. A competence that is supported by multiple functions within an organization, that rests on deeply held cultural norms and values, and draws on employees' tacit knowledge of tasks, processes and organizational routines, will be more time consuming and difficult to replicate. The degree to which a core competence is distinctive depends on how difficult it is for competitors to replicate it. Core competencies are unique to a specific organization because they are 'a combination of complementary skills and knowledge bases embedded in a group or team that results in the ability to execute one or more critical processes to a world-class standard' (Coyne *et al.*, 1997:43).

However, as mentioned by Leonard-Barton (1995:55), 'the flip side of core competencies, or core capabilities, is core rigidities. Core rigidities

Table 2.6 Key questions on successful core competencies

Key questions	Interpretation/Understanding
Are our skills truly superior?	If a core competence is the basis of a strategy, the company must demonstrate that it is better at it than all or most of its actual and potential competitors.
How sustainable is the superiority?	It means that such competence is not only rare and then difficult to imitate, but also it takes time to develop, and it is difficult to understand its sources of nurturing. The time it takes to develop a competence is a function of its complexity.
How much value can the competence generate in comparison to other economic levers?	The competence must be more powerful than other strategic levers relevant to the industry, such as structural advantage or access to cheap resources. It can be obtained by assessing how much of the total value in the industry chain is added by the company.
Is the competence integral to our value proposition?	If a company wants to extract value of its core competence, the investment in superior skills must be tied to actions that will be rewarded by the marketplace. Such competence must be capable of generating future value propositions.

Source: Adapted from Coyne *et al.* (1997).

inhibit innovation and are activated when companies fall prey to insularity or overshoot an optimal level of best practices'. Core competencies must have a dynamic nature in order to prevent them from becoming core rigidities, mainly in turbulent environments.

2.4.5 Knowledge-based view

The knowledge-based view (KBV) is sometimes considered an extension of the resource-based view. The KBV of the firm suggests that the primary rationale for the firm is the creation and application of knowledge (Grant, 1996; Spender, 1996). Within the KBV, the organization is seen as an institution for integrating knowledge, the critical input in production, and the primary source of value. All human productivity is knowledge dependent, machines are simply embodiments of knowledge (Grant, 1996) and organizational capabilities are based on knowledge. Knowledge is then a resource that forms the foundation of the company's capabilities (Marr *et al.*, 2004).

This knowledge perspective stresses that performance differences between firms are a result of their different knowledge bases and differing capabilities in developing and deploying knowledge. The firm's knowledge-based resources are often tacit, personal, or implicit and non-codified, thereby creating knowledge barriers and making them difficult for competitors to imitate (Miller and Shamsie, 1996). Because knowledge is the only resource that provides sustainable competitive advantage, the firm's attention and decision making should focus primarily on knowledge and the competitive capabilities derived from the way we exploit such knowledge (Leonard-Barton, 1995).

This emerging view of the firm may require a fundamental shift in the way we think about organizations. IFAC (1998) lists some of major points of departure to understand the differences between an industrial management perspective and knowledge management perspective

- The KBV of the firm sees people as revenue generators, whereas within the industrial paradigm, people are seen more simply as costs or factors of production.
- The purpose of learning within the knowledge organization is to innovate or create new assets or processes instead of simply applying new tools or techniques.
- Within the knowledge organization, production flows are idea-driven (how new knowledge is created and transferred) as opposed to machine-driven and sequential in the industrial scenario.
- The law of diminishing returns is replaced with increasing returns to knowledge, and economies of scale in the industrial paradigm are replaced with economies of scope in the knowledge paradigm.
- The power base of management rests on their competencies and knowledge sharing as opposed to their hierarchical position within the organization.
- Information flows via networks versus via the organizational hierarchy (Sveiby, 1997).

Based on these assumptions, Sveiby (2001) presents a knowledge-based strategy formulation, emphasizing the role of the competence of people, which will be developed in Chapter 4. The essence of his theory is that the primary intangible resource is the competence of people, because all tangibles and intangibles are the result of human action, and depend ultimately on people for their continued existence.

2.5 Intangibles and intellectual capital as key value drivers: the value creation process

All perspectives based on IC (for example, accounting, reporting, market efficiency) are very important, but perhaps the most valuable is the strategy view because it helps to understand how IC creates value. Indeed, if we cannot demonstrate that IC creates value other perspectives will not be worth much.

There is a consensus amongst researchers and managers that intangibles and the IC of organizations are of strategic importance because they are the engines of value creation. Hall (1992) used the concept of intellectual assets or intangible assets as critical value drivers and more recently, several others (Marr, 2005; Cabrita and Bontis, 2008; Cabrita, 2009) have attempted to understand the nature of IC interrelationships and the value creation process. These interrelationships are difficult to grasp since IC is a complex and dynamic phenomenon. This dynamism of IC is especially demonstrated in the company's ability to renew itself and innovate.

Andriessen (2001) argues that the basis of sustainable competitive advantage resides in a unique bundle of intangible assets. Adopting this perspective, we use the terms 'core competencies' and 'core capabilities' interchangeably and also consider the term 'intellectual capital' to be an equivalent expression.

As IC is 'knowledge that can be converted into value', business strategies require a longer-term focus on IC. Firms with this broad focus tend to have the dual perspective of both value creation and value extraction. We argue that a management approach based on values may help to understand what a value driver is and how IC may be viewed as a strategic driver with significant impact on performance and competitiveness.

2.5.1 Value-based management

A plethora of new management approaches for improving business performance has emerged in the last decades (for example, total quality management (TQM), business process engineering (BPE), empowerment, flat organizations, organized *kaizen*, re-engineering, and so on), but only some of them have succeeded. A reason normally given in the literature for explaining the failure of such tools relates to the lack of alignment between performance targets and the goal of creating value.

Value as a construct has been the subject of particular attention from several disciplines (for example, economics, finance, accounting, marketing, strategy, social psychology and organizational behaviour). To the economist, 'value' is a measure of the utility that ownership of an item brings to the owner. This utility is normally measured in monetary terms. Economists assume 'value' as a future stream of benefits expressed in monetary terms and can discount and sum these amounts to determine the current monetary currency equivalent of a future stream of income. This discounting and summing calculation is the determination of the net present value of a future stream of benefits.

However, to focus effectively on the value creation process it is crucial to rely on a framework or a model that helps to identify and relate value drivers. When the business changes, the framework or model needs to change with it. As we move toward a KE, interest in understanding how value from knowledge is created, has been widely demonstrated not only in the activities of private and public entities, but also in those of governments and international communities (Martin, 2004).

The most usual route in following the idea that knowledge is the key driver that produces value is value management. Value-based management (VBM), focusing on value creation, provides an accurate metric – value – upon which the whole organization may work and develop. VBM has been defined as a philosophy that focuses on the identification of the required functions that produce value at the lowest possible monetary amount. In this sense, VBM can be thought of as a system that seeks to enable management to formulate, design, control and adapt the business processes that are interconnected to create value. In turn, this allows the firm to understand its investments, whether they are in resources, technology, or tangible assets, among others. This value management system is dynamic, which means that value is created, updated and modified over time.

The principles that support the VBM are very simple. The value of a company is determined by its discounted cash flows (DCF). Value is created only when companies invest capital at returns that exceed the cost of that capital. VBM extends these concepts by focusing on how companies use them to make both strategic and operational decisions. If properly implemented, VBM is a management approach that aligns a company's intent and management processes to focus management decision-making on the key drivers of value (Koller, 1994). The key point is that VBM uses value as a performance metric and decision-making tool. It calls on managers to use value-based performance metrics for making better decisions.

As put forward by Koller (1994:89), 'VBM can best be understood as a marriage between a value creation mindset and the management processes and systems that are necessary to translate that mindset in action'. Taken alone, either element is insufficient, because it takes part of the system. Taken together, they can have a relevant and sustained impact on the organization's management system.

Excellent companies are value-driven. We believe that value is the only correct criterion of performance. In an economy of intangibles:

> these values are almost always stated in qualitative, rather than quantitative terms . . . . Furthermore, financial and strategic objectives are always discussed in the context of other things the company expects to do well. The idea that profit is a natural by-product of doing something well, and not an end in itself, is almost always universal (Peters and Waterman, 1982:284).

The concept of value drivers suggests the existence of causal relationships between variables because the alignment of certain variables has systematic implications for organizational performance. But what is a value driver? A value driver is any variable (resource, activity or both) that affects the value of the company. However, value drivers need to be identified, organized and prioritized so that managers can identify which have the greatest impact on value and assign responsibility for them to individuals who can help the organization meet its targets. Those value drivers that have the greatest impact on value, or, in other words, those that actually create the value of the business, are the key value drivers.

Identifying key value drivers is not an easy task as it requires the organization to think about its process as a whole, and also because value drivers cannot be considered in isolation from each other. This perspective shows the relationship between strategic objectives and value. Another interesting point is that, in the context of KE, a VBM requires both an economic and social perspective. This means that value creation is also a social responsibility and a collective task.

Therefore, assessing the VBM requires a deep understanding of those performance variables or the key value drivers. It is crucial to understand which variables influence value creation because a company cannot act directly on value. It has to act on things it can influence – customer satisfaction, employees' motivation, employees' commitment, quality of information, organizational trust, and so on. It is through these drivers of value that top management learns to understand the relationship between strategy and value. They are not static and have to be regularly reviewed. Providing sustainable value requires that the firm moves its business focus to where the value is, learning from a knowledge of its customer base that become more and more sophisticated. The key purpose of VBM is that the firm knows what drives its business, what combinations of tangibles and intangible resources facilitate the performance, and what configurations and coordination mechanisms are used to enable superior performance.

2.5.2   The value creation process in the knowledge economy

The purpose of a value chain analysis is to identify the elements of the activities and the organizational processes and link them to the firm's value creation process. Identifying the firm's value creating process – the way in which knowledge is created, integrated, transformed, and utilized – will mean viewing the organization as a whole in its cross-functional relationships. In our context, the value creation process is related to the shaping of information, knowledge and innovations (Edvinsson, 2000).

As mentioned by Eustace (2003), value chains have always had a limited life in competitive markets, but are now eroding much faster than in the past. This forces firms to look for new factors of differentiation, namely 'non-price' factors of competition. Value is now directly related to the intelligence, speed, agility, attitudes, and commitment that are part of a set of latent intangibles that nurture talent, creativity and innovation, the source of sustainable competitive advantage. This set of intangibles or IC creates value when its elements are combined and put into action, and degrades when left unused (Roos, 2005). This suggests that the value generated is a function of the way in which resources are managed. In other words, having a resource is not enough to create value. In order to create or leverage value, the resources have to be deployed effectively and efficiently.

Sveiby (2001) explains that the key to value creation lies with the effectiveness of knowledge transfers and conversions. The more knowledge a firm possesses, the more it will be in the position to create new knowledge and transfer to others. In fact, knowledge creation is a process of value addition to previous knowledge through innovation (Narayanan, 2001).

If we look at an organization from the point of view of creating value from transfers and conversions of knowledge, the concept of a value chain tends to fall down because knowledge shared between people generates a value network that grows each time a transfer takes place, doubling the organizational knowledge. This is because, in contrast to the value chain, the intangible value in a value network grows each time a transfer takes place since knowledge does not leave the creator. In this sense, knowledge shared is knowledge doubled (Sveiby, 2001). The concept of a value chain is giving way to global value networks, such that it is the knowledge capital of the network as a whole that enables it to combine external and internal sources of intangibles to exploit commercial opportunities. This perspective has been extended beyond the traditional value chain to other more complex ways of creating value, such as *value networks, value constellations,* and *value shops* (Haanes and Fjeldstad, 2000)

- *Value networks* create value by making different products and services available to customers. The value is derived from the network giving buyers access to sellers of what they want, and by putting suppliers in contact with customers who want their products. As value should be added at every point along the value network, when a participant receives a value input he should find ways to use that input to provide greater value in the form of products and services. If a participant in a network can both gain value for him- or herself and also leverage that input for a greater value output, than that is really creating value. Examples of companies creating value through networks include commercial banks, airlines, postal agencies, insurers, brokers, and stock exchanges.
- *Value constellations* can be considered to be linked sets of different value networks.
- *Value shops* create value by solving unique problems for customers by using relevant competencies. Examples of companies that create value as 'shops' include accountants, academics, physicians, designers, lawyers, investment bankers, business consultants, and consulting engineers.

2.5.3 Intangibles and intellectual capital as key value drivers

IC has been identified as a set of intangibles (resources, capabilities and competences) that drive business performance and value creation (Roos and Roos, 1997; Bontis, 1998; Cabrita and Vaz, 2006). This argues the relevance of causal relationships between IC and organizational value (Marr *et al.,* 2004). However, intangible assets seldom affect performance directly. Instead, they act indirectly through relationships of cause and effect (Kaplan and Norton, 2004) and, rather than uni-directional causality, a bi-directional causality relationship between financial and non-financial indicators can be expected.

None of the elements of that set of intangibles is *per se* sufficient for successful performance. These key elements need to be combined and configured to generate value. Recent studies (Bontis, 1998; Cabrita and Bontis, 2008; Cabrita, 2009) found out that IC is a phenomenon of inter-actions, connections and complementarities, meaning that a resource's productivity may improve through investments in other resources. IC is a renewable resource that must be nurtured; an organic process that can be facilitated but not controlled. In this sense, IC is a matter of creating and supporting connectivity between all sets of expertise, experience and competencies inside and outside the organization.

What is really important is that companies know how they use their knowledge to create value for their customer. The answer should be found in deliberate reflection and choices about what the company's package of intangibles should be and how it should be produced, acti-vated, mobilized and delivered to the customer, because it is when IC elements are combined and put into action that value is created.

Carlucci *et al.*, (2004) demonstrate that the generated value is the result of an organization's ability to manage its business process, to make its choices, and that the effectiveness and efficiency of perform-ing organizational processes are based on organizational competencies. Knowledge assets interact with each other to create competencies and capabilities, and it is often these interactions that provide a competitive advantage because they make these assets difficult for competitors to replicate (Barney, 1991; Teece *et al.*, 1997; Marr, 2005). These value driv-ers are bundled together, and the interactions between them are var-ied, complex and dynamic, making it difficult to demonstrate the cause and effects relationships and their linkage to value outcomes. Returns and outcomes are deeply dependent on the connectivity that has been established between the networks of bundled assets.

Taking the notions of stocks and flows may help to understand the role of intangibles or IC as key value drivers. Roos *et al.*, (1997) stress the conceptual distinction between stocks and the flows, and introduce the concept of influence, which is defined in the dictionary as the ability to produce an effect. A stock is something that we have (for example a resource) and a flow is a transformation of one resource into another. This view places the emphasis on the value creation process in flows, meaning that we need to be good at transformations. It makes it clear that there is no correlation between having a resource and being able to transform it.

Therefore, it is vital to identify which resources are net value creators (sources) and which are net value destroyers (sinks). We argue that if it is crucial to identify intellectual capital assets, companies must also be aware of their intellectual capital liabilities.

2.5.4 Intangible liabilities

Whilst intellectual assets attract many references in the literature, intellectual liabilities are virtually ignored. Only a limited number of studies have shown that intellectual liabilities even exist (for example, Harvey and Lusch, 1999; Caddy, 2000; Dzinkowski, 2000; Abeysekera and Guthrie, 2004).

Abeysekera (2006:61) refers to the matter when arguing that, within the traditional accounting system perspective, the IC held by a firm can be viewed as 'unaccounted capital', which can be described as the knowledge-based equity that supports the knowledge-based assets. This is only one side of the story because the knowledge-based equity is only a part of the second element of the balance sheet. Liabilities must also be considered.

Leonard-Barton (1992) argues that firms are faced with the dilemma of both utilizing and maintaining their capabilities. Paradoxically, core capabilities both enable and impede innovation, in the latter case becoming core rigidities. Projects lacking alignment with the four dimensions of a firm's core capability (employee knowledge and skills, technical systems, administrative systems, values and norms) are inhibited. This means that, over time, 'core incompetencies' grow around the firm's core competencies.

2.6 In search of a comprehensive theory of intellectual capital

The development of intellectual capital theory has been guided primarily by the ideas and thoughts of a handful of influential practitioners, including Sveiby (1997) and Edvinsson and Malone (1997). These pioneers established the foundations of the way in which intangible factors determine the success of companies. In the words of Andriessen (2001), the pioneers established the basis of the 'intellectual capital standard theory'. Their respective models – 'Intangible Assets Monitor' (IAM) (Sveiby, 1997) and 'Skandia Navigator' (Edvinsson and Malone, 1997) – are representatives of the assumptions, principles, and foundations of the intellectual capital standard theory.

However, later contributions from other academics and practitioners have developed and refined the standard theory. Today, this theory is the pre-eminent guide to the management of intangible assets, and has facilitated success through sustainable competitive advantage for leading companies and organizations.

2.6.1   Assumptions and principles of the prevailing paradigm

As IC is the key source of wealth creation, it is logical that firms devote particular attention to the effective management of such capital. Therefore, the ability to identify, audit, measure, renew, and increase these intellectual assets is a key factor in the success of companies in the modern environment. In this respect, significant effort has gone into the search for methodologies and models to improve the management of IC, although, it must be said, with mixed success. The main reason for this is the nature of these assets and the fact that each business has its own particular knowledge mix, specific objectives, and market environment. Three authors have been of special significance in this search for useful models of intellectual capital:

- Sveiby (1997), who designed the first intellectual capital model – the 'Intangible Assets Monitor' (IAM);
- (Kaplan and Norton, 1996a, 1996b), who devised the 'Balanced Scorecard' methodology (with respect to effective strategy implementation); and
- Edvinsson (Edvinsson and Malone, 1997), who was the architect of the 'Skandia Navigator' (followed by Ross *et al.* 1997, whose 'Process Model' gave a strategic perspective to the 'Skandia Navigator').

Although these models and methodologies will be discussed in the next chapter, they are briefly mentioned here because they have actually inspired a number of works that nurture and support the basis of the 'intellectual capital standard theory'. Those models mirrored the assumptions, principles and foundations of the prevailing paradigm.

The main assumptions and principles that support the standard theory (or the prevailing paradigm) can be summarized in eight points:

1. the accounting view;
2. the strategy implementation view;
3. breakdown of IC;
4. cause and effect relationships;
5. relatively static approach to value-creation processes;
6. limitation of concept of intellectual capital;
7. use of the same models and methodologies to manage and produce reports; and
8. attempts to treat intangible assets as if they were tangible.

Each of these assumptions is discussed briefly below.

1 The accounting view

Among representative models of the standard theory there are some that try to explain the causes of the difference between the company market value and the company book value. The aim is to establish an intangible assets accounts plan that allows identification of the relevant intangible assets and their later valuation. This points to an accounting perspective on IC. It identifies the company's intangible assets and enters them into the books – complementing the financial balance sheets with another kind of balance sheet (of intangibles).

2 The strategy implementation view

The majority of the representative models corresponding to the standard theory follow a strategy implementation approach. In fact, it is assumed that in the company where the IC model will be applied there is a strategy already formulated in clear and explicit terms. In this case, the IC model takes the strategic formula as given and concentrates on successful strategy implementation through managing intangibles in a systematic and continuous way.

3 Breakdown of intellectual capital

This is a common denominator of all models. Despite the different terminology that they each use, the models presented in the literature all break down IC into its distinct elements. These elements can be summarized as human capital, structural capital, and relational capital. For each of these elements, the company establishes a set of indicators that is used to take account of, assess, and manage each specific type of capital. That is, each type of capital is evaluated independently from the rest in the model's intrinsic processes. At the same time, the set of indicators is linked with the strategic objectives through the key success factors. Using the tree metaphor it is possible to visualize the links among the three constructs – human capital, structural capital and relational capital – the roots (hidden values) of the tree (see Figure 2.13).

However, the actual daily operations of firms show that this division is artificial because in the value-creation processes all three types of IC act together and such a division never arises. Furthermore, physical and financial assets act together with the intangible assets in the value-creation processes. These are all entwined resources or assets and are not separated.

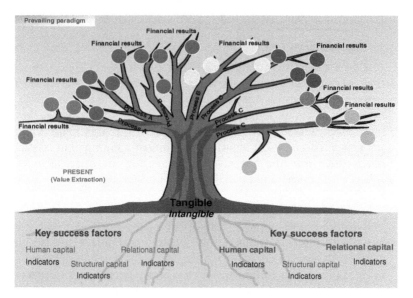

Figure 2.13   Company value creation tree – Prevailing paradigm

4   *Cause and effect relationships*

The models mentioned above examine cause and effect relationships between each of the three types of capital (human, structural, and relational) and each of the objectives (strategic and financial). These are extremely difficult to establish – due mainly to the artificial division of the model's intangible assets. In the value-creation processes, the human assets act together with the structural and relational assets, making it difficult for directors and managers to determine such cause and effect relationships. In addition, beyond the cause and effect relationships there also exist complementary relationships.

5   *Relatively static approach to value-creation processes*

The artificial categorization of IC lacks a consideration of how firms actually deploy their resources through their organizational core activities. Because of this, a great number of IC models (as we will see in the next chapter) fall short in explaining how firms effectively compete, and how they recreate the sustainable competitive advantages that give rise to value creation.

Indeed, the most common reason for failure in firms today is inadequate strategy implementation – which actually demands paying close attention to what the firm *does* (rather than what it *has*). In short, the prevailing paradigm lacks an activity-based view.

6   Limitation of concept of intellectual capital

Existing models limit discussion of IC to ideas about the means of production, and do not take proper account of other non-intellectual intangibles – such as values, organizational culture, and so on. Mostly, IC models consider intangible assets as being mainly intellectual assets or knowledge assets. However, other intangible assets (such as values, attitudes, organizational culture, talent, and employee commitment) also exist. As Hofsted (1991) demonstrates, the *values* of the organization's founders become the *practices* of the employee, and are embedded in the organization's collective attitude.

We argue that even if these other affective assets cannot be labelled as 'intellectual', they are of great importance to the success of companies and organizations. However, because the emphasis is on *intellectual* assets, other relevant intangible assets are neglected.

7   Use of the same models and methodologies to manage intangibles and produce external reports

The models above are too often identified with the reports of intangible assets that they generate – reports that supplement the balance sheets of the company's tangible assets. Usually, the same models and methodologies that are used to prepare such external reports of intangible assets are also used to *manage* the same intangibles, even though the requirements of management are quite different from those of preparing an external report. One exception is the 'Balanced Scorecard', which *was* conceived specifically as a management tool. Moreover, the end users of intangibles reports are shareholders, suppliers, financial institutions, and so on – that is, external stakeholders in general. In contrast, the end users of management models and methodologies are the organization's internal managers.

8   Attempts to treat intangible assets as if they were tangible

The use of the term 'intangible *assets*' is dangerous in that it induces people to think of 'intangibles' as assets that can be entered in the books as if they were tangibles, using the extended double entry accounting system.

Several efforts have been made to assimilate intangible assets with tangible assets. For example, there have been attempts to establish a sort of general accounting plan in line with traditional accounting methods – including the utilization of universal indicators that might serve to address almost any situation. The most comprehensive list of such indicators is the 'Universal Intellectual Capital Report' of Edvinsson and Malone (1997). These authors attempted to apply to intangible assets procedures similar to those that have been universally applied to tangible assets – with the aim of generating balance sheets and earnings statements that could be used to make comparisons in any type of company, no matter its nature. Caddy (2000) followed a similar approach in his attempt to discover and assess not only intangible *assets* but also intangible *liabilities*.

2.6.2   Assumptions and principles of the new paradigm

Viedma (2003a) developed the main assumptions and principles that support the new intellectual capital theory (or the new paradigm), which can be summarized in seven points:

1. the complete strategic view (strategy formulation as well as strategy implementation);
2. not breaking down intellectual capital into its constituent parts;
3. core competencies as the only intangible assets to manage;
4. reality and dynamism in the value-creation processes;
5. breaking down core competencies into their constituent intangible assets;
6. core competencies linked with core capabilities of professionals who work independently or in teams; and
7. evaluation and assessment of the value-creation potential of future core competencies.

Each of these assumptions is discussed below.

1   The complete strategic view

The models of this new paradigm (as described in the next chapters) support decision- making, both in the process of strategy implementation and in the key process of strategy formulation. According to this approach, it is not important to determine and appraise every intangible asset because only a few are relevant to a firm's strategy formulation and implementation. These few relevant intangible assets are usually grouped according to the firm's core competencies or core capabilities, which are the true IC and are therefore the key variables to manage.

The theoretical background to the significance of core competencies is grounded in resources and capabilities theory (Barney, 1991; Grant,

1991, 1998; Teece *et al.*, 1997). In short, this view focuses on the fact that in turbulent and changing environments, competitive sustainable advantages are due mainly to resources and capabilities – in particular, the core competencies or capabilities that Andriessen (2001) describes in terms of a 'coordinated bundle' of intangible assets that constitute the roots of the firm's competitive sustainable advantage.

2 Not breaking down intellectual capital into its constituent parts

The new theory – freed from production of annual reports and statements, and accounting principles and rules conditionings – focuses on a strategic view in achieving the firm's mission and objectives and in surpassing its 'best in class' competitors. Thus, the artificial division of IC into human, structural, and relational capital is of little use because the products and services that result from a specific strategy have no relationship at all with these three types of capital considered independently. Rather, those products and services are the result of an integrated bundle of assets reflected in core competencies and capabilities (Figure 2.14). As entwined networks of resources exist in the form of competencies, and work in connection with each other, they cannot be seen as being distinct.

3 Core competencies as the only intangible assets to manage

From the above discussion, it can be concluded that for each business unit in the operations value chain, and for each project in the innovation value chain, the only assets to manage are those grouped in the core competencies. A firm's specific core competencies are not usually very numerous. Moreover, because a relationship between products and services and the core competencies that enable them is easily established, an appraisal of core competencies can be made by estimating the expected returns from the products in which they participate.

4 Reality and dynamism in the value-creation processes

One of the main issues that has always been at the core of strategy theory is how firms compete in their industries or, more broadly, in the global markets. This raises another question, 'How do firms create and exploit value?' This leads to an examination of what is deemed to be the essence of the entrepreneurial success – good strategy formulation and implementation. Seeking answers to these sorts of questions leads back to both the resource-based view and the activity-based view (because implementation is mainly about activities) to try to explain how firms deploy resources in order to create sustainable competitive advantages and achieve superior performance.

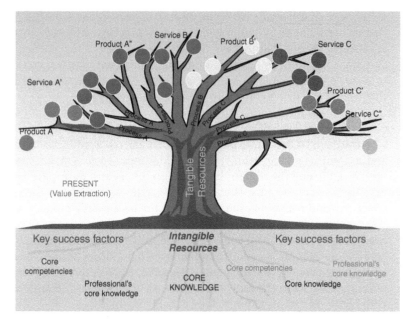

Figure 2.14   Company value creation tree – New paradigm
Source: Viedma (2004a: 42).

From a knowledge perspective, this is possible only with IC models that focus on a firm's core competencies. Such models allow consideration not only of which intangible resources are crucial to achieving success, but also which core activities must be acted upon (if it is accepted that value creation and exploitation are both intrinsically resource-oriented and activity-oriented). As Haanes and Fjeldstad (2000) have observed, it is not only what the firm *has*, but what the firm *does*, that matters in value creation.

The concept of sustainable competitive advantages, which underlies the processes of value creation and exploitation, presupposes a certain dynamism that is extremely difficult to capture if attention is paid only to resources, and if an assessment tool based on a false division of IC into three artificial categories is used in the analysis. As Man *et al.* (2002:128) have stated, '... the dynamic nature [of the concept of competitiveness] involves the dynamic transformation of competitive potentials through the competitive process into outcomes'. Both resources (tangible and intangible) and activities exist in *competitive* and *non-competitive* processes, and this makes it impossible to appraise the firm's intangible forces if only a resource-based view is taken – a view that requires the creation of *competitive* advantages for attaining superior performance and market value, but fails to take adequate consideration of the *non-competitive* processes.

5   Breaking down core competencies into their constituent intangible assets

Once the principle that core competencies constitute the firm's authentic IC has been accepted, the improvement, strengthening, and enrichment of the intangibles 'bundle' is enhanced if they are broken down into their constituent parts. This should be undertaken in a broader sense, including not only intangibles that are intellectually based but also intangibles that are affective in origin.

6   Core competencies linked with core capabilities of professionals who work independently or in teams

Core competencies are the result of aggregating intangible assets of different types. But each asset is made up of knowledge and skills, and skills are always generated by human beings – working either independently or in teams. Thus, core-competencies management is essentially dependent upon the effective management of the core competencies of professionals who work either individually or in coordinated teams.

7   Evaluation and assessment of the value-creation potential of future core competencies

Finally, the strong relationship between future products and services and the competencies that support them allows an assessment of the future potential of each core competency or core capability. As we will see in the next chapter, Andriessen (2001) suggested in his model – the 'Value Explorer' – appraising the strength of each core competency by means of the following four criteria: (i) value-added to customers; (ii) future potential; (iii) sustainability; and (iv) robustness.

2.6.3   Other new views and contributions

It is now important to synthesize both of these theoretical approaches with other new views and contributions. The new views and contributions considered in this context are:

1. the essential role of commitment and action;
2. intellectual capital as the difference between intangible assets and intangible liabilities;
3. intellectual capital as a dynamic concept;

4. intellectual capital identified with the concept of a 'business recipe' in action;
5. benchmarking as a strategic tool.

Each contribution is discussed below.

1   The essential role of commitment and action

Commitment and action have an essential role in the process of wealth or IC creation. Firm competencies are the ultimate creators of intellectual wealth or intellectual capital. As such, they are a necessary but not sufficient condition for wealth creation. However, firm competencies must be established with the incorporation of certain personality characteristics and attitudes that reflect a strong commitment to convert competencies into competitive and profitable products and services. This positive emotionality embedded in the concept of commitment, together with an appropriate bundle of competencies, is what ultimately accounts for differences in human and organizational behaviour. Commitment is the 'copper wire' that leads human competencies through to superior organizational performance. It is the element that enables these competencies, purposefully aligned with the firm's strategy and objectives, to find their way to market considerations.

Furthermore, commitment accounts for the sustainability of the firm's competitive advantages. The challenge of consistently delivering superior performance requires extraordinary effort and sustained commitment on the part of the key people in an organization. The demands for innovation that the KE has exerted on firms has in turn, emphasized *talent* as the main value-driver of capital creation (both wealth and intellectual capital). Given that talent is acknowledged as a key source of competitive advantage, the ability of a firm to manage this intangible also becomes a core competence that adds to the firm's value. In such an environment, *commitment* needs to be managed as well as *competencies* (Mayo, 2001; Gubman, 1998).

This view of commitment and action draws upon Jericó's (2001) conceptualization of talent as being the result of:

competencies × commitment × action

It also draws upon Ulrich's (1998) definition of IC as being:

competencies × commitment

This view is also in accordance with the work of Man *et al.* (2002) and Mayo (2001), whose contributions emphasize that competencies alone cannot deliver superior performance in isolation from a more complex bundle of human capabilities (including personal values and attitudes).

It is therefore apparent that IC theory needs to develop new ways of systematically including *commitment* in its appraisals. It has long been recognized by theorists in organizational behaviour that commitment is a basic driver of a firm's performance, and its explicative power has been clearly demonstrated in entrepreneurship research (Beattie, 1999; Hood and Young, 1993). In particular, the concept of 'utility', as adopted in the economic views of entrepreneurship theory (Douglas and Shepherd, 2000), is important in this. Perhaps what is missing is an integration of entrepreneurial and strategic thinking.

2   Intellectual capital as the difference between intangible assets and intangible liabilities

Practically all models (both those of the prevailing theory and those of the new paradigm) make reference only to intangible *assets*. Caddy (2000) was the first to consider the existence of both intangible assets *and* liabilities in organizations. Whereas intangible assets are oriented toward wealth creation, intangible liabilities are oriented toward its destruction.

The systematic application of the available IC measurement tools should provide hints as to what is going wrong in a given organization, and should thus point to the presence of certain flaws (or intellectual liabilities) that are undermining the firm's potential for intellectual value creation. According to Powell (2001), any assessment of a sustainable competitive advantage should consider competitive advantages and competitive disadvantages simultaneously.

It is apparent that IC should be defined as the difference between intangible assets and intangible liabilities, in such a way that positive and negative drivers of value creation are both considered – thus allowing effective IC management. Given that managing intangible assets is a difficult task, identifying and measuring intangible liabilities would appear to be an even more difficult task. However, IC theory is mature enough to undertake this exercise.

3   Intellectual capital as a dynamic concept

Most models approach IC in terms of a static concept only, without reference to how intangible categories create and destroy wealth. They fail to consider wealth creation and destruction as taking place through virtuous circles (Knight, 1999) and vicious circles.

A virtuous circle can be said to be in place when there is a good alignment between the personal and professional objectives of key people and those of the organization, thus leading to an environment of creativity and a positive approach to life. In contrast, vicious circles reflect a misalignment of the objectives of employees and those of the organization. It is possible to identify and manage these circles only through a *dynamic* approach to intellectual capital assets and liabilities. This identification of virtuous and vicious circles must be combined with the identification of intellectual assets and liabilities (as noted above).

Vicious circles and virtuous ones can take a long time to become apparent and, once they are identified, it can take time for an organization to influence their effects. This is significant in a competitive global environment. Once the market starts giving signals of a misfit between its value parameters and the firm's value offer, time for adjustment can be very short. The presence of strong competition, together with the time required to adjust internal vicious circles and intellectual liabilities, can mean that firms are simply unable to adjust in a timely fashion.

All of this emphasizes the need to include activity-based views (ABVs) within the new general theory of IC.

4   Intellectual capital identified with the concept of 'business recipe' in action

Core knowledge and core competencies are brought to bear in creating value through a successful business recipe. The difference between a successful business *formula* and a successful business *recipe* is the same as that between a successfully *formulated* strategy and a successfully *implemented* strategy. Superior performance that ends in value creation is a natural consequence of a firm's success in bringing a superior business formula *to the market.*

This emphasis on *implementation* is thus significant for any new general theory of IC – especially in light of the comments already made (above) about the importance of activity-based views in identifying intellectual liabilities and vicious circles.

5   Benchmarking as a strategic tool

Recognizing the importance of *benchmarking* as a strategic tool allows early identification of virtuous and vicious circles and facilitates the management of IC in accordance with the new views and contributions outlined thus far. The only IC measurement tools that introduce benchmarking techniques in their appraisals are those of the Operation Intellectual Capital Benchmarking System (OICBS) (Viedma 2003b), the Innovation Intellectual Capital Benchmarking System (IICBS) (Viedma, 2003c), and the Social Capital Benchmarking System (SCBS) (Viedma, 2004b), all developed in Chapters 5, 6 and 7 respectively. The objective of the OICBS and the IICBS is to determine whether the firm possesses superior core competencies in relation to the world's best competitor, whilst the SCBS, complementing the IICBS and the OICBS, determines amongst alternative clusters the best location to develop the specific network organization that each particular business model requires. These management and measurement tools can be used to account for sustainable competitive advantages that might lead to superior performance and wealth creation.

In terms of assessing world competitiveness, OICBS and IICBS benchmark a firm's business recipe against that of its world's best competitor. A firm will be able to create value in the long run as long as its business recipe has proven to be superior to the world's best. A detailed and thorough process of benchmarking will enable the identification of superiority (or inferiority) – signalling the presence of virtuous (or vicious) circles that will have to be subsequently managed.

Markets are changing with increasing rapidity, making it very difficult for firms to keep track of the innovations and performance of competitors. In this context, strategic benchmarking, if applied systematically, becomes an effective and efficient tool to track the firm's value-creation processes in creating sustainable competitive advantages. Benchmarking is effective because it focuses on what is strictly relevant to value creation: a superior business recipe and core competencies. It is efficient because it fosters a better assignment of organizational resources as long as the unit of analysis is essentially the firm's business recipe. Although recognizing the difficulties on benchmarking intangibles, we argue that top management team should benchmark the firm's business recipe with the best competitor's business recipe, because it informs key people about how well they have been doing and whether an in-depth analysis is required.

However, a firm's intellectual assets and liabilities, together with its virtuous and vicious circles, remain a matter for the firm's internal management. The effectiveness of management will obviously influence performance – either transforming the firm's business recipe to reach the point of being a superior business recipe that creates value, or never reaching that point and failing to create extra value.

2.6.4   The formulation of a comprehensive theory of intellectual capital

The discussion above raises the main ideas of a general theory of IC, as can be depicted in Figure 2.15.

The general theory of IC proposed rests on the following principles:

1. A firm's success is always the result of both *well-formulated* and *well-implemented* strategies (Grant, 1998).
2. Successful strategy formulation and execution crystallizes into a successful business recipe (SBR) that offers customers competitive and good-quality products and services. Ultimately, an SBR is the market's validation of the firm's competitive quality offer.
3. Strategy formulation and execution are always human tasks. They are in the hands of the top management team (TMT) and the firm's most important technicians and managers – its key professional people (KPP).
4. The TMT and the KPP start from a business formula (that is, a formulated strategy), work through the operations and innovation value chains, and finally settle on an SBR (as an implemented strategy). These activities can be performed in a superior way due to the core knowledge and core competencies of the KPP.

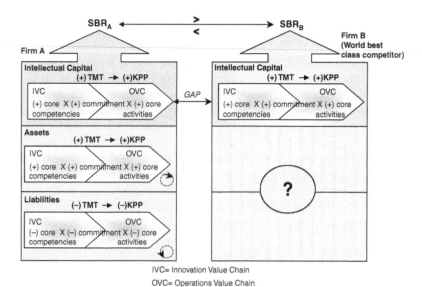

IVC= Innovation Value Chain
OVC= Operations Value Chain

Figure 2.15   Formulating a comprehensive theory of intellectual capital
Source: Viedma (2003a: 223).

5. Apart from the core knowledge and competencies of the TMT and KPP, the process also requires commitment from the TMT and KPP to convert the business formula into an SBR, and thus carry the firm forward to success. Such a commitment fosters a climate of positive attitudes and trust that is essential for knowledge sharing, organizational learning, and value creation. In short, this is an extended version of one of the most relevant principles of leadership effectiveness – that of 'engaging people' (Ulrich *et al.*, 1999).

6. A firm's business recipe can be judged successful (that is, an SBR) only when it has been proven to be clearly superior to those of the best international competitors as a consequence of a complete and detailed process of benchmarking.

7. For analytical purposes, core knowledge and core competencies can be broken down into their constituent parts of human assets, structural assets, and relational assets.

8. The engine of the process leading to an SBR is the core knowledge, core competencies, and strong commitment of the TMT and KPP, who strategically manage value-chain activities in a motivating and knowledge-sharing environment. This is the dynamics of IC creation through virtuous circles. An effective SBR must constantly transform itself to fit the demands of an ever-changing environment.

9. It should not be assumed that the TMT always develops certain activities and actions that are perfectly aligned with the firm's strategy and objectives. Frequently these top managers coexist with others whose professional and personal strategies are not aligned with those of the organization – thus producing vicious circles.

10. The engine of the process leading to wealth destruction (business recipe deterioration) starts in the TMT – in those managers whose personal objectives prevail against the organization's strategic objectives. These managers put their core knowledge, core competencies, and commitment into effect in a way that does not produce value creation. Rather, they foster internal conflict for power, intrigues, and a culture that is negative regarding the firm's requirements for innovation and competitiveness.

11. The above description of virtuous and vicious circles represents two extremes in a continuum of typologies. For a given firm, it is to be expected that several circles of both types might coexist, each of them important to a greater or lesser degree, thus placing the firm into an intermediary position between the two extremes of 'virtuous' and 'vicious'. These configurations evolve through time.

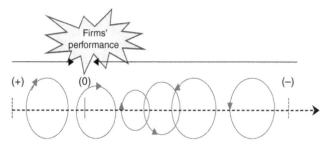

Figure 2.16   The coexistence of virtuous and vicious circles
Source: Viedma (2003a: 224).

They change, expand, and contract – depending on the firm's abilities to manage them effectively. It is worth noting that the negative effects of vicious circle are generally more pervasive than the positive effects of virtuous circles – causing a given firm's performance to shift to the left (thus invading the virtuous positive zone). Figure 2.16 illustrates these ideas.

2.7   Conclusions

One can argue that intellectual assets have existed in organizations from the dawn of civilization. However, to achieve entrepreneurial excellence in this innovation-driven economy, characterized by increasingly global markets and fierce competitiveness based on IC, organizations need to be able to earn economic returns from developing, leveraging and using those intellectual assets.

As change becomes the standard, organizations can no longer find stability in their products and customers. Rather, firms succeed because they are able to develop a range of unique products and services based on a repertoire of unique – or at least difficult to replicate – capabilities and competences. A firm is made up of a number of competencies, based on resources, embodied in a configuration of various forms of capital (financial, human, social), which to a great extent is idiosyncratic to the firm. It is such unique capabilities of firms that provide the basis for profit.

IC, defined as the knowledge and other intangibles that produce or create value (or have the potential to create value in the future), is actually a source of sustainable competitive advantage in the context of KE.

We discuss the concepts of business formula and business recipe as the foundation of a firm's successful strategy. Successful strategy formulation and execution crystallizes into a successful business recipe that offers customers competitive and good-quality products and services. Ultimately, a successful business recipe is the market's validation of the firm's competitive quality offer.

The principles and foundations of the prevailing IC theory have been analysed above, together with those of the alternative new theory. A synthesis of the two and the integration of new views and contributions have enabled us to advance a first comprehensive theory of IC. By conceptualizing IC as the difference between intellectual assets and liabilities, this new general theory attempts to unravel and tackle the fundamentals of the value-creation process in firms. At the core of this analysis is the concept of the management of virtuous and vicious circles and the importance of the personal objectives of top management and key personnel being aligned with the objectives of the organization in a spirit of strong commitment.

The general theory of IC introduces a new concept of the successful business recipe (SBR) to emphasize the importance of successful *implementation* in a context of a *dynamic* understanding of IC.

3
The Practice of Entrepreneurial Excellence in the Knowledge Economy Context

3.1 Introduction

In Chapter 2 it was said that an excellent business is one that achieves growth and extraordinary profits over a long period of time because it has sustainable competitive advantages.

According to the basic principles of strategic management literature, excellence in organizations has always been mainly due to good strategy formulation (business formula) and excellent strategy implementation (business recipe). In the KE context, this fundamental statement is still valid. Nevertheless, in this context, building excellent business formulas and first class business recipes requires the contribution of intangibles as the key building blocks for gaining and sustaining competitive advantage. So, intangibles or IC become the key ingredient to manage in order to achieve entrepreneurial excellence.

The purpose of this chapter is to provide the readers with an overview of the existing models for achieving excellence. It is not our intention to make an exhaustive assessment of all non-financial methodologies that have emerged over the last years. Instead we provide an illustrated description of the state of the art of IC methodologies.

We start with the EFQM and Malcom Baldridge models, which are closely linked to the Total Quality Management (TQM) movement, and then we follow with the more significant IC models. We classify IC models into two groups:

1. The models within the first group focus on strategy formulation;
2. The models within the second group focus on strategy implementation.

The majority of IC models belong to the second group.

This chapter is dedicated to the strategy implementation IC models, leaving the strategy formulation models for Chapter 4. Figure 3.1. sums up the main ideas that have been discussed so far.

3.2 The state of the art of intellectual capital management and reporting

Today, organizations compete on opportunity recognition, innovation cycle time, learning speed, flexibility, responsiveness and quality. Competition is more and more based on how managers think about their business and how they invest their time, their creative energy and their resources. The present and future of organizations is dependent on their hidden values, frequently referred to as IC.

Therefore, firms have to bring their IC to the surface, to care for it, and disseminate it throughout the business. If managers can measure it, they will value it. To care for their IC, managers can benefit from new work being done in the field of IC to measure, manage and communicate the value of these non-financial aspects of their businesses.

Over the past decades many authors have written extensively about the failure of traditional accounting systems to assist managers with the management of their organizations. The recognition of the relevance of

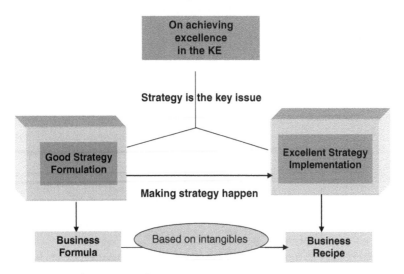

Figure 3.1 Making strategy happen

knowledge in the process of value creation has given rise to a variety of different approaches to the firm's management.

Debate no longer centres on whether or not knowledge assets exist but on their measurement. Perhaps the number of high-profile financial collapses, and the inability of the markets to estimate their worth with safety, have created the urgency needed to focus on the disclosure of non-financial information. At the same time, the internet and e-commerce have changed the business world, urging business to run at internet speed with compressed innovation cycles and real time information about stakeholders, and imparting urgency in adopting new business scenarios to respond to rapid changes. Although recent studies state that companies that measure and report intangibles may experience substantial gains, there is still no consensus about what kind of information should be provided to the market.

3.2.1   Measuring and reporting intellectual capital

Measuring intangibles is nothing new. Management has always been the application of knowledge to knowledge (Drucker, 1993). One of the main problems in understanding the importance of intangibles appears to be that, while there is still a heavy reliance on financial information, there is a general lack of information on intangibles. It is also recognized that the incorporation of information about IC in firm's statements is important in the capital market's assessment of the value of the company, because it affords an opportunity for investors to gain a perspective on these companies' future potential for growth.

Differences between financial accounting and IC measurement rely much more on the perspectives driving the analysis than on the utility of their reports. Table 3.1 illustrates the major differences between financial accounting and the measurement of IC.

Table 3.1   Differences between financial accounting and measurement of IC

Scope	Financial accounting	Measurement of IC
Orientation	Looks backward	Toward the future
Focus	Hard facts (quantities)	Soft facts (qualities)
Dynamics	Outcomes of value creation	Causes of value creation
Reporting perspective	Historic	Predictive
VALUE PERSPECTIVE	REALIZATION OF VALUE	CREATION OF VALUE

These two perspectives are complementary. Perhaps the most important distinction between them is that, whilst the financial accounting perspective reports the realization of value, the IC perspective concerns the creation of value. So, measuring and reporting IC is not meant to be a substitute for the traditional measurement and accounting practices but a supplement. If IC reports were publicized together with the financial reports, stakeholders would have a better foundation and ability to make the right decisions about a company, whether these stakeholders were potential investors, government institutions, banks, customers or potential employees. To some extent, this would close the gap between internal and external information on the company's abilities.

Financial statements will remain an important tool for organizations since they ultimately evidence whether improvements in quality, innovation, training, employee loyalty and customer satisfaction are leading to improved financial performance and value created for stakeholders. However, as we have seen, these metrics are of little help in providing early indications about the business' problems or opportunities. While financial statements provide an excellent review of a firm's past performance, we need to balance this information with the drivers of their future financial performance. It is, then, important to recognize the importance of reporting both predictive and historic information on performance.

3.2.2 Why, what and how to measure intangibles

Generally speaking, IC management and reporting is about the non-physical and the non-financial resources of a company, how they are built and retained, and how they contribute to value creation. Knowledge, competencies, customer relations, brands and other intangibles are the basic factors for identifying and analysing the company's value drivers and key business processes.

A range of questions around measuring intangibles are described in the literature. Figure 3.2 illustrates the most relevant questions in the field

- *Why* managers decide to embark on measuring IC
- *What* aspects should be enhanced, and
- *How* the process ought to be carried forward – that is, obtain people's understanding, trust and commitment, use the influence of culture, other organizational features, and so on.

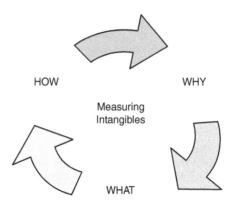

HOW   WHY

Measuring
Intangibles

WHAT

Figure 3.2   Why, what and how to measure intangibles

Why measure?

The reasons behind the decision to measure IC can vary but, ultimately, we can classify them into two groups:

- internal purposes; and
- external purposes.

Internal perspective is concerned with the identification of the firm's intangible components in order to manage them so they can be efficiently applied to create value, whilst external perspective is related to the importance of communicating the real value of an organization to the market.

In this sense, internal measurement of IC is about knowledge management activities, and the external perspective seems to be particularly relevant for accounting purposes, as it allows organizations to place and communicate a value for their intangible assets. As explained by Skyrme (2003), often external reasons (for example, better public image, an increase in market value, reducing the difference between market and book value, additional information for potential investors and the market) outweigh the internal ones (for example, business success, the connection between investments in intangibles and business goals, as well as the necessity of managing them).

Marr *et al.* (2003), conducting a review of over 700 papers, concluded that five main purposes for measuring IC dominate the literature:

a) To help organizations formulate their strategy;
b) To assess strategy execution;

c)   To assist in diversification and expansion decisions;
d)   For use as a basis for compensation; and
e)   To communicate with external stakeholders.

The first three of these purposes relate to internal decision-making: the aim is maximizing performance. When using compensation as the reason to measure IC, concerns are related to the executive incentive scheme. The fifth purpose refers to evidencing motivations for external stakeholders. These disparate motivations have the common goal of managing the firm's resources in such a way as to maximize earnings performance and its value.

One of the most important and widely referenced empirical researches is by DATI – Danish Trade and Industry Development Council's (1998). This study of ten firms identifies three reasons for measuring IC. The first relates to supporting management's strategic direction and to promoting the diffusion of knowledge. The second reason is about upgrading the work of human resources. The third reason for measuring IC is to support or maintain various parties' awareness of the company.

In contradiction, other authors enumerate some disadvantages from the firm's perspective in measuring and reporting IC. According to Van der Meer-Kooistra and Vosselman (2000), the disadvantages of disclosing IC information include cost, confidentiality, subjectivity, lack of standardization, tax, the creation of undue expectations, and increased constraints on management. The literature offers many arguments advocating that the increase of information about intangibles contributes to the reduction of uncertainty, which is reflected in lower risk premium and, thereby, a more accurate valuation of the company.

Summing up, we may say that beneficial effects will derive from measuring and reporting intangibles, both in terms of the effects on external reputation, market valuation and the ability to raise capital, and internally in the esteem that internal stakeholders (staff) will hold the company and its management.

What to measure?

Although knowledge assets and business processes can be of crucial importance to an organization, a misdirected strategy can lead to a poor future. Looking at the processes in an organization, it is possible to see what IC resources can be usefully measured. The resources that are created and the benefits that are generated, in terms of the value they add to the organization, need to be identified so that a judgment can be made on whether they have been good investments. A company should only measure what is strategically important for growth – the things that will guide the company into the future. To do this requires an understanding of how IC resources are transformed from one type to another and then into cash. Therefore, it is of paramount importance that IC measures focus on the way a firm creates value.

Nevertheless, it is accepted that it is very difficult for managers to assess the relative contribution of those IC elements and knowledge management practices to the firm's success. In view of this, O'Dell and Grayson (1998) recommend an approach that aims to measure both outcomes and activities. Measuring outcomes aims to focus on the extent to which a firm achieves its stated objectives. The success of the firm may serve as a proxy measure for the success of its IC management practices. For example, outcomes might be measured in terms of the reduced cost of a process, improved efficiency, the reduction in time taken to do it, the improved quality of delivery, time to market, etc.

Measuring activities, on the other hand, shifts the focus onto the specific IC management practices that were applied. They focus on the specific knowledge management activities behind this practice and on their effects or influences. Some of these measures are quantitative ('hard') measures as, for example, the number and frequency of hits to an intranet site per employee. However these measures represent only a part of the picture, that is, they say nothing about why people are doing what they are doing. To complete the picture, we also need qualitative ('soft') measures, such as by asking people about the attitudes, commitment and behaviours behind their activities.

This perspective is in line with that developed in Chapter 2. To build on an IC system solely focused on indicators 'blocked' into IC components is similar to drawing a corporate strategy with the resource-based view (RBV) as the only theoretical foundation. In fact, what the market values is the outcome or the result of the deployment of these unique resources and capabilities through the firm's specific actions. This means that the activity-based view (ABV) of the firm as a main theoretical approach is an integrated and balanced approach for building an IC management system.

So, answering the question *what to measure* should be led by two key considerations

1. To measure IC requires a focus on the relationships between tangibles and intangibles
2. The choice of indicators depends on the company's strategy.

Finally, given that the whole point of IC management is to improve the performance of the organization and help it to achieve its objectives, the best and most logical approach is to tie the measurement of IC into the firm's overall performance measurement systems.

How to measure?

How does a company identify and measure assets they cannot see? Reporting IC takes into consideration the knowledge management activities, and discloses indicators for IC, based on the managerial activities in the firm. In practice, IC statements contain both financial and non-financial information, as well as a narrative view, where indicators and their interconnectedness, as an integral part of the framework, help to understand the value creation process of the firm.

In general, investors and analysts request more reliable information on, for example, managerial qualities, expertise, integrity, experience, customer relations, personnel creativity and competencies. All these components are related to IC. However, empirical research on the disclosure of IC indicators tends to focus on the value relevance of specific indicators, such as R&D expenses, advertising, patents and brands.

Another important element to consider when implementing IC management systems and reporting is that every company comes with a cultural heritage which contributes to the successful implementation and operation of IC management and practices. There may be a cultural barrier to the understanding and appreciating of information on intellectual resources. According to Johanson (2003), there are four types of problems that inhibit the using of IC information, which are mainly related to the ability of people to understand how knowledge resources are to work in a knowledge society. Those problems are:

- knowledge about how knowledge works;
- uncertainty about the validity of information;
- lack of ownership of intellectual resources, in particular in the area of human capital; and
- lack of insight into problems of implementation.

Such assumptions emphasize the view that measuring IC becomes important when seen in a context. While IC measurement may help to visualize the paths the company can follow to create competencies, it is typically used to link the company with the strategy.

A point to stress is that there is no universal solution. What is valuable for one company may be worthless for another. Hussi and Ahonen (2002) studied nine Finnish companies and found that each company not only puts emphasis on one type of intangibles at a time but also shifts that emphasis to other intangibles over time. This reveals that IC or knowledge-based competition is a highly context-dependent and idiosyncratic phenomenon because, ultimately, it deals with social processes and people's beliefs, values and life experiences. At the same time, if the value of the intellectual resources is context-dependent and the returns increasing, the ability and opportunity to use and transform such resources into others becomes very important, and thus must be considered in any model for reporting on IC.

3.3   Non-strategy focused models

The European Foundation for Quality Management (EFQM) and the Malcolm Baldrige Award are associated with the Total Quality Management (TQM) movement, and both models are linked with quality awards. They are used as practical tools for encouraging organizations to self-assess their progress toward excellence, examining the *softer* dimensions of their performance such as leadership, employees and impact on society.

Both models are based on the concept of excellence, defined as the 'outstanding practice in managing the organization and achieving results'. It is assumed that excellent organizations are those that strive to satisfy their stakeholders by what they achieve, how they achieve it, what they are likely to achieve, and the confidence they have that the results will be sustained in the future. But being 'excellent' requires total leadership commitment and the acceptance of a set of principles – the 'Fundamental Concepts' – on which an organization bases its behaviour, activities and initiatives. When an organization turns them into practice, it opens the way to 'sustainable excellence'.

These models have been largely used by organizations across the world to help them to improve their performance. However, to offer fair comparison and a system of benchmarking to companies, these models must be applied consistently in their structure, criteria, approach and context.

These models adopt an operational view and believe that improving enablers within the business model leads to an improvement in results but they do not consider innovation and substantial transformation of the existing business model because they do not have a strategic perspective.

3.3.1   The EFQM Model

The EFQM Excellence Model was introduced at the beginning of 1992 as the framework for assessing organizations for the European Quality Award. The EFQM Excellence Model is a generic framework for quality management, which can be used as a self-assessment instrument. According to the model principles, quality management should focus on all activities, on all levels in an organization, and should be a continuous process to improve performance, which has to meet expectations and needs of stakeholders. The essence of the model is based on nine dimensions, which are called criteria as shown in Figure 3.3. These nine criteria are grouped in 'enablers' and 'results'. Enablers cover the processes, the structure and the means of an organization. The results criteria refer to the aspects of performance.

The model's nine boxes represent the criteria against which to assess an organization's progress toward excellence. Five of these criteria are 'enablers' and four are 'results'. The 'enabler' criteria cover what an organization does, while the 'results' criteria cover what an organization achieves. 'Results' are caused by 'enablers', and 'enablers' are improved using feedback from 'results'.

Excellent results with respect to performance, people, customers and society are achieved through leadership driving policy and strategy that is delivered through people, partnerships and resources, and processes. The arrows emphasize the dynamic nature of the model. They show innovation and learning helping to improve enablers that in turn lead to improved results. Many IC approaches use similar indicators for customer and employee satisfaction. EFQM is different from most of these in using standard weightings to rate the indicators, and pursuing a concept of quality standards in process and targets.

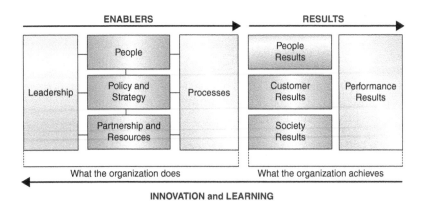

Figure 3.3   The EFQM excellence model

Source: Adapted from the EFQM readings based on http://www.efqm.org/en/

Table 3.2   Fundamental concepts of excellence

Criterion	Excellence definition
Results Orientation	Excellence is achieving results that delight all the organization's stakeholders and, where relevant, exceed them
Customer Focus	Excellence is creating sustainable customer value, by understanding and anticipating their needs and expectations.
Leadership and Constancy of Purpose	Excellence is visionary and inspirational leadership, coupled with constancy of purpose.
Management by Process and Facts	Excellence is managing the organization through a set of interdependent and interrelated systems, processes and facts to create sustained results.
People Development and Involvement	Excellence is maximising the contribution of employees through their development and involvement.
Continuous Learning, Improvement and Innovation	Excellence is generating increased value and improved level of performance through systematic innovation by harnessing the creativity of their stakeholders
Partnership Development	Excellence is developing and maintaining value-adding partnerships.
Corporate Social Responsibility	Excellence is exceeding the minimum regulatory framework in which the organization operates and to strive to understand and respond to the expectations of its stakeholders in society.

Source: Adapted from the EFQM readings based on http://www.efqm.org/en/

The fundamental concepts of excellence in the model are defined in terms of each criterion in Table 3.2, and the interaction of fundamental concepts is presented in Figure 3.4.

3.3.2   The Malcom Baldrige Award

The Malcom Baldrige Award is a practical tool that assists organizations to develop their management systems by measuring whether or not they are improving in the area of excellence. Seven categories make up the award criteria as presented in Table 3.3, providing a holistic diagnosing tool for sustaining business excellence

Figure 3.4   The interaction of fundamental concepts
Source: Adapted from the EFQM readings based on http://www.efqm.org/en/

The Criteria for Performance Excellence have evolved significantly over time to help organizations address a dynamic environment, focus on strategy-driven performance, and address concerns about customer and workforce engagement, governance and ethics, societal responsibilities, and long-term organizational sustainability. The Criteria have continually progressed toward a comprehensive, integrated systems perspective of organizational performance management.

The criteria are built on the following set of inter-related core values and concepts: visionary leadership; customer-driven excellence; organizational and personal learning; valuing employees and partners; agility; focus on the future; managing for innovation; management by fact; social responsibility; focus on results and creating value; and system perspective. These values and concepts are embedded beliefs and behaviours found in high-performing organizations. They are the foundation for integrating key performance and operational requirements within a results-oriented framework.

Figure 3.5 shows how those criteria are connected and integrated. The organizational profile (top of the figure) sets the context in which

Table 3.3   The Malcom Baldrige Award criteria

Categories	Definition	Questions
Leadership	Examines how senior executives guide the organization and how the organization addresses its responsibilities	- How do your senior leaders lead? - How do you govern and fulfill your societal responsibilities?
Strategic Planning	Examines how the organization sets strategic directions to address its strategic challenges and leverage its strategic advantages.	- How do you develop your strategy? - How do you implement your strategy?
Customer and market focus	Examines how the organization determines requirements and expectations of customers and markets; builds relationships with customers; and captures, satisfies, and retains customers.	- How do you obtain information from your customers? - How do you engage customers to serve their needs and build relationships?
Measurement, analysis, and knowledge management	Examine the management, effective use, analysis, and improvement of data and information to support key organization processes and the organization's performance management system.	- How do you measure, analyze, and then improve organizational performance? - How do you manage your information, organizational knowledge, and information technology?
Workforce focus	Examines how the organization enables its workforce to develop its full potential and how the workforce is aligned with the organization's objectives.	- How do you build an effective and supportive workforce environment? - How do you engage your workforce to achieve organizational and personal success?
Operations focus	Examines aspects of how organization designs, manages, and improves its work systems and work processes to deliver customer value and achieve organizational success and sustainability.	- How do you design, manage, and improve your work systems? - How do you design, manage, and improve your key work processes?

(Continued)

Table 3.3 (Continued)

Categories	Definition	Questions
Results	Examine the organization's performance and improvement in its key business areas: customer satisfaction, financial and marketplace performance, human resources, supplier and partner performance, operational performance, and governance and social responsibility. It also examines how the organization performs relative to competitors.	- What are your product performance and process effectiveness results? - What are your customer-focused performance results? - What are your workforce-focused performance results? - What are your senior leadership and governance results? - What are your financial and marketplace performance results?

Source: Adapted from Baldrige Performance Excellence Program. 2011–12 Criteria for performance excellence. [Online] http://www.nist.gov/baldrige/publications/upload/2011_2012_Business_Nonprofit_Criteria.pdf

the organization operates. The system operations are composed of six Baldrige categories in the centre of the figure that define the organization's operations and results. Leadership, strategic planning and market focus represent the leadership triad, whilst workforce focus, process management and results represent the result triad. The leadership triad emphasizes the importance of senior leaders for setting the organizational direction and seeking future opportunities. The organization's workforce and key processes accomplish the work that yields the overall performance results. All actions point toward results that are a composite of products and services, customers and market, financial, and internal operational performance results, including workforce, leadership, governance and social responsibilityresults.

The Malcom Baldrige criteria have been used by thousands of organizations of all kinds for self-assessment and training and as a tool to develop performance and business processes. According to a report by the Conference Board, a majority of large U.S. firms have used the criteria of the Malcolm Baldrige National Quality Award for self-improvement, and the evidence suggests a long-term link between use of the Baldrige criteria and improved business performance.

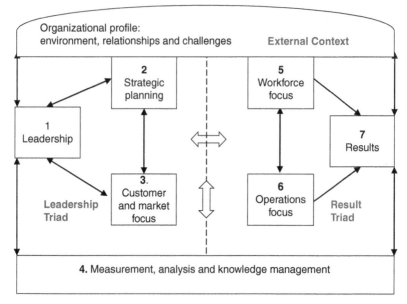

Figure 3.5   Baldrige criteria for performance excellence framework: A system perspective

Source: Adapted from http://www.nist.gov/baldrige/publications/upload/2011_2012_Business_Nonprofit_Criteria.pdf

3.4   Strategy formulation models that do not break down intellectual capital into its constituent parts

Despite the merit of all IC measurement models conceived in the last decade, in the late 1990s some difficulties arose, particularly with SMEs, when trying to put into practice the prevailing IC models and methodologies. This led to the development of new methodologies. Among those are the 'Value Explorer' (Andriessen, 2001), and the 'Intellectual Capital Benchmarking System' (Viedma, 2004), which become especially successful among SMEs. These two models share similar goals and, taken together, propose some new approaches that constitute an alternative theory to the IC standard theory, as demonstrated in Chapter 2.

Two common elements characterize those models:

1. The first is that they are mainly suitable for strategy formulation, while the majority of IC models focus on the strategy implementation;

2. The second is that they do not break down the IC into its constituent parts but instead they manage only core competencies and core capabilities.

3.4.1 The Value Explorer Model

The Value Explorer Model (Andriessen, 2001), inspired on the Prahalad and Hamel's (1990) theory of core competencies, aims to measure the value of a company's intangible assets in terms of their future earning potential. The model does not include all intangible assets but only those that have a key role in the company's strategy formulation and implementation. In this model IC is equivalent to the set of core competencies, or the bundle of intangible assets responsible for building the firm's competitive advantages. Figure 3.6 shows the structure of the model with core competencies at the centre and the major intangible assets within the core competencies, around them. A core competence is then defined as a unique bundle of intangible assets and is conceived in terms of 'the ability to ...'

The success of a firm is the result of the interactions of many assets, some tangibles and others intangibles, often hidden. To identify these hidden assets, the model classifies those core competencies into five components

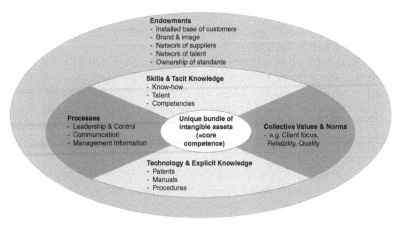

Figure 3.6 The value Explorer Model
Source: Andriessen *et al.* (1999).

- Endowments – include the assets related to the installed base of customers, brand and image, network of suppliers, network of talents and ownership of standards
- Skills and tacit knowledge – comprising know-how, talent and competencies
- Technology and explicit knowledge – representing the knowledge organized in patents, manuals and procedures
- Collective values and norms – consist of a company's norms and procedures, culture, quality and reliability requirements
- Management and operational processes – consisting of processes related to leadership and control, and communication and management information.

The importance of these assets for the success of a company is growing in the context of KE. It is therefore becoming increasingly important to provide more insight into their quality, scale, and potential value to the firm. Management is seen as a 'mirror' that reflects the quality of the company's intangible assets (Andriessen *et al.*, 1999).

The aim is to encourage management to think about the firm's strengths and the strategic options for the future. The Value Explorer method starts by distinguishing between relevant and non-relevant intangible assets. Relevant assets are those that provide substantial added value to the company, and therefore they are of strategic importance. Because intangible assets do not have a separate value but provide added value to the company only in combination with each other, the company has to identify the interrelationships between those intangible assets that are strategically important. The company should then follow the steps defined in Table 3.4.

Andriessen *et al.* (1999) explains how the Value Explorer model works. The first step is to define the intangible assets by determining the company's core competencies. As demonstrated in Figure 3.6, each core competence is a combination of intangible assets (e.g. knowledge and skills, management processes, technology and explicit knowledge, values, and relationships), and is determined by a combination of various techniques.

In the first step the company aims to define its core competencies, each explained in terms of the intangible assets of which they consist of, namely:

- Skills and tacit knowledge
- Collective values and norms

Table 3.4 The Value Explorer method application

Steps	Description
1. Determine the core competencies	Examination of customer needs, analysis of products/services
2. Determine the strength	Development of five tests provides insight into the strength of the competencies
3. Determine the value	Determination of the value of each individual core competence and of all core competencies combined.
4. Monitor progress	Using of a dashboard showing the results of the tests and valuation, and a management agenda with points for attention.

Source: Andriessen *et al.* (1999).

- Technology and explicit knowledge
- Processes
- Endowments such as image, customer relationships, and networks.

The second step is to estimate the strength of each of those core competencies with the aid of a checklist providing a score on a scale from 0–5. The model uses five criteria to determine whether a competence is really a core competence. To accomplish this aim five tests are developed, as described in Table 3.5.

The answers are given on the basis of information gathered, such as annual reports, market analysis, customer satisfaction surveys, and so on.

The third step consists of determining the value of a core competence using the relationship between the strength of a core competence and its value to the company. Because all five factors are essential for the value of a core competence, its total value is determined by multiplying the five indicators by each other:

Value of core competence V_{cc}= Added value × competitiveness × potential × sustainability × robustness

The authors demonstrate that the value of a core competence (V_{cc}) is equal to the added value of the core competence for the customer, given current competitive relationships, the growth that can be expected in the coming years (potential), and the number of years for which it can

Table 3.5   Testing core competence strengths and weaknesses

Criteria	Indicator	Checklist
A core competence must provide a clear benefit for customers;	Added value	Added value test
The firm must be demonstrably better at it than its competitors;	Competitive advantage	Competitiveness test
The competence must offer potential for new products and services in the future;	Potential	Potential test
The competence must be difficult to imitate;	Sustainability	Sustainability test
The competence must be firmly embedded in the company.	Robustness	Robustness test

Source: Andriessen *et al.* (1999).

be exploited (sustainability). This is then corrected by a factor showing whether there is a risk that the company will lose the core competence prematurely (robustness).

Considering that a core competence itself is not saleable in the market, how can we evaluate those five indicators? The authors suggest that we consider the products or services that can be realized thanks to the core competence in order to determine the gross profit. The gross profit of these products can be divided as a function of the underlying core competencies (see Figure 3.7). The added value factor and the competitiveness factor of a core competence are demonstrated by calculating the gross profit of the products to which the core competence contributes.

Finally, the fourth step consists of monitoring progress. For managing a core competence two tools can be used: a dashboard showing the results of the tests and valuation, and a management agenda with points for attention.

The results of the checklists give indications of why the strength of each core competence is high or low and allow management quickly see the reasons and the areas on which it should focus.

This model was developed in collaboration with the consultant company KPMG and according to the authors this method appears to be best suited for SMEs. For large companies this approach seems more complex because often they have a large range of activities and the wider the

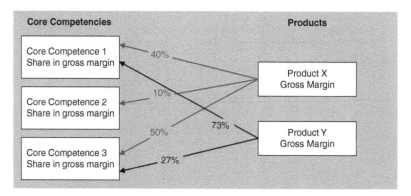

Figure 3.7   Products and underlying core competencies
Source: Adapted from the work of Andriessen et al. (1999).

range, the larger the number of different core competencies. However, the method can be applied to individual business units of large companies, providing that individual core competencies can be distinguished for these units.

Finally, the authors argue that the method should be applicated to firms with some history. It must be a firm with core competencies and one or more products for which a gross profit can be determined. This means that the method is not suitable for new businesses.

3.4.2   Intellectual Capital Benchmarking System

Developed by Viedma at the Technical University of Catalonia, the Intellectual Capital Benchmarking System (ICBS) has a strategic view based on managing core competencies – as does the 'Value Explorer'. Sustainable competitive advantages are mainly due to the company resources and capabilities or, being more specific, to the core capabilities that are in practice, equivalent to the core competencies or to IC, as shown in Figure 3.8.

Core competencies form the basis of a firm's strategy, which should be compared with those of 'best in the class' competitors in the same business activity. If our company (A), for example, is operating in the fast food sandwich industry and we consider McDonald's as the international 'best in class' company (B), the relevant core competencies or core capabilities, or IC of McDonald's will be the model's constituents to benchmark. In this case, our firm should benchmark the McDonald's core competencies.

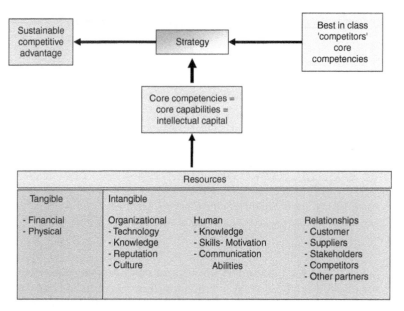

Figure 3.8   Firm's resources and capabilities
Source: Viedma (2004).

Nevertheless, there is a substantial difference between ICBS and the rest of the IC models. ICBS focuses mainly on strategy formulation whereas the other IC models essentially consider strategy implementation.

Two important characteristics distinguish the ICBS model

1. The first is that the model considers that sustainable competitive advantage is based both on what the firm *has* (resource-based view) and on what the firm *does* with what it has (activity-based view). The prevailing paradigm – included the majority of IC models – lacks an activity-based view, or company's ability to create and use its core capabilities.
2. The second is that the ICBS model focuses on the value chain activities of both the operations and innovation processes.

The ICBS is both a new management method and a new management tool that allows companies to benchmark their core innovation and operational capacities against the world-class competitors in their sector. It is a framework built around the key factors and criteria that determine competitiveness in the context of global markets. It identifies the specific competitiveness factors which are relevant in a given business sector, and audits and benchmarks the core capabilities or key IC that the company needs to develop to reach its future goals and successfully compete with 'best in class' competitors.

We further discuss these models and methodologies in Chapter 4 as tools that support the new theory of IC.

3.5   Strategy implementation models which break intellectual capital down into its constituent parts

Attempts at universally classifying and valuing IC have raises serious problems because knowledge is context-dependent and intangibles are dynamic rather than tangible assets. As already mentioned, IC is commonly regarded as having three components: human capital; structural capital; and relational capital. There are a number of key models for measuring the value of IC. In this section we describe some of the best known.

3.5.1   Classification of strategy implementation models

A great number of systems focusing on non-financial measures have been devised to help managers measure business performance. Basically, they fall into two categories

1. *Measurement methods*, which give managers more insight into their company's intangible resources. Measuring IC is based on defining components or categories of intangible assets. Each component is measured using both quantitative (for example, market share or number of skilled employees) and qualitative (for example, competence of employees) indicators
2. *Valuation methods*, which attempt to place a value in monetary terms on the intangibles within a company. This perspective evaluates IC using financial ratios (e.g. return on assets, return on equity) or market capitalization ratios as providing insights into the progress of an organization's IC.

Sveiby (http://www.sveiby.com/articles/IntangibleMethods.htm) provides a structured approach of more relevant methods, as presented in Table 3.6. The methods are categorized into five groups based on the method of evaluation. These are: Direct Intellectual Capital (DIC) methods; Market Capitalization (MC) methods; Return on Assets (ROA)

Table 3.6 Methods for measuring intangibles

Market Capitalisation Methods	Scorecard Methods
• The Invisible Balance Sheet • Market-to-Book Value • Investor assigned market value (IAMV™) • Tobin's q • Calculated Intangible Value Financial	• ICU Report • Regional Intellectual Capital Index (RICI) • IAbM • SICAP • National Intellectual Capital Index • Topplinjen/Business IQ • Public Sector IC • IC-dVAL™ • Intellectus Model • IC Rating™ • Value Chain Scoreboard ™ • Meritum Guidelines • Intangible Assets Statement • Knowledge Audit Cycle • Value Creation Index (VCI) • IC Index™ • Holistic Accounts • Skandia Navigator™ • Intangible Asset Monitor (IAM) • Balanced Scorecard • German Guideline – ICS Made in Germany* • Holistic Value Approach (HVA)* • Intellectual Capital Benchmarking Systems (ICBS) * • Measuring and Accounting IC (MAGIC)* • InCaS*
Return on Assets Methods	**Direct Intellectual Capital Methods**
• Economic Value Added (EVA™) • Value Added Intellectual Coefficient • (VAIC™) • Calculated Intangible Value (CIV) • Knowledge Capital Earnings	• EVVICAE™ • Dynamic Monetary Model • The Value Explorer™ • Intellectual Asset Valuation • Total Value Creation (TVC™) • Inclusive Value Management (IVM™) • Accounting for the future (AFTF) • Technology Broker (IC Audit) • Citation-Weighted Patents • HR statement • Human Resource Costing & Accounting (HRCA) • Inclusive Value Management (IVM™) • Financial Method of Intangible Assets Measuring (FiMIAM) –DIC/MCM

* Methods were added to the original Sveiby's list from other sources.
Source: Adapted from http://www.sveiby.com/articles/IntangibleMethods.htm

methods; and Scorecard (SC) methods, to which Pike and Roos (2004a) add what they call Proper Measurement Systems (MS).

1. *Direct Intellectual Capital Methods* (DIC) estimate the monetary value of intangible assets by identifying their various components. Once these components are identified, they can be directly evaluated, either individually or as an aggregated coefficient.
2. *Market Capitalization Methods* (MCM) calculate the difference between a company's market capitalization and its stockholders' equity as the value of its IC or intangible assets.
3. *Return on Assets Methods* (ROA) are used to compare the relative ROA of different companies. Average pre-tax earnings of a company are divided by the average tangible assets of the company. The result is a company ROA which is then compared with its industry average. The difference is multiplied by the company's average tangible assets to calculate an average annual earnings from the intangibles. Dividing the above-average earnings by the company's average cost of capital or an interest rate, one can derive an estimate of the value of its intangible assets or IC.
4. *Scorecard Methods* (SC). Various components of intangible assets or IC are identified and indicators and indices are generated and reported in scorecards or as graphs. SC methods are similar to DIC methods, except that no estimate is made of the monetary value of the intangible assets. A composite index may or may not be produced.
5. *Proper Measurement Systems* (PMS). Everything of value in or about the company is broken down into attributes which can be measured. These are built into a measurement system, usually a conjoint hierarchy, and real data is used to produce reliable calculations of value. These can be combined with financial data to provide value for money and related outputs. Examples of these are the Holistic Value Approach (HVA) and the Inclusive Value Measurement (IVM™).

The literature describes various advantages and disadvantages associated with each major group. The MCM and ROA methodologies tend to be based on industry comparisons rather than the company itself and many of the MCM approaches view IC as a separable entity from book value. Whilst DIC and SC measures provide a more comprehensive perception of a firm's IC performance than that of financial metric MC and ROA approaches (Sveiby, 2004). They are aimed at management support and DIC is intended to be holistic. Pike and Roos (2004a) argue that DIC and SC methods are more detailed and can be easily applied at any level of an organization.

Van den Berg (2005) provides a different perspective on the way to classify IC models. He classifies them according to temporal orientation, system dynamics, and causal direction characteristics (see Table 3.7). Through this categorization, the author emphasizes three of the most relevant aspects that an IC model ought to conform to. The first is to evaluate to what extent it supports future-oriented managerial decisions, that is, those concerned with improving the firm's innovation potential and competitiveness. The second aspect refers to its systemic and dynamic view. The third aspect concerns the ability to establish cause and effect relationships that allow the firm easily to identify the true causes of its strengths and weaknesses.

Under *temporal orientation*, Van de Berg (2005) distinguishes the models that provide a historic report of performance from those that mostly include measurements designed to manage future firm performance. Future-oriented measurements are preferred over historic reports because they provide information that can be incorporated into decision-making, while the historic reports confine management to a retrospective assessment.

For *system dynamics*, each model is examined to determine whether it has a stock or resource focus versus a flow or process focus. Both stocks or balance sheet amounts, and flows affecting stocks are important to the management of a firm. Most organizations focus primarily or almost exclusively on the stocks or resources because they are easier to measure than flows. However, managers must also focus on measuring the transformation process or flow, which is more complicated but also more useful. As Van de Berg (2005) rightly states, the measurement of growth, or the rate of change of a flow, could also be important to the management of a firm.

For *causal direction* models the classification is based on whether it has a causal focus or value-creating direction, versus an effect or valuation focus. It is important to know both the cause and the financial and economic outcome of management decisions affecting IC, linking a given effect to various causes.

3.5.2   Intangible assets measuring models

In recent years, a number of models have been proposed to measure intangible assets. IC models are tools that management can use to develop and monitor how the company uses its competencies, resources and capabilities to create value. As IC management is forward-looking and has a strategic purpose, the models will further the long-term goals

Table 3.7   Intellectual Capital models classification

Models	Temporal orientation		Systems dynamics		Causal direction	
	Historic	Future	Stock	Flow	Cause	Effect
Economic Value Added (EVA™)	✓		✓			
Market Value Added (MVA)	✓		✓			
Tobin's Q	✓		✓			
Balanced Scorecard (BSC)	✓		Both	Both	No evidence	✓
IC Navigator	✓		Mostly	Few included	No evidence	✓
IC-Index	✓		Mostly	Few included	No evidence	✓
IC Audit	✓		Mostly	Few included	No evidence	✓
Intangibles Asset Monitor (IAM)	✓		Mostly	Few included	No evidence	✓
Real options		✓	Both	Both		
Citation-weighted Patents (CWP)	✓		✓		✓	
Holistic Value Approach (HVA)	✓		Both	Both	✓	✓
Meritum Guideline*	✓		Both	Both	✓	✓
Danish Guideline*	✓		Both	Both	✓	✓
German Guideline*	✓		Both	Both	✓	✓
Holistic Value Approach (HVA)*	✓		Both	Both	✓	✓
IC Benchmarking System (ICBS) *	✓		Both	Both	✓	✓
IC Dynamic Value*	✓		Mostly	Few included	No evidence	✓

(Continued)

Table 3.7   (Continued)

Models	Temporal orientation		Systems dynamics		Causal direction	
	Historic	Future	Stock	Flow	Cause	Effect
Value Explorer*	✓		Mostly	Few included	✓	✓
InCaS*	✓		Mostly	Few included	No evidence	✓

* Methods that were added to the original van den Berg's (2005) source.
Source: Adapted from Van den Berg (2005).

of the company. The Nordic Industrial Fund (2003) lists some common features of the IC models:

(i) strategic, forward-looking and furthering long term goals;
(ii) management tool to develop, communicate and monitor how the company's knowledge resources create value;
(iii) give a structured picture of the competencies available to the company;
(iv) focus on competitiveness and how knowledge contributes to business performance;
(v) value is created in the relations between employees, the organization, the customers and other external partners.

An overview of some international, advanced models is given below. In some aspects they differ, in others they overlap.

Economic Value Added (EVA^{TM})

Introduced by Stern Stewart, Economic Value Added (EVA^{TM}) is a tool to assist managers to pursue their prime financial objective by aiding in maximizing the wealth of its shareholders. The EVA^{TM} method of value measurement has its basis in traditional accounting. As defined by Stewart, EVA^{TM} is the difference between a company's net operating income after taxes and its cost of capital of both equity and debt:

$$EVA^{TM} = \text{Net sales} - \text{operating expenses} - \text{taxes} - \text{capital charge}$$

In summary, the goal in calculating EVA^{TM} is to arrive at earnings that are close to cash and compare this return to a capital base that is also expressed in cash equivalent terms.

Even though the increase in EVA^{TM} may result from the effective management of intellectual assets, it does not explicitly refer to the management of intangible resources.

Market Value Added (MVA)

Market Value Added (MVA), like EVA^{TM} also has its origins in the concept of economic profit. MVA is the difference between the market value of a company (both equity and debt) and capital that lenders and shareholders have entrusted to it over the years in the form of loans, retained earnings and paid-in-capital. Thus, MVA is a measure of the difference between 'cash in' (what is invested by the investors) and 'cash out' (what they could get by selling at today's price). If MVA is positive, the company has created wealth for the shareholders. If MVA is negative, the company has destroyed wealth.

$$MVA = \text{Market Value of Debt} + \text{Market Value of Equity} - \text{Total Adjusted Capital}$$

The total outstanding debt of a company multiplied by the market value of that debt is the market value of a company's debt. The total outstanding number of shares multiplied by the share price is the market value of a company's equity. Total adjusted capital is the balance sheet total adjusted for the accounting principles.

Calculated Intangible Value (CIV)

Developed by Stewart, CIV is a general approach to measuring the intangible value of a company. It is calculated by determining the difference between the company's value and the value of its tangible assets.

The company's value is determined by the book value of the company's assets and the discounted cash-flow of residual operating income, whilst the value of its tangible assets represents the book value of these assets and the discounted cash-flow of residual earnings using the average industrial rate of return. This difference characterizes the company's capability in using the intangible assets in order to 'outrun' competitors in the industry.

Human Resource Costing and Accounting Model (HRCA)

Human Resource Costing and Accounting (HRCA) comprises Human Resource Accounting (HRA) and the costing of human resources.

The literature has several studies about how to evaluate human assets. The objective of HRA is to quantify the economic value of people to an organization (Sackmann *et al.*, 1989) in order to provide information for managerial and financial decisions.

In their simplest forms, HRA models attempt to calculate the contribution of human assets to the firms by capitalizing salary expenditures. However, all these models tend to be subjective and uncertain and thus lack reliability, as their measures cannot be verified with any assurance.

Based on the literature, Johanson and Nilson (1996) state three goals of HRCA models

- An ambition to improve the management of human resources from an organizational perspective by increasing the transparency of human resource costs, investments and outcomes in the management accounting reports, such as profit and loss accounts, balance sheets and investment calculations
- Attempts to improve the basis of valuing a company for investors, also increasing transparency
- Aspirations from human resource specialists to use monetary arguments when suggesting investments in human resources (internal perspective).

The Balanced Scorecard (BSC)

The Balanced Scorecard (BSC) is the world's most popular and widely used model for strategy implementation. The web sites – Balanced Scorecard Collaborative, Inc (*http://company.monster.com/tbsc/*) and Palladium Group, Inc (*http://www.palladiumes.com/redirect.html*) – have facilitated the worldwide awareness, use, enhancement, and integrity of the Balanced Scorecard as a value added management process.

The BSC has evolved from performance measurement (Kaplan and Norton, 1992) through strategy implementation (Kaplan and Norton, 1996) to strategy management (Kaplan and Norton, 2001), and more recently to a framework to manage the readiness of intangibles (Kaplan and Norton, 2004). The BSC has generated a large and growing literature and is now widely diffused in business and also to some degree in public management (Brignall and Modell, 2000; Kloot and Martin, 2000).

The BSC is a management model which is used to translate an organization's mission and strategy into a comprehensive set of performance measures that provide the framework for a strategic measurement and management system. The components of an effective BSC are the organization's mission, core values, vision, and strategy, as illustrated in Figure 3.9.

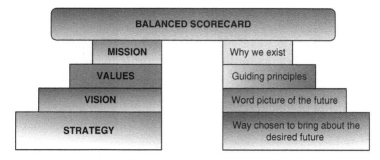

Figure 3.9   The components of an effective Balanced Scorecard
Source: Adapted from Niven (2006).

The mission defines the core purpose of the firm – why it exists. Values are the deeply held beliefs within the organization. The vision represents a word picture of what a firm ultimately intends to become. The vision statement balances the interest of multiple stakeholders in describing how the firm will create future value.

To make strategy happen firms have to mobilize their members' attention and action towards the drivers of value.

The BSC method as a strategic approach and performance management system enables organizations to translate a company's vision and strategy into implementation, working from four perspectives

- From the *financial perspective*, managers include traditional accounting measures yet use selectively chosen measures designed to fit the different parts of the company and their Strategic Business Units (SBUs)
- From the *customer perspective*, managers identify the customer and market segments in which the SBU will compete and the measures of the business unit's performance in these targeted segments. The customer perspective typically includes several generic measures of successful outcomes, such as customer satisfaction, customer retention, new customer acquisition, customer profitability, and market share
- From the *internal business process perspective*, managers identify the critical internal processes in which the organization must excel. Metrics provide insight to managers on how efficiently and effectively the business is performing. The key issue is the correlation between this set of metrics and the mission of the company. The internal

business process perspective typically includes generic measures of efficient performance and operational management processes such as the delivery of goods and services, processes improvement and cost reduction. Metrics for the organizational processes must be focused on performance, specifically within the context of how managers execute the strategy

- From the *learning and growth perspective*, managers identify the infrastructure that the organization must build to create long-term growth and improvement. The customer and internal business process perspectives identify the most critical factors for current and future success. Learning and growth come from three principal sources: people, systems and organizational procedures. The financial, customer and internal business process objectives in the BSC typically reveal gaps between existing capabilities of people, systems, and procedures and what will be required to achieve performance targets. To close these gaps, managers will have to invest in training employees, improving information systems, and aligning organizational procedures, routines and culture.

As explained by Kaplan and Norton, the four perspectives, which are illustrated in Figure 3.10 (below), can be framed as:

- *Financial*: How do we look to our shareholders?
- *Customer*: How do our customers see us? Are we meeting their needs and expectations?
- *Internal processes*: What do we need to do well in order to succeed? What are the critical processes that have the greatest impact on our clients and our financial objectives?
- *Learning and growth*: How can we develop our ability to learn and grow in order to meet our objectives in the above three areas?

According to Kaplan and Norton, an effective strategic learning process requires a shared strategic framework that communicates the strategy and allows all participants to see how their individual activities contribute to achieving the overall strategy. The BSC provides a representation of an organization's shared vision. The use of measurements as a language helps to translate complex and nebulous concepts into a more precise form that promotes consensus among senior management.

Kaplan and Norton (2001; 2004) also stress the importance of visualizing causal relationships of measures and objectives in so-called strategy maps (Figure 3.11). Strategy maps are essentially communication tools

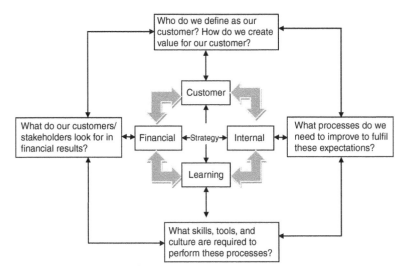

Figure 3.10 The Balanced Scorecard method
Source: Adapted from Kaplan and Norton (1996).

that visualize an organization's strategy and the processes and systems needed to implement it. It is a useful tool to chart how intangibles translate into corporate goals and how the four perspectives are interlinked.

The scorecard should, then, incorporate the complex set of cause and effect relationships amongst outcome measures and the performance drivers that describe the history of the strategy of those outcomes. Outcome measures without performance drivers fail to communicate how the outcomes are to be achieved. Conversely, performance drivers without outcome measures give managers the route for achieving short-term operational improvements but they will fail to describe how operational processes have been translated into financial performance. As discussed by Olve *et al.* (1998), financial measures are normally outcome-oriented, whereas renewal and development measures contain performance drivers. The customer and the process focus comprise a mixture of outcomes and performance drivers.

Some critics emerge in the literature. For example, Neely *et al.* (2002) argue that the four perspectives fail to address the needs of multiple stakeholders, some of them with great influence in the value creation process. In the same vein, Hansson (1998) claims that BSC indicators are too restricted because they do not capture the unique drivers and process that

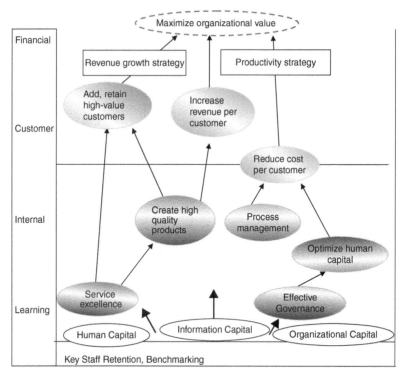

Figure 3.11   Strategy map

are critical to the firm's output. Examples of such drivers are identified as feelings, values, beliefs and relationships. In addition, Chen *et al.* (2004) point out that the BSC does not consider the importance of employees, overlooking the significance of knowledge management in the context of the knowledge economy. Whilst Marr *et al.* (2004:555) point out that, although the learning and growth perspective implicitly incorporates measures about innovation capability and staff development, it does not provide 'detailed guidelines on which knowledge dimensions should be measured'. In turn, Lank (1997) argues that, although some measures (for example, training days per employees or total time spent in training) demonstrate management's engagement with the importance of learning, the development of IC (or the process of knowledge management) requires a different perspective. As IC follows a strategic view it is crucial to understand how an organization develops its IC and how value drivers are linked to the organization's mission.

In order to address the dynamic environment that organizations face today, Kaplan and Norton (2004:13) tried to adapt their framework to more complex choices, identifying in its 'learning and growth perspective three categories of intangible assets that are essential for any strategy implementation'. They introduce the concept of 'intangible assets' as the content of the learning and growth perspective, including the following elements:

- human capital (employees' skills, talent and knowledge);
- information capital (databases, information systems, networks, and technology infrastructure); and
- organizational capital (culture, leadership, employee alignment, teamwork, and knowledge management).

Though the integration of these three sub-components into the learning and growth perspective may represent an attempt to adapt the use of the BSC to recent developments in the context of intangibles' management, Marr and Adams (2004) criticize the way Kaplan and Norton use the concept of intangibles to fit their model. The authors emphasize the fact that the presence of relational capital – a category of the IC concept – in the work of Kaplan and Norton is confined to the customer perspective, not taking into consideration a set of relationship assets that constitute a major category of intangible assets. In this sense, Marr and Adams argue that they ignore much of the earlier work developed by other authors specialized in this subject.

Many elaborations of the BSC model can be found in the literature, and the concept of BSC has inspired the development and application of a variety of IC models. Despite the criticism of the consideration of intangibles, both the BSC and IC models can achieve the same goal by different means. They are not only tools for measuring intangibles, but also share the vision of continuous learning and improvement to create value for the future. Marr and Adams (2004) explain that perhaps the most important aspect that differentiates BSC and IC is found in the different strategic perspectives on value creation upon which they are based, which, consequently, shape the selection of indicators. Whilst the competitive advantage perspective followed by the BSC elects markets, customers and rivals as primary elements of value creation, the competency perspective followed by the IC models focuses on internally-generated competencies and capabilities (Figure 3.12). These two perspectives constitute different routes to drive the value creation process as mentioned by Mouritsen *et al.*, (2005:24):

According to the competitive advantage approach value comes from manoeuvring the marketplace, while for competence strategy, value

derives from techno-organizational capabilities. This has consequences, one being that the balanced scorecard indicators are said to
cohere in a sequential structure of cause-and-effect, while for intellectual capital, the indicators are bundles and form a network around
capabilities and their development.

The literature refers to other management tools – such as Navigator
(Gupta and Roos, 2001), success maps (Neely *et al.*, 2002) and value
creation map (Marr *et al.*, 2004) – to visualize the causal links and connections between intangible value drivers and organizational performance outcomes.

These value creation maps allow the organization to identify and map
the key knowledge assets and show how the pathways intersect each
other to deliver organizational value. Knowledge assets are represented
in bubbles linked with arrows. Individual bubbles represent stocks of
particular knowledge assets and their size signals their strategic importance. Individual arrows of different thickness show the transformations
and relationships between knowledge assets and stakeholder needs.
These maps can be used to visualize the static (stocks) and dynamic
(flows) nature of IC, allowing managers to gain a deeper understanding
of core competencies and the dynamics of value creation.

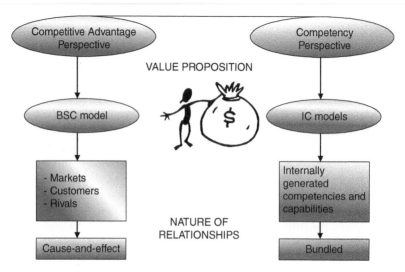

Figure 3.12 "Value creation" approach followed by BSC and IC models

Intangible Assets Monitor (IAM)

Developed by Sveiby (1997), the Intangible Assets Monitor (IAM) considers that the total market value of a company consists of its visible equity and three kinds of intangible assets. The visible equity is the book value of the firm. The intangible assets are categorized into:

(1) individual competence (the individuals: education, experience);
(2) internal structure (the organization: management, legal structure, manual systems, attitudes, R&D, software); and
(3) external structure (market: brands, customer and supplier relations).

Both indicators – non-financial indicators to measure intangible assets and financial indicators to measure visible equity – provide a complete indication of financial success and shareholder value.

Measurement of each of the three intangibles can be divided into three groups, as in the following:

(1) growth and renewal;
(2) efficiency; and
(3) stability.

Organizations should develop one or two indicators for each intangible under each of the measurement groups, constructing a table based monitor. Table 3.8 represents the basic structure of the IAM and includes some measures to use for each of the intangibles, by measurement group. Other measures have also been added to this list by authors other than Sveiby. Selected indicators should be adapted to the reality of each company, reflecting its strategic objectives.

The literature points out many similarities between the BSC and the IAM models and their underlying theories:

1. both theories develop non-financial measures that must complement the financial indicators;
2. both models categorize the non-financial areas (intangibles) into three;
3. both models use the strategy as the driver of the design of the metrics;
4. both theories argue that change is the most important aspect to measure;
5. both models agree that the measuring approach should essentially be used for improving learning and communication.

Table 3.8   Intangible Assets Monitor

Indicators	Individual Competence	Internal Structure	External Structure
Growth and Renewal	- Years in profession; - Education level; - Turnover; - Training costs	- Proportion of support staff; - Sales per support staff; - Investments in internal structure	- Profit per customer - Sales per employee - Organic growth
Efficiency	- Proportion of professionals in the company; - Value-added per professional	- Investment in IT; - Time devoted to R&D; - Sales per support person; - Corporate culture poll.	- Sales per customer; - Growth in market share; - Satisfied customers; - Quality index.
Stability	- Average age; - Seniority; - Professional turnover rate.	- Age of organization; - Support staff turnover rate; - Rookie ratio.	- Proportion of big customers; Age structure; - Frequency of repeat orders

Source: Adapted from Sveiby's works.

Some important differences between the two models are also stressed in the literature

1. The IAM theory assumes that knowledge or people's competencies are the only source of profit generation or wealth creation, whilst this assumption is not so evident with the BSC
2. The IAM theory is a stock-flow theory that perceives intangible assets as real assets and tries to find metrics indicating changes in the assets such as the growth, renewal, efficiency and stability. BSC is not a stock-flow theory
3. The IAM is based on the knowledge-based view of the firm, whereas the BSC regards the notion of the firm as given by its strategy.

To sum up both, the BSC and the IAM have a strategic focus and are strategy driven, but the latter has, in addition, a knowledge perspective that places people at the heart of wealth creation.

The IAM has been used by various organizations such as the VM-Data, a Swedish consultant company, the Celemi or the PLS-Consult.

The Skandia's Intellectual Capital Navigator and its associated Value Creation Model.

Skandia's Intellectual Capital Navigator, developed in 1994, is one of the earliest frameworks used in practice (Edvinsson, 1997) and it is probably one of the best known of all the systems for measuring IC.

The Skandia Navigator is based on the classification of market value (see Figure 3.13). Market value is split into financial capital and IC. The latter is equivalent to intangible assets. The components of IC are subdivided into human capital and structural capital. Structural capital can be further subdivided into customer capital and organizational capital. The latter can be further broken into process capital and innovation capital that represents the enablers in the innovation of products and processes.

Skandia Navigator reflects five key dimensions (see Figure 3.14) and Edvinsson explains that the Navigator can be viewed as a house. The financial focus is the roof. The customer focus and process focus are

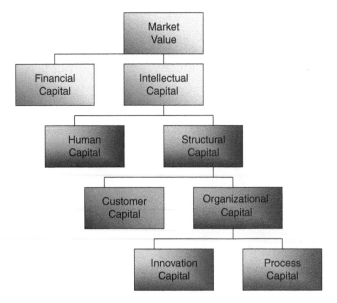

Figure 3.13   Skandia' value scheme
Source: Edvinsson and Malone (1997).

the walls. The human focus is the soul of the house. The renewal and development focus is the platform.

Each of the five focuses has critical success factors that are quantified to measure change. The financial focus captures the financial outcomes of an organization's activities. The indicators used to measure financial focus are largely represented in monetary terms. Customer focus concentrates on assessing the value of customer capital and uses both financial and non-financial indicators. Customer intellectual capital measurement should capture the effectiveness of the company/ customer relations. Process focus puts the emphasis on the effective use of technology to support the company's value creation. Edvinsson (1997) states that the wrong technology or technology that has failed should not be recorded on the IC statement as an asset. The renewal and development focus attempts to capture innovative capabilities of the organization, measuring the effectiveness of its investment in training programmes and its expenditures in R&D and strategic partnership. Finally, the human focus comprises measures that reflect the human capital of the organization. External stakeholders are interested in how human capital contributes to value generation and how organization culture supports the intended strategic direction of the company.

The Skandia IC report is based on 164 different indicators, of which up to 91 are new IC metrics and the remaining 73 traditional metrics are used for measuring the five areas of focus. Monetary measures are combined using a pre-determined weighting to calculate an overall

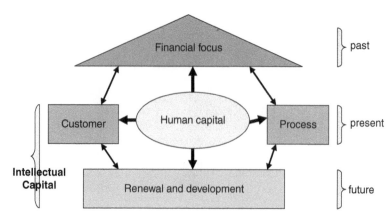

Figure 3.14   Skandia Navigator
Source: Edvinsson and Malone (1997).

IC value (C) for the company. Percentages, that are considered measures of incompleteness, are combined to produce the coefficient of IC efficiency (*i*) which captures the organization's velocity, position and direction. An organization's IC is represented by a multiplicative function of two sums, C and *i*.

Organizational IC = *i* C

The Skandia Navigator model has been used by a great number of companies. (For more information see, *http://www.unic-net*.) The model was also adapted for evaluating the national intellectual capital of Israel (Pasher and Shachar, 2005) and Arab Region (Bontis, 2004).

Intellectual Capital Services' IC-Index^{TM}

Originally developed in Scandinavia and Australia by Roos and Roos (1997), the IC-Index aims to construct an index representative of IC. This index consists of a percentage that gives an indication of how IC contributes to the organization's financial results.

The model defines intangible assets as a set of resources and flows contributing to the organization's value creation processes. The basic structure of the model identifies two categories of IC (Figure 3.15). The human capital which includes the competencies, attitudes and intellectual agility of employees in an organization. The structural capital that comprises the set of relationships (customers, suppliers and partners), organizational infrastructure (including processes and information systems) and, finally, renewal and development represent new processes, innovation in new products, and so on.

This notion of IC-Index^{TM} includes identifying not only the resources necessary to create value (stocks) but their utilization, or the transformations from one resource into another (flows) as well as their relative importance for attaining the desired future position. The IC-Index^{TM} consolidates all individual indicators representing intellectual properties and components into a single index. Changes in the index are then related to changes in the firm's market valuation. Roos *et al.* (1997) suggest that the selection of IC forms, indicators and weightings can be decided by knowing the company's strategy, the characteristics of the industry where the company operates, and the relative importance of each capital form in the creation of value in the particular business of the company as shown in Table 3.9.

The IC-Index model looks at the relative importance of each category as well as the impact of changes in IC. Each of these indices is, in turn,

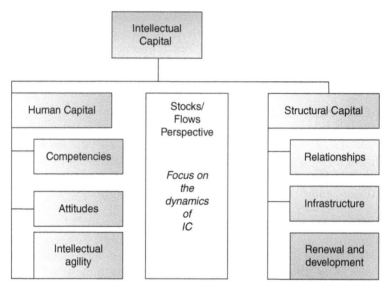

Figure 3.15 Intellectual Capital Index Model
Source: Adapted from Roos *et al.* (1997).

Table 3.9 Factors affecting the selection of IC forms, weightings and indicators

	Selection of capital forms	Selection of indicators	Selection of weights
Strategy	X		
Industry		X	
Business			X

Source: Adapted from Roos et al. (1997).

aggregated into a single index that can be used to compare the same unit over time, or other business units.

So, the IC forms that help the firm achieve its strategic goals should be the drivers in deciding which structural, human capital or other capital form to emphasize in an index. The weights assigned to the IC forms should be the relative importance each capital form has in the particular business of the company. Finally, the firm should be aware of its day to day operations in order to know which specific indicators to choose.

Based on a stock-flow perspective, the IC-Index allows managers to 'understand the effects a particular strategy has on the IC of a company and compare two alternatives to understand which one is preferable from an IC point of view' (Roos *et al.*, 1997:92).

The model has been used and tested in some organizations such as Battery Ltd, Mec-Track and SkandiaLink, a subsidiary of Skandia group.

Knowledge management lifecycle

Some organizations measure the progress of their knowledge management activities in terms of their maturity. The American Productivity and Quality Centre has developed a framework known as 'Road Map to Knowledge Management Results: Stages of Implementation'. The aim is to provide organizations with a map to guide them in getting started, right through to 'institutionalizing' knowledge management – embedding it in the organization and making it an integral part of the way an organization works. The map has five stages: a) getting started; b) developing a strategy; c) design and launch of a knowledge management initiative; d) expansion and support; e) institutionalizing knowledge management. There are IC measures associated with each stage.

More information is available at: http://www.apqc.org/portal/apqc/ksn?paf_gear_id=contentgearhome&paf_dm=full&pageselect=detail&docid=110624

Technology Broker's IC Audit

Developed by Annie Brooking (1996), the Technology Broker's IC Audit categorizes IC into four component areas, as defined in Figure 3.16:

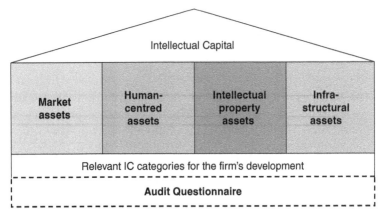

Figure 3.16   The Technology Brokers' IC Audit
Source: Adapted from Brooking (1996).

The model uses an audit questionnaire to identify all the firm's IC categories that are important to its development, whether they are owned or not by the firm. These categories are:

- market assets which consist of such things as brands, customers, distribution channels and business collaborations;
- intellectual property assets which include patents, copyrights, and trade secrets;
- human-centred assets which refer to education, experience, motivation, competencies and work-related knowledge;
- infrastructure assets which comprise management processes, information technology systems, networking, and financial systems.

The model works as a diagnostic to help managers to develop IC indicators initially through a 20-question survey touching on a range of issues regarding intangible assets. Each component of Brooking's IC model is then examined via a number of specific audit questionnaires that ask questions specific to those variables thought to contribute to that asset category. The results of this test suggest that the less a company is able to answer in the affirmative to the 20 questions, the more it needs to focus on strengthening its intellectual capital. In total, the Technology Broker IC Audit is comprised of 178 questions. Following the survey, it is calculated a monetary value for the IC using traditional valuation approaches (market, income, or cost) to each category. The market approach uses market comparables as a benchmark for asset value. The income approach estimates the income-producing capability of the asset. The cost approach estimates value based on the asset's replacement cost.

The model has been implemented in some consultant and technology companies.

Value Creation Index (VCI)

The Value Creation Index (VCI) was devised by Ernst & Young and according to Pike and Roos (2004b), the model helps to understand financial and non-financial contributions to market value which are frequently seen as separable when they are not. The VCI drivers of value are derived from an extensive literature survey and advanced statistics. A set of nine key areas with statistically proven significance were found. Metrics were weighted and combined to give a Value Creation Index. The index is compared and combined with financial data.

The ARCS model for IC reporting

The ARCS model is the result of a work of Austrian Research Centres Seibersdorf (ARCS) which carries out research and development services for the economy and realizes an important function linking basic research at universities and applied research carried out by companies.

ARCS published the first Intellectual Capital Report in 1999. It provides information on the products and services supplied by ARCS and the resulting value added. It is based on a model that reflects the cycle of knowledge within the company. The process of acquiring, applying and exploiting knowledge starts with the definition of knowledge goals, which can be derived from the corporate strategy. The IC at ARCS comprises structural capital, human capital and relational capital. Projects are carried out at the operating level, and value added by utilizing these intangible assets, which need to be constantly developed and maintained. There are numerous interactions and spill-over effects in the process, which give ARCS its unique interdisciplinary character. A specific attribute of the ARCS model is the integration of intangible results or non-financial results with respect to the economy, research and society. In addition to these results, there are also some financial returns that appear in the ARCS annual report (Koch *et al.*, 2000).

Philip M'Pherson's Inclusive Value Methodology (IVMTM)

Developed by Philip M'Pherson, the IVM is a model in which users create hierarchies of intangibles to which they assign value ratings according to priorities. A computer model then determines the overall value rating and tests for areas of risk. The IVM is essentially a multi-dimensional accounting system that measures and combines financial and intangible contributions using the value contexts of all stakeholders individually. For more information see *www.systemsvalue. co.uk*

Holistic Value Approach (HVA)

The HVA is a combination of Göran Roos' IC Index and Philip M'Pherson's IVM™ and also draws on substantial contributions from Stephen Pike. Also referred to as the 'Business Value Model', the HVA distinguishes between the value generated internally by the organization's activities and the value originated externally

Pike and Roos (2000) consider that typically the organization generates value internally through:

1. the values and quality of the corporate Governance;
2. effectiveness of the deployed intellectual capital;
3. effectiveness of the resulting activities, processes and operations;
4. quality of compliance with regulatory standards;
5. costs (negative value) = operational costs + costs of information to and from the external environment + costs of negative environmental and social impacts.

Value generated externally comes from:

1. revenue from the sale of products and services;
2. customer value added after purchase (over the life-cycle of use);
3. employee value added after receipt of salary and financial benefits;
4. stakeholder value added;
5. assessments of regulators and professional interests, namely financial analysts;
6. the environmental and social impacts resulting from the existence of the organization, its activities, its outputs and discharges;
7. awareness rising by special interest groups concerned with ethical and environmental matters;
8. reports from the media and public opinion.

Internal and external values are then grouped within the definition of Inclusive Value, integrating two main categories: financial value and non-financial value.

As described in Figure 3.17, the HVA displays a navigator that visualizes how value is really created in the organization. It starts by identifying key stakeholders and outlining the organizations strategic intent, the role it plays and the values it delivers. The development of the value hierarchy and the measurement of attributes can be completed only by operational staffs that carry out day-to-day business operations. This activity is then used to identify two sets of variables for each stakeholder: one is the set of weights that represents the relative importance of each objective to the stakeholder; the other is the behaviour of the measuring attributes. The flows and influences between these attributes represent the business' value-creating pathways. The strategic alignment is the stage when the previous phases are brought together and the indicators are attached to the value-creating path, this means assigning the

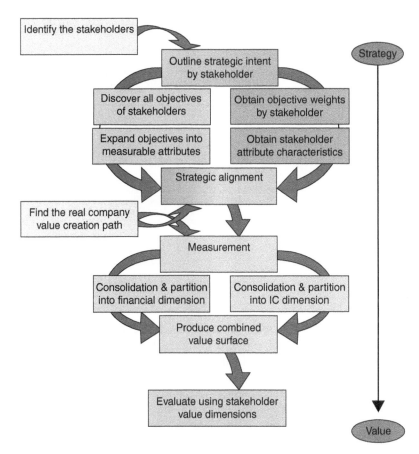

Figure 3.17 The HVA approach in the context of valuing a business
Source: Adapted from Pike and Roos (2000).

different key performance indicators to the different stocks and flows in the navigator. This reveals whether the previously articulated strategy is in alignment with the way the organization creates value on a daily basis.

Value Added Intellectual Coefficient (VAIC^{TM})

The Value Added Intellectual Coefficient (VAIC^{TM}), developed by Ante Pulic (1998) is an output-oriented process methodology, designed to provide an indication of a business unit's IC efficiency, by measuring the performance of physical capital and that of IC.

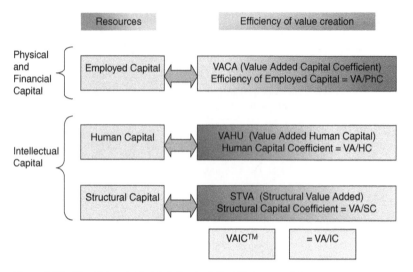

Figure 3.18   The Value Added Intellectual Coefficient model
Source: Adapted from Pulic (1998).

Physical capital includes all necessary financial funds, calculated as a sum of the following positions from the balance sheet: equity; open reserves; funds for general banking risks; supplement capital; participation capital; and lower ranking capital. Profits after tax are then added to this. This is the total amount of physical capital a company has at its disposal. IC includes human capital and structural capital. Human capital can be described as labour expenses, and structural capital represents the value-added obtained from business processes (difference between sales and expenses) subtracted from the human capital. Under this concept, labour expenses are not only seen as compensation for invested time but as compensation for knowledge inputs.

These two kinds of capital can create new value. The calculation of the efficiency of value creation has three steps:

a) 1st step: calculation of value added (VA):

$$VA = OUT - IN$$

VA = value added
OUT = sales
IN = inputs (all expenses except labour expenses)

b) 2nd step: calculation of value added capital coefficient (VACA)
VACA relates value added (VA) and employed physical capital (PhC). This ratio determines how efficiently that value added is

created. The goal is to create as much value added as possible with a given amount of intellectual and physical capital.

$$VACA = VA/PhC$$

c) 3rd step: calculation of VAIC™

$$VAIC™ = VA/IC$$

This equation demonstrates how successful IC creates value.

The higher the VAIC™ value the better a business unit's management utilizes the potential value creation from the available physical capital and IC.

VAIC™ views a firm as a dynamic system of connected relations highly sensitive to external inputs and the most important aspect of the Pulic's methodology is its focus on value creation, value creators and value generation activities.

VAIC™ model was applied to various organizations such as Siemens and Ericsson and also to Croatian and Austrian banks. It was also used to measure the efficiency of value creation in the Croatian economy.

Nordika

Nordika project aimed to promote Nordic and international collaboration while helping companies to acquire and develop reliable methods for assessing the value of their IC resources. The concept of IC reporting represented one of the most important issues tackled by the Nordic Industrial Fund. The concept became necessary as the total worth of a company's collective skills, experience and other intangibles became increasingly dominant in determining product success and market share.

IC reporting is a management tool providing the company, its customers and its partners with crucial knowledge and understanding of what the company stands for and how successful it is in maintaining and developing its position and capabilities. Nordika's report is itself a management tool for companies wishing to carry out IC reporting, since it provides basic definitions, an overview of mainstream approaches to IC, and pointers to what to look for and what lessons to draw from the experience of other companies in the Nordic countries.

More information is available at: http://prosjektweb.nordicinnovation.net/news/default.asp?proID=10.

The Meritum Guideline

Project MERITUM – Measuring Intangibles to Understand and Improve Innovation Management – started in 1998 and was conducted in six countries (Denmark, Finland, France, Norway, Spain and Sweden).

The MERITUM project emerged as the result of a number of OECD conferences that were held to encourage a focus on accounting for intangibles. The OECD initiatives were based on the notion that intangibles appear to be increasingly important.

The project was organized around four themes:

- Establish a classification scheme for intangibles. In the 1990s there was no common classification of intangibles. A useful classification was devised dividing them into human, structural and relational capital;
- Document company management and control systems for identifying European best practice in measuring intangibles. One of the main findings here is that there was a difference with respect to the experience of measuring, reporting and managing intangibles in different participating countries;
- Assess the relevance of intangibles in the functioning of capital markets by means of market data analysis. The analysis conducted under this activity supported the general idea that intangibles are relevant to the financial market;
- Produce guidelines for the measurement and reporting of intangibles. Since the Meritum guidelines were neither known outside the inner circle nor as well developed as they needed to be, the work by the researchers involved was continued in another EC project, E*KNOW-NET, started in September 2001 with the main objective of creating an European Research & Communication arena on intangibles.

The guidelines describe the management of IC as taking place through the identification, measurement and monitoring of intangible resources and intangible activities (Figure 3.19).

Identification aims at visualizing the key intangibles in the organization. Therefore, the identification process starts with an analysis of the current situation of the company and its ability to reach its strategic objectives. These abilities are considered as critical intangibles. To formulate the strategy, it is important to identify critical intangibles, otherwise there are no criteria for what is critical for the firm and what is not. The critical intangibles are the main factors, the key drivers that contribute the most to the value creation process and those that might maintain the company's competitive advantage. Once the critical intangibles have been established, the company has to identify the intangible resources and activities that affect the critical intangibles. The result becomes a network of intangible resources and activities in human, structural and relational capital, which are linked to the company's strategic objectives.

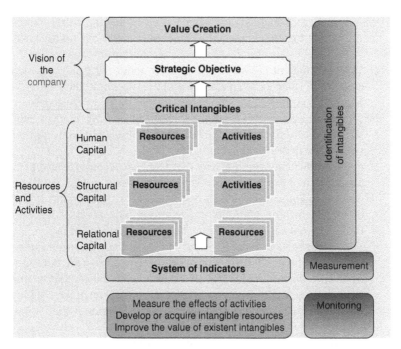

Figure 3.19 Global perspective of Meritum Guidelines
Source: Adapted from Meritum (2001).

Specific indicators should then be identified to measure each intangible resource and activity. Indicators may be financial and non-financial.

Reporting will encompass the vision of the company, its strategic objectives and critical intangibles, a summary of intangibles resources and activities, and a system of indicators.

The Danish Guideline

Some of the most extensive experience of IC reporting is probably to be found in Denmark where the Danish Agency for Development of Trade and Industry (DATI), in collaboration with researchers, companies, industrial organizations, consultants and government officials, initiated a project in 1998 in which all the firms involved in the project published annual IC reports. The first version of the Danish guidelines (DATI, 2001) was developed on the basis of the experiences of 17 Danish companies as part of the government's initiative to encourage the transition from the industrial economy to the knowledge economy.

The aim of the project was to provide a set of guidelines for the development and publication of IC statements. The Danish Guideline is a management tool oriented to external reporting, and it consists of four elements, which together express the company's knowledge management:

a) The first element is a *knowledge narrative* about the firm's ambition to create (use) value for its customers, and the types of knowledge resource required and the relationship between value and knowledge resources;
b) The second element is a set of *management challenges* which emphasize the role of the knowledge resources that need to be strengthened within the firm's business model;
c) the third element comprises a set of *actions and indicators* related to management challenges. Actions relate to the efforts needed to compose, develop and procure knowledge resources, while indicators are the means of monitoring the portfolio, development and effects of k-resources. Indicators make actions visible by making them measurable;
d) The fourth element is the *IC report*. When the knowledge narrative and the management challenges have been defined, they are put together in an IC report. As well as the external intellectual capital statement, more detailed internal reports might be needed. The process of preparing intellectual capital statements is shown in Figure 3.20.

These four elements together represent the analysis of the company's knowledge management. They are interrelated: the knowledge

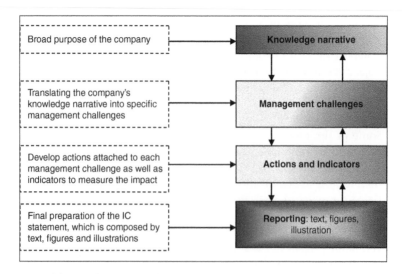

Figure 3.20   The framework of Danish intellectual capital reporting
Source: Adapted from DATI (2001).

narrative communicates what the company's skills and capacity do or must do for customers, and which knowledge resources are needed to satisfy their needs. The management challenges emphasize what has to be done if knowledge resources are to be developed. The actions formalize the problems identified as management challenges and the indicators show how initiatives are launched and put into effect. Once fully completed, the analysis can be presented in the IC report.

More information is available at: *http://www.pnbukh.dk/site/10186.htm.*

The German Guideline (ICS – Made in Germany)

'Wissensbilanz – Guideline on the Preparation of an IC Statement' is a German guideline supported by the German Federal Ministry of Economics and Labour. The Guideline targets SMEs, as well as other forms of organization which have a comparable structure. In particular, it targets all decision-makers in an organization, from the managing director via the controller and those responsible for personnel matters, to the quality management commissioner, strategy managers, and knowledge managers, as well as the heads of sales and marketing.

The model is drafted in six steps with four milestones. The milestones evolve from the simplest form of an IC statement (Milestone I), whose target is the management of an organization to extract measures of improvement based on the results, to a full IC statement (Milestone IV) that integrates correlation analyses and assessments which provide information on how long it will take until measures which have been initiated ultimately lead to business success.

More information is available at: http://www.akwissensbilanz.org/ Infoservice/Infomaterial/Leitfaden_english.pdf.

Summarizing, the objective undertaken by MERITUM and E*Know-Net, the Danish projects and the German Guidelines was to develop a new language, which could help external parties like banks, policy makers, investors, financial analysts, and so on, to understand the IC process. Further, the ambition of the projects was to help firms to manage the IC process. Both guidelines are based on the assumption of looking upon the firm as a knowledge-based system and thus share the insight that companies need to develop their knowledge resources.

3.5.3   InCaS-Made in Europe

During the period 2006–8, a consortium comprising 25 companies in five European countries, several experts and research institutions developed an Intellectual Capital Statement (ICS) methodology called, InCaS, 'Intellectual Capital Statement – Made in Europe' for the implementation of ICS, especially in European SMEs. The InCaS management tool aims to provide a practical guide to a comprehensive and trustworthy internal and external report, contributing to a more competitive Europe by way of disclosing harmonized information on SMEs' true innovative capacity and competitive capabilities.

The ICS structural model

InCaS methodology is based on the ICS structural model described in Figure 3.21, a strategic management tool for developing the IC 'language', that is, the vocabulary (terms/ elements) and grammar (interrelation of terms/ elements) to be used when talking about IC and ICS.

The ICS structural model considers that organization embedded in the business environment guides its decisions and strategic position, based on the vision of founders and owners. Depending on the business strategy, managerial decisions lead to the choice of operational measures. Such measures serve to improve business processes and the utilization of IC components in those processes.

InCaS divides IC into three categories: 'human capital' (HC); 'structural capital' (SC); and 'relational capital' (RC). All intangible resources are considered in these categories. Business processes (BP) are chains of activities within an organization, which provide the output of the organization to the customers. BP describes the interaction of people, information, knowledge and resources. Core processes or those that create value

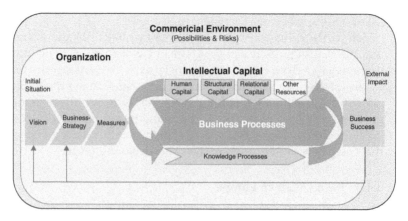

Figure 3.21   ICS structural model
Source: InCaS http://www.psych.lse.ac.uk/incas/page114/files/page114_1.pdf

are supported by all others. Business success (BS) is the operating result which is achieved through the employment of resources (tangible and intangible) in the business processes. Business success includes tangible (for example, growth, profitability, revenue) and intangible (for example, customer loyalty, reputation) business results.

InCaS methodology solves the conceptual conflict of 'individualization vs. standardization' (Figure 3.22). For internal management purposes, it uses an individualized approach, allowing the company to define the specific elements of strategy and IC according to its specific business model. For external reporting purposes, on the other hand, it allows external stakeholders, namely, customers, partners, banks and investors, to compare the IC statements of different companies.

The ICS Procedure

The ICS was designed as a scalable approach, in five steps, leaving the user to decide the extent to which the company's IC was to be analysed. The ICS implementation is a workshop-based procedure involving members of the ICS project team – from representatives of the top management to staff from the operational level – and an external person to moderate the ICS workshops.

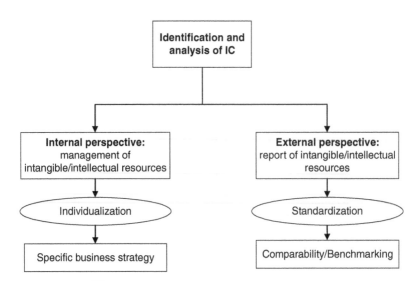

Figure 3.22   Fields of use of ICS
Source: Based on http://www.incas-europe.eu/

Step 0: Pre-arrangement
In order to ensure that the management meeting is effective and productive, some basic information is gathered bearing in mind the following prerequisites:

- analysis of the initial situation;
- analysis of the enterprise's 'fitness' level for ICS;
- establishment of project management.

Documents and further considerations regarding developments and trends in the market should be studied in advance. The initial situation of the organization is measured and documented (several strategic management tools can support and facilitate this process). This helps to identify internal and external possibilities and risks as well as opportunities and threats. This is particularly important in the development of any further strategies, especially the IC strategy which should be in line with the business strategy. Discussion on the current situation and future orientation of the organization forms the basis for all further steps.The involvement of management in the team has proven to be decisive to success.

Step 1: Business model
During the initial visit – the management meeting (Step 1) – some basic issues concerning the ICS project should be addressed. Since the ICS may be adapted to specific cases, it is necessary to conduct an interview on the company's background and the business model. Some important points are then defined by the management team

- Definition of the system boundaries
- Definition of the value creating model
- Definition of the business environment
- Definition of the main strategic objectives
- Business Processes (BP) and Business Success (BS)

Step 2: IC analysis
In the first workshop the intellectual capital (IC) will be examined and analysed in detail. This analysis can be broken down into three subcategories:

- IC definition;
- QQS-assessment;
- impact analysis.

IC Definition

In addition to the performance identified in Step 1, there are a large number of further (intangible) influencing factors which affect the efficiency and effectiveness of performance and the success of the organization on the market. They are part of the organization's intellectual capital.

IC is divided into three categories: Human Capital (HC), Structural Capital (SC), and Relational Capital (RC) It describes the intangible resources of an organization.

To speed-up and simplify the process of defining the individual IC factors, it is suggested to use to use the list of common IC factors as starting point, always bearing in mind that the factorr' name and definition should be adjusted to the company's specific needs

QQS-Assessment

It is important to cover the influencing factors from the areas of human, structural and relational capital (in other words the intangible assets) in the intellectual capital statement. In order to identify the strengths and weaknesses of IC factors, the influencing factors are evaluated on the basis of three given dimensions in a self-assessment. The evaluation dimensions are: Quantity; Quality; and Systematic (QQS-assessment).

Impact analysis

Impact analysis is a simple way of assessing the IC factors' impact on a company's business success. This consists of understanding and analysing the complex contexts in which intangible resources move and their interdependencies (cause and effect relationships) in the intellectual capital field.

Step 3: Measurement

In Step 3 indicators need to be identified to allow a measurement in order to validate the assessment. In order to measure the IC factors, the ICS project team has to determine related indicators. It is advisable to use 2–6 indicators per IC factor for the measurement.

After the evaluation, the influencing factors of the intellectual capital statement are validated – measurable indicators, in the shape of numbers and facts, are attached to each influencing factor.

Step 4: Strategy refinement and measures

In the second workshop the strategy should be refined and measures should be derived from the results of the previous steps (Figure 3.23).

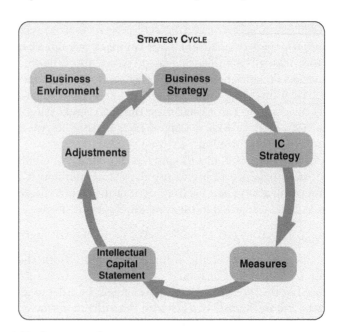

Figure 3.23   Strategy cycle
Source: http://www.incas-europe.eu/

ICS Step 4 is broken down into major parts:

- interpretation of results;
- strengths and weaknesses analysis;
- impact analysis;
- identify fields of intervention.

The considerations regarding the business environment (opportunities and risks from the previous steps) should be related to the organization's vision and strategy. The business strategy needs to be refined and should take into account the new information gathered in the previous steps. The knowledge strategy derived from the business strategy describes the organization's position with regard to sub-areas of intellectual capital.

The IC strategy is derived from the business strategy and steers the measures to develop intellectual capital. The success of the steps taken is measured and evaluated in the intellectual capital statement, and in addition to changes in the business environment, forms the starting point of a new cycle.

Step 5: Final ICS Document
Two finalized ICS versions, an internal and an external version, are prepared. In the internal version all results should be disclosed as it is used as an internal management tool, whereas the external version might not show all results due to the fact that the ICS contains sensitive data and the company may not wish to disclose all the results and findings of the ICS process.

The data acquired in Steps 1–4 make it clear that the results can only sensibly be interpreted in context. Depending on the starting situation, and on the strategic goals set, completely different conclusions can emerge. The ICS, which is used for communication, must therefore provide a description of this context and an interpretation which, in addition to the numbers and facts, also shows the consequences from the point of view of the organization.

The InCaS tool still provides 7 extra modules (advanced) that represent an attempt to overcome the knowledge gaps and management weaknesses commonly observed in average organizations when implementing an ICS. The gaps refer to the business model concept, or some of its elements such as the vision, the core business processes and the assessment of the external environment.

Benefits of the ICS implementation
The ICS is an instrument for assessing, reporting, developing and communicating the IC of an organization and contributing to enhancing the firm's innovation competencies and capabilities. As a result, the implementation of ICS in a company can bring the following benefits:

- helps you determine strengths and weaknesses of strategic IC factors (diagnosis);
- prioritizes improvement opportunities with the highest impact (decision support);
- supports measures in favour of organizational development (optimization and innovation);
- enhances transparency and the involvement of employees (internal communication);
- diminishes strategic risk and improves the success rate (monitoring);
- facilitates the communication of corporate value to stakeholders (reporting).

Relevance of the objectives of InCaS

Some of the major business constraints on SMEs are a lack of skilled labour, access to finance, implementing new technologies and implementing new organizational structures. Moreover, acquiring equity or debt capital for future-oriented investments (at reasonable costs and risks) becomes a critical factor in sustainable business success. This is even more the case as it is driven by the Basel III Agreement, which demands the evaluation of 'soft factors' in order to assess credit ratings, and by international accounting standards (the International Accounting Standards Board and Financial Accounting Standards Board) that suggest reporting intangible assets as a supplement to the conventional business report. For these reasons, not only managers and employees demand transparency about the IC within SMEs, but so also do external stakeholders, such as investors, lenders, customers and partners. In this context, ICS guidelines help European SMEs, a primary target group, to:

- Improve productivity by maximizing exploitation of existing intellectual resources;
- Develop and sharpen unique selling propositions by strengthening their strategic core competencies;
- Manage and retain their relations to customers, partners and staff;
- Acquire loans for future-oriented investments more easily and at reduced costs by reporting intangible assets to banks and investors;
- Reduce operational and strategic risks by monitoring critical success factors systematically.

InCaS methodology is a practical guide to a comprehensive method of identifying, measuring, and managing intangibles. It is a trustworthy tool to report intangibles for both internal and external purposes. Also, it provides an ICS Audit module. All these important features will certainly make InCaS an important strategic tool for the future success of European SMEs. More information material on the InCaS method and related topics can be downloaded from the InCaS website, *www.incas-europe.org.*

3.6   Conclusions

In this chapter we reviewed the most significant strategy models. Models that are not focused on strategy are useful for improving and upgrading the existing business models but they are not adequate for guiding the innovation and radical transformations required in a global and hypercompetitive environment.

By contrast, intellectual capital models, because of their strategic nature, are more suitable for guiding business models in the face of the challenges mentioned above.

We have classified intellectual capital models into two groups:

- strategy formulation models which do not break intellectual capital down into its constituent parts; and
- strategy implementation models which do break intellectual capital down into its constituent parts.

Practically, all the existing intellectual capital models fall into the second group. The more significant ones have been described, and we have paid more attention to some of them, such as the BSC and InCaS-Made in Europe, because of their practical relevance.

With respect to the first group, we have described, in a summary way, the two main models corresponding to this group. These two models are Value Explorer and ICBS. The rest of the book will be specifically dedicated to the ICBS.

In summary, we conclude that a strategic perspective is the most relevant approach. Business excellence is always due to good strategy formulation and excellent strategy implementation. In order to achieve business excellence, there are some models and methodologies that can guide organizations in the two fundamental processes of strategy formulation and strategy implementation. Among these models the most relevant are the following:

- ICBS for strategy formulation;
- BSC and InCaS-Made in Europe for strategy implementation.

With the ICBS we contribute to filling the gap that existing IC models do not cover because their focus is on strategy implementation, as we will see in Chapter 4.

4
Building an Integrative Methodology and Framework for Strategy Formulation

4.1 Introduction

Globalisation and the incredible technological advances, particularly in the areas of information and communications technology, created a "new era" that has reshaped the global economic environment. Those trends are changing the competitive structure of markets in such a way that the effectiveness of traditional sources of advantage is blurred. A new paradigm economy emerged in which knowledge is seen as the critical factor of production, the vehicle of economic benefits and the source of the nation's prosperity and sustainable competitive advantage. In response, new models of business are emerging where the value chain have their hard nucleus in the creation, transformation, dissemination, application and leverage of intellectual resources.

Despite these critical changes in our societies – as in the past – all success business stories are based on a soundly formulated and effectively implemented strategy.

Good decisions are based on well-formulated strategies. This chapter focuses on the formulation phase of strategy (Figure 4.1). The crux of strategy formulation is to define a strategy that makes the best use of the organization's intellectual resources and capabilities.

The basic purpose of strategic management is to match the company's strategy with the environment where the organization is operating in. Because the environment is constantly changing, effective strategic management requires a continuous flow of new theories suitable to the new scenarios. Structural changes transform the traditional business frameworks into insufficient and incomplete tools for developing

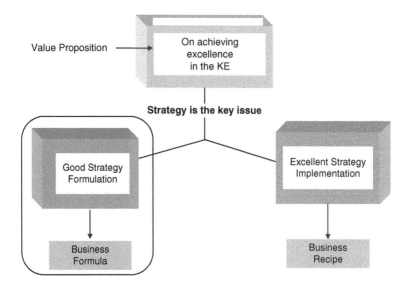

Figure 4.1 Formulating good strategies

a strategy. Traditional frameworks such as the BCG matrix, the Porter's Five Forces and the SWOT analysis have had a lasting influence on strategic management and have been especially valuable for managers to develop and implement long-term strategy for organizations so as to build and sustain competitive advantage. However, those frameworks are becoming insufficient because their assumptions rely on the economic situation characterised by more stable market structures, and where changes are not so rapid and profound as today. Because most models were developed in an era of stable markets, they also lack the perspective of intangibles.

One of the main challenges for the KE is how to use SWOT analysis efficiently and effectively in the present context. An approach of the "extended Swot analysis" is here discussed. This chapter develops the theoretical principles that support the Extended SWOT analysis as a framework for formulating strategies at business level in an efficient and effective way to achieve success in the new context in which the main features are: *(i)* the importance of knowledge as the main source of sustainable competitive advantage; and *(ii)* the world-wide hyper-competition. The challenge is to move SWOT analysis away from the generalities of "strengths", "weaknesses", "opportunities", and "threats" to more concrete factors and characteristics appropriate to the new reality.

A specific methodology and information system framework – Intellectual Capital Benchmarking System (ICBS) –, focused on the value chain activities of both the operations and innovation processes, is developed.

Deploying scarce resources to create superior value when dealing with the innovation process is a very different task from that involved when dealing with the operations process. To create value the two processes require different resources and different core knowledge. For this reason, the ICBS has a specific methodology and information system framework for each of the processes. Relying on the principles of the resource-based view and activity-based view, and the concepts of business intelligence and strategic competitive benchmarking, the general model of ICBS can be divided into three partial models. The Innovation Intellectual Capital Benchmarking System (IICBS) which is mainly focused on the value chain activities of the innovation process. The Operations Intellectual Capital Benchmarking System (OICBS) which is mainly focused on the value chain activities of the operations process. Finally, the Social Capital Benchmarking System (SCBS) complements the two others IC models, focusing on the social capital existing in a cluster location.

In order to build this strategic management tool we rely on the design science research methodology, whose main purpose is to solve practical problems that have no solutions within existing frameworks, by creating a new methodology that later on will be scientifically validated through practical applications and using the reflective cycle. (More information on the design science research methodology can be found in Andriessen (2004b) and Van Aken (2004)).

4.2   Strategy formulation frameworks

Organizations have relied on some frameworks and theories over time, to support and nurture the process of strategy formulation.

The most popular frameworks and theories for strategy formulation are:

- The Acnur and Englyst Model (Acnur and Englyst, 2006)
- The Boston Consulting Group Matrix (Ansoff, 1987; Ansoff and McDonnell, 1990)
- The *Five Forces* (Porter, 1980)
- *A Knowledge-Based Theory of the Firm to Guide Strategy Formulation* (Sveiby, 2001)
- The Strengths Weaknesses Opportunities and Threats (SWOT) Analysis.

- The Intellectual Capital Benchmarking System (ICBS) (Viedma, 2004).

Some of the frameworks that have been extensively used in business practice have revealed their limitations. Namely, they neglect the role of intangibles, the turbulence of environments, and linkage with the implementation phase.

More recently, Sveiby (2001) has developed the key concepts of a knowledge-based strategy formulation. Despite the merit of his model, Sveiby only focuses on internal knowledge, or the knowledge created and converted within the firm. ICBS methodology goes beyond this, assuming that modern business has to compete by exploiting capabilities which competitors find hard to imitate. Those distinctive capabilities are knowledge, skills and creativity applied to satisfy customers, exploit market opportunities and meet society's aspirations for a better environment.

These two approaches represent an important contribution to modern strategic thinking because they improve our understanding of strategy formulation.

4.2.1 The Acnur and Englyst model

Acnur and Englyst (2006) consider that a well-formulated strategy process will lead to a good strategy; this occurs in three phases (Figure 4.2)

(1) *Strategic thinking* – this phase works through strategic priorities and creative strategies.

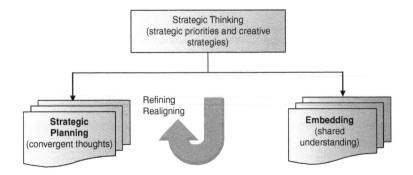

Figure 4.2 Phases of strategy formulation process
Source: Adapted from Acnur and Englyst (2006).

(2) *Embedding* – this phase refers to building a shared understanding and acceptance of strategic choices throughout the organization. It aims to support continuous change, that is, continuous learning and adapting.
(3) *Strategic planning* – this phase centres on planning for the future – predicting for organizational performance – incorporating the outcomes of strategic thinking.

Finally, to face these changes in a successful way, the strategy might need to be refined and realigned. A key condition of the model is that employees are convinced that the business goals will be achieved. This indicates that a formulated strategy is not just an ambiguous document containing detailed responsibilities, but a plan for action.

4.2.2   The Boston Consulting Group (BCG) matrix

Introduced by the Boston Consulting Group (BCG), the BCG matrix offers a useful method for comparing a firm's strategic business units (SBUs). An SBU is a unit of the company that has a separate mission and objectives and that can be planned independently from the other businesses. An SBU can be a company division, a product line, or even individual brands – it all depends on how the company is organized.

Using the BCG box, a company classifies its SBUs in two dimensions:

- *horizontal axis* (relative market share), which reflects the measure of SBU strength in the market;
- *vertical axis* (market growth), which provides a measure of market attractiveness.

By dividing the matrix into four areas, four types of SBUs are traditionally distinguished. Figure 4.3 relates businesses' or products' position with the flows of investment to nurture the firm's portfolio of businesses or products.

'Question marks' refer to businesses or products with low market share but which operate in higher growth markets. This means that they have potential to become stars, but they require substantial investment in order to grow market share at the expense of competitors.

'Stars' refer to high growth businesses or products competing in markets where they are relatively strong compared with their competitors. In general, they need heavy investment to sustain their growth. It is assumed that they will become 'cash cows'.

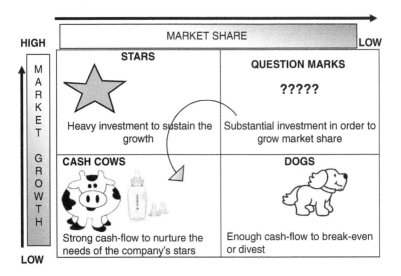

Figure 4.3   The Boston Consulting Group Box ("BCG Matrix")
Source: Adapted from Acnur and Englyst (2006).

'Cash cows' are low-growth businesses or products with a relatively high market share. These are mature, successful businesses with relative little need for investment. These cash cows provide a strong cash flow to nurture the needs of the company's stars.

'Dogs' represent businesses or products that have a low relative share in unattractive markets or low-growth markets. Dogs may generate enough cash-flow to break-even, but they are rarely worth investing in.

Once an organization has classified its SBUs, it must decide what strategy should be adopted, as detailed in Figure 4.4.

The BCG matrix has been extensively used in business practice because it has the advantage of simplicity, and has proven to be an effective tool for analysis of a firm's business portfolio. The business portfolio is the collection of businesses and products that make up the company. The best business portfolio is one that fits the company's strengths and helps exploit the most attractive opportunities.

The BCG matrix is considered a useful tool for two purposes:

(1)   For making decisions on desirable market share positions; and
(2)   For assigning strategic funds among the SBUs.

HOLD The company invests just enough to keep the SBU in its present position; maintain the status quo	**BUILD MARKET SHARE** The company should invest to increase market share.
HARVEST The company reduces the investment and uses the cash flow generated to nurture other SBUs.	**DIVEST**** The company can divest in order to use the resources elsewhere

Figure 4.4   Choosing strategies based on the BCG matrix

* For instance enjoy positive cash flow and maximize profits from a Star or a Cash Cow.
** For example, get rid of the Dogs, and use the capital to invest in Stars and Question Marks.

The BCG matrix is especially suitable for a portfolio of businesses in a SBU but it does not consider inter-related businesses developed in different SBUs. This over-simplification of reality limits the application of the BCG matrix.

4.2.3   The five forces framework

The dominant paradigm for strategy during the 1980s was the competitive forces approach. Porter (1980), one of the most influential authors on business strategy, is clearly identified with the market-driven view of strategy, which believes that the main drivers for strategic choices are external to organizations.

The essence of Porter's model is that the structure of an industry, defined as the interaction of five forces (that is, buyers, substitutes, suppliers, entrants, and existing competition) determines the state of competition within that industry and sets the context for companies' conduct – that is, their strategy. This perspective sees the essence of competitive strategy formulation as a matter of choosing an appropriate industry and positioning the firm within that industry according to a generic strategy of either low cost or product differentiation.

In addition, the Five Forces framework assumes that some industries, or sub-segments of industries, are competitive because they have structural impediments in the form of entry barriers that provide firms with better opportunities for creating sustainable competitive advantage (Teece *et al.*, 1997). Hence, the source of value is a structural advantage, that is, it is creating barriers to entry (Coyne and Subramaniam, 1996). In this scenario, industry structure plays an important role in determining the firm's strategic action.

Using concepts developed in Industrial Organization (IO) economics, Porter's (1979) Five Forces framework determines the attractiveness of a market and offers important insights into the forces at work in the business environment of an SBU. The 'Five Forces' framework (Figure 4.5) emphasizes the actions a firm can take to create defensible positions against competitive forces and provides insights into developing strategic options to improve relative performance in industry or to influence relative position in industry.

Porter's framework relies on developing the competitive advantages from strengthening the parameters within the 'Five Forces' framework. The five industry-level forces focused on entry barriers, threat of substitution, bargaining power of customers, bargaining power of suppliers, and rivalry among an industry's existing competitors,

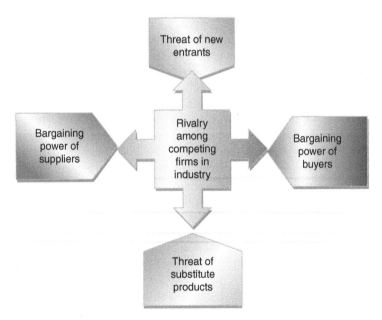

Figure 4.5   Five Forces framework
Source: Adapted from Porter (1979).

determine the inherent profit potential of an industry or a sub-segment of an industry.

The significant contributions of Porter's framework can be summarized:

- It can be used to compare the impact of competitive forces on the own organization with the impact on competitors. Competitors may have different options in reacting to changes in competitive forces. This may influence the structure of the whole industry and some industries may be more attractive than others. Industry structure defines who is more attractive but firms can influence the five forces through their own strategies;
- It helps managers build up a shared understanding of the threats and opportunities facing the firm to gain competitive advantage. A strong competitive force can be viewed as a threat, since it depresses profits, while a weak competitive force can be regarded as an opportunity for organizations to earn profits. This approach provides a systematic way of thinking about how competitive forces work at the industry level, how these forces determine profitability, and helps the firm find a position in an industry from which it can best defend itself against competitive forces or influence them in its favour.

Although a relevant tool in strategic decisions, the Five Forces framework has been criticized due to some major limitations. One of the strongest criticisms of the Five Forces framework is that the model addresses the profitability of industries rather than individual firms, and therefore does not help particular firms to identify and leverage unique capabilities and therefore sustainable advantages (Teece, 1984, Barney, 1991).

A second limitation for which it has been criticized is that the model assumes relatively static market structures. It does not take into account new business models, the dynamics of markets and the turbulence of environments.

A third limitation of the Five Forces is that, although providing a good framework for analysis, it does not consider the dynamism and complexity of the relationships in the new economy, such as those developed in the structure of networks and clusters, and does not accommodate new strategic options like strategic alliances or virtual networks (Prahalad and Hamel, 1990).

However, Five Forces analysis is just one part of Porter's complete strategic models. The other elements are:

- the value chain;
- generic strategies.

The importance of the 'value chain' as a tool is that it shows the contributions by different functions of an organization to the value-adding process. In addition, the value chain helps to understand the linkages better between activities leading to more optimal 'make or buy' decisions that can result in either a cost advantage or a differentiation advantage.

Like the Five Forces framework, the value chain also has some limitations, including the difficulties associated with complex calculations (among others, for example, isolating key cost drivers, identifying linkages across activities, and the value added from interrelated activities) between a series of value-adding activities. Another weakness of the value chain is that it ignores the role of information in leveraging maximizing value for organizations. A virtual value chain, in addition to any pre-existing physical value chain, can be established and that new value chain may create value not through physical components, but also by capturing, analysing, incorporating and utilizing information, giving rise to innovation. So, any present value chain should accommodate the role of information to meet the requirements of the KE.

In addition, Porter (1985) suggests that, a firm needs to make a choice about the type and scope of its competitive advantage. The basis for building a competitive advantage is related to a company's choice to focus on the advantages either in terms of costs or based on differentiation (Figure 4.6).

Generic strategies, as depicted in Figure 4.7, are related to the extent to which the scope of a business' activities are either narrow or broad and the extent to which a business seeks to differentiate its products or services. A firm's relative position within an industry is decided by its choice of com-

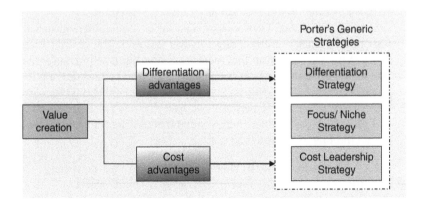

Figure 4.6 Basis for building competitive advantage

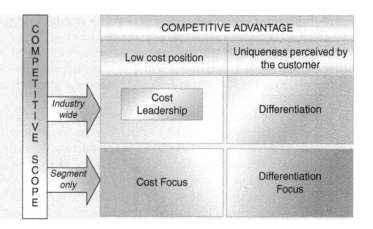

Figure 4.7   Porter's generic strategies
Source: Adapted from Porter (1985).

petitive advantage (cost leadership vs. differentiation) and the choice of competitive scope. Competitive scope distinguishes between firms targeting broad industry segments and firms focusing on a narrow segment.

Differentiation is about charging a premium price that more than covers the additional production costs, and about giving customers clear reasons to prefer the product over other, less differentiated products.

Cost leadership is usually associated with large-scale businesses offering standard products with relatively little differentiation that are perfectly acceptable to the majority of customers.

In the cost focus strategy, a business seeks an advantage from a lower cost in just one, or a small number of market segments.

In the differentiation focus strategy, a business aims to differentiate within just one, or a small number of target market segments. The special customer needs of the segment mean that there are opportunities to provide products that are clearly different from competitors who may be targeting a broader group of customers. The main issue for any business adopting this type of strategy is to ensure that customers really do have different needs and wants – or that there is a basis for differentiation – and that existing competitor products are not meeting those needs and wants.

4.2.4   A knowledge-based theory of the firm to guide strategy formulation

Developed by Sveiby (2001), from the Swedish School of Economics and Business Administration, this theory puts the competence of people at the heart of strategy formulation. People are seen as the only true agents in business. All tangible and intangible relations are the result of human activity, and depend ultimately on people for their continued existence.

When considering the competence of people as the firm's primary intangible resource, Sveiby's central issue of strategy formulation is related to the basic knowledge transfers or conversions that have the potential to create value for the organization.

Three families of intangible resources are considered in Sveiby's theory (Figure 4.8)

- The *External* structure is the family of intangible relationships with customers and suppliers which is seen as the basis of the reputation and image of the firm
- The *Internal* structure includes patents, templates, models, computer systems and other administrative processes. The organizational culture also belongs to the internal structure. These are created and nurtured by employees and are 'owned' by the organization
- The *Individual Competence* consists of the competence of the professional and technical staff, the experts, the R&D people, the factory workers, sales and marketing. In short, all those who have a direct contact with customers and whose work directly influences the customers' view of the organization.

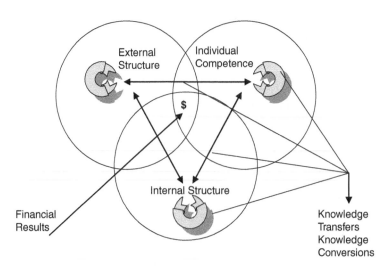

Figure 4.8   A knowledge-based perspective of the firm
Source: Sveiby (2001).

The interactions between people in different roles and relationships create both intangible value (knowledge, ideas, culture, insights, values, and so on) and tangible value, usually measured in monetary terms. The strategy formulation based on the knowledge-based perspective is concerned with how to use resources, competencies and capacities in order to leverage knowledge and how to avoid the blockages that prevent the sharing and creation of new knowledge. The key to value creation lies in the effectiveness of such transfers and conversions.

The essence of Sveiby's theory is that knowledge transfers between persons tend to enhance competence and teams. Based on such assumptions, the author distinguishes nine basic knowledge transfers or conversions that have the potential to create organizational value. Activities that represent the backbone of a knowledge strategy are those that improve the capacity to act of people both inside and outside the organization. Sveiby describes ten knowledge strategy issues as shown in Table 4.1.

While Ten Knowledge Strategy Issues relies on the capacity of people to create and share knowledge both inside and outside the organization, the process of learning from the best competitors is a forgotten issue in Sveiby's approach. Indeed, when examining the best practices of others and drawing comparisons, an organization can perform what is called a 'gap competitive analysis'. This is a way to identify the performance or operational differences between the company's process and that of its benchmarking partners, to understand why the differences exist, and to address the process of organizational learning. The benchmarking process is accomplished in the ICBS model, to be developed later in this chapter.

4.2.5   The SWOT analysis

SWOT analysis (Strengths, Weaknesses, Opportunities and Threats) has its origin in the work of business policy academics at Harvard Business School and other American business schools from the 1960s onwards.

Recognized by Andrews (1971) as the best way to begin a discussion of strategy, it is perhaps the most well-known approach to formulating strategy, having influenced both practice and research over past decades. As a methodology for strategic planning its use has been extended beyond companies to industries and nations, and even individuals. It is a systematic way of identifying and analysing a firm's relationships between internal capabilities – strengths and weaknesses – and external environment – opportunities and threats – providing the basis for formulating strategies from these relationships (Figure 4.9).

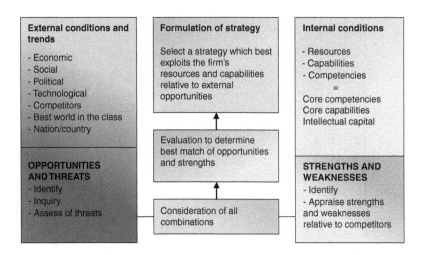

External conditions and trends	Formulation of strategy	Internal conditions
- Economic	Select a strategy which best exploits the firm's resources and capabilities relative to external opportunities	- Resources
- Social		- Capabilities
- Political		- Competencies
- Technological		=
- Competitors		Core competencies
- Best world in the class		Core capabilities
- Nation/country		Intellectual capital

	Evaluation to determine best match of opportunities and strengths	
OPPORTUNITIES AND THREATS		**STRENGTHS AND WEAKNESSES**
- Identify		- Identify
- Inquiry		- Appraise strengths
- Assess of threats	Consideration of all combinations	and weaknesses relative to competitors

Figure 4.9   SWOT analysis as a tool in the formulation of strategy

Strengths are defined as the company's core competencies and describe the positive attributes, tangible and intangible, internal to the organization. Weaknesses are the company's drawbacks. Opportunities are the characteristics within the larger marketplace that can offer the company a competitive advantage. Threats are conditions in the same market that pose a threat to or block an opportunity for these firms.

Organizations are advised to take strategic action to preserve or sustain strengths, offset weaknesses, avert or mitigate threats, and capitalize on opportunities. The aim is to realize the extent to which there are relevant weaknesses, be able to cope with changes occurring in the business environment, and assess the opportunities to exploit using the organization's bundle of resources (Johnson and Scholes, 2002).

This analysis consists of a technique specifically designed to help identify suitable business strategies for an organization to follow. The first step in a SWOT analysis is to list the specific items of internal strength and weakness related to a problem (in the top row of the 2 × 2 grid) with external opportunities and threats in the bottom row of the SWOT grid, as exemplified in Figure 4.10. Internal analysis can include questions focused on structure, image, capacity, efficiency, and access to markets or resources. External analysis assists in the identification of various environmental issues including customers, suppliers, competitors, and partners. Johnson *et al.* (1998) recommended that the list of answers to the questions be limited to ten or fewer points per heading and to

Table 4.1 Ten knowledge strategy issues

Type of knowledge strategy	Description	Strategic questions	Answer
Knowledge transfers/ conversions between individual professionals	How best to enable communication between employees within the organization and determine what types of environments are most conducive to creativity.	*How can we improve the transfer of competence between people in our organization? How can we improve the collaborative climate?*	Activities focused on trust building and collaborative actions
Knowledge transfers/ conversions from individuals to external structure	How the organization's employees transfer their knowledge to the stakeholders	*How can the organization's employees improve the competence of customers, suppliers and other stakeholders?*	Activities focused on empowering the employees to help the customers learn about the products.
Knowledge transfers/ conversions from external structure to individuals	How the organization's employees learn from the external structure.	*How can the organization's customers, suppliers and other stakeholders improve the competence of the employees?*	Activities focused on creating and maintaining good personal relationships between employees and the people outside the organization.
Knowledge transfers/ conversions from competence to internal structure	How information repositories should be shared with the whole organization.	*How can we improve the conversion of individually held competence to systems, tools and templates?*	Activities focused on tools, templates, processes and systems so they can be shared more easily and efficiently.
Knowledge transfers/ conversions from internal structure to individual competence	How a competence is made available to other individuals in such a way that they improve their capacity to act.	*How can we improve individual's competence by using systems, tools and templates?*	Activities focused on improving the action-based learning processes.

Knowledge transfers/ conversions within the external structure	What the customers tell each other about the services/products of a supplier.	*How can we enable conversations among the customers, suppliers and other stakeholders to improve their competence to serve their customers?*	Activities focused on partnering and alliances.
Knowledge transfers/ conversions from external to internal structure	What can organizations gain from the external world and how such new knowledge can be converted into action.	*How can competence from the customers, suppliers and other stakeholders improve the organization's systems, tools and processes and products?*	Activities focused on creating alliances to generate ideas for new products, R&D alliances, etc.
Knowledge transfers/ conversions from internal to external structure	What knowledge the outside world can gain from the organization.	*How can the organization's systems, tools and processes and products improve the competence of the customers, suppliers and other stakeholders?*	Activities focused on making the organization's systems.
Knowledge transfers/ conversions within internal structure	This is concerned with the backbone of the organization.	*How can the organization's systems, tools and processes and products be effectively integrated?*	Activities focused on building integrated IT systems, improving the office layout, etc.
Maximize value creation – see the whole	This is concerned with the coordination of activities in a coherent strategy.	*How can we integrate all activities in a strategic framework?*	Activities focused on providing a knowledge-based perspective.

Source: Adapted from Sveiby (2001).

Internal Analysis (structure, image, capacity, efficiency, access to resources, financial resources)	
Strengths What do we do well? What advantages do we have? What do we better than our competitor? What do people in our market see as our strengths? What unique or lowest-cost resources do we have access to?	*Weaknesses* What could we improve? What should we avoid? What do people in our market see as our weaknesses?
GOAL: PRESERVE	**GOAL: ELIMINATE**
External Analysis (customers, suppliers, partners, competitors, economic and social environment, technological changes, political and regulatory issues)	
Opportunities Where are the good opportunities facing us? What are the interesting trends we are aware of?	*Threats* What obstacles do we face? What is our competition doing?
GOAL: ACHIEVE	**GOAL: AVOID**

Figure 4.10   A SWOT worksheet

avoid over-generalizations. In the context of the SWOT grid, Nickols and Ledgerwood (2006) suggest that the four basic categories should be: preserve (strengths); eliminate (weaknesses); achieve (opportunities); and avoid (threats).

To complement the classical SWOT analysis, Lee and Sai On Ko (2000) and Sai On Ko and Lee (2000) establish four pairs of combination strategies, namely:

(1) *Maxi-Maxi (S/O):* in essence, the organization should strive to maximize its strengths to capitalize on new opportunities. This combination shows the organization's strengths and opportunities.

(2) *Maxi-Mini (S/T):* essentially, the organization should strive to use its strengths to parry or minimize threats. This combination shows the organization's strengths in evaluating threats, for example, from competitors.

(3) *Mini-Maxi (W/O):* Essentially, the organization should attempt to minimize weaknesses by taking advantage of opportunities. This combination shows the organization's weaknesses in tandem with opportunities.

(4) *Mini-Mini (W/T):* this is most definitely a defensive strategy to minimize an organization's internal weaknesses and avoid external threats. This combination shows the organization's weaknesses by comparison with the current external threats.

For the authors, the purpose of SWOT is to match (by a process of exploration) specific internal and external factors (the environment of an organization based on its strengths, weaknesses, opportunities and threats), which create a strategic matrix that supports balanced decisions. The internal factors (for example, operational, financial, marketing) are within the control of organization, while the external factors (for example, political, legal, economic, demographic, technological or competitive) are out of the organization's control.

Although the SWOT analysis remains popular, it faces some criticisms about its intrinsic nature. For some, SWOT analysis is seen merely as list making because the outputs do not constitute analysis at all, as they do not go beyond description. For Barney (2002), for instance, the SWOT analysis is only an organizing framework, a 'snapshot' of a point in time, whilst Warren (2002) argues that the methodology does not match today's complex market-led economies. The main concern is that this framework does not suggest how questions about a firm's strategic theories can be answered. Other authors argue that, though the SWOT framework represents a very common approach to distinguishing between the external environment and the internal forces, it seems of little help, even irrelevant or useless, either in a two-way classification (internal vs. external factors) or a four-way classification (strengths, weaknesses, opportunities and threats). Furthermore, since the SWOT analysis usually reflects a person's existing position and viewpoint, threats can sometimes be viewed as opportunities, and *vice versa*, depending on the people or group involved. In addition, at some point in time, a given strength may become a weakness and *vice versa*.

Despite these limitations, the SWOT analysis is recognized as an intelligent tool for formulating strategies. In view of this, some attempts to refine the SWOT framework have recently emerged in the literature. Helms and Nixon (2010) reviewed the state of art in this field and found that it is crucial to link SWOT analysis to other strategic tools and methodologies for further theory building.

The Swot framework has been evolving in order to integrate the two complementary perspectives of the strategy discipline. An approach that takes on an organization's position within the industry which helps it to understand its competitive environment (it is the market-driven theory) and the resource-based view (it is the RBV theory) which helps it to evaluate its ability to exploit opportunities and respond to threats.

Traditional models for strategic management have defined the firm's strategy in terms of the products it makes and the markets it serves – product/market positioning. The resource-based approach suggests, however, that firms should compete based on their unique, valuable and inimitable resources and capabilities rather than the products and services derived from those resources and capabilities. As argued by Kogut and Kulatilaka (1994), resources and capabilities can be seen as the platform from which the firm derives various products and services for its markets.

These two views of strategy may be seen as complementary when combined and integrated in the SWOT framework. Indeed, 'the resource-based perspective complements the industry analysis framework' (Amit and Schoemaker, 1993:35). Roos (2005:130) has provided an important contribution to this field in developing the 'Amit and Schoemaker's theory of integrated strategy' (Figure 4.11), a theoretical approach that

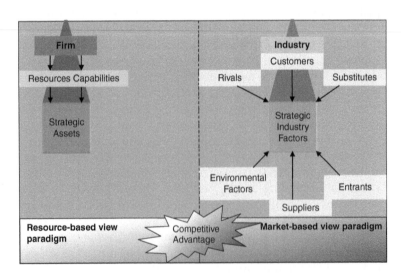

Figure 4.11   Amit and Schoemaker's theory of integrated strategy
Source: Adapted from Roos (2005).

seeks to integrate the competitive forces and the resource-based paradigms of competitive advantage.

In the same vein, Zack (2002) analysed the sources of advantage (inside and outside the company) that come from knowledge as a strategic resource and developed a knowledge-based SWOT framework, a K-SWOT (Figure 4.12), relating the 'SW' side and 'OT' side of SWOT analysis to knowledge.

The 'SW' side of the K-SWOT framework looks at knowledge from an internal resource-based perspective to explain why knowledge may be a firm's most strategic resource. The 'OT' side of the K-SWOT framework looks at knowledge as the basis for describing, evaluating and choosing strategic positions within industries and related knowledge-based opportunities and threats. The two sides form an integrated K-SWOT showing how both strategic views (that is, the resource-based view and the market-based view) are complementary and reinforcing.

With this framework, the author attempts to show how each of these perspectives can be applied to knowledge-based competition. The knowledge-based view of the firm focuses on the organization's ability to acquire, develop and share knowledge resources to formulate and execute its strategy. The view of knowledge as an approach to strategic positioning suggests how those organizations face opportunities and threats based on how the knowledge driving their strategy compares with that of their competitors.

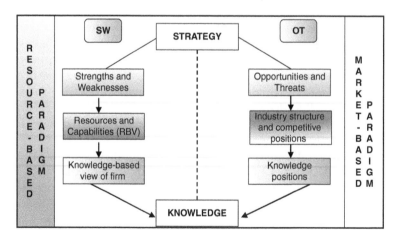

Figure 4.12 The K-SWOT Framework
Source: Adapted from Zack (2002).

It is noteworthy that, from a knowledge-based perspective, competition is seen as being about how one organization's strategic knowledge compares to that of another defending a similar knowledge position, regardless of whether or not they are currently producing similar products or selling to the same markets. As argued by Zack (2002:8):

Two firms having the same knowledge may, in fact, choose to use that knowledge (appropriately or not) to produce different products for different markets. Knowledge as the driving underlying resource for producing and marketing products, however, means that these strategic knowledge positions represent potential (if not current actual) product/market competition. A strategic knowledge map offers a more forward-looking view to identify those firms who have the greatest potential to become a strategic threat.

The two perspectives are integrated to form the K-SWOT by the realization that it is the organization's knowledge and learning strengths and weaknesses that enable it to locate and move to strategic knowledge positions in order to manage its knowledge-based opportunities and threats. Zack *et al.* (1999) go further, explaining how, based on its existing knowledge, an organization may articulate its strategic intent, identifying the knowledge required to achieve its intended strategy and, comparing that with its actual knowledge, identify strategic knowledge gaps (Figure 4.13).

These include internal knowledge gaps, that is, what the organization needs to know to execute its strategy successfully. This internal knowledge gap represents the knowledge strengths and weaknesses side of the K-SWOT. The external knowledge gaps, that is what competitors know, that will be necessary for the organization to know to compete successfully, represent the knowledge opportunities and threats of a K-SWOT. Knowledge management (KM) and learning programmes must be aligned with these two strategic knowledge gaps, in order to add strategic value.

In addition, Viedma (2004) suggests an extension of the Grant's (1998) framework depicted in Figure 4.14, which considers strategy to be a link between the firm and its industry environment, and distinguishes between two features of a firm's internal environment (its strengths and weaknesses) and two features of its external environment (opportunities and threats). As considered by Grant, a modern firm can be said to embody three sets of key characteristics: its goals and values; its resources and capabilities; and its organizational structure and systems. The external

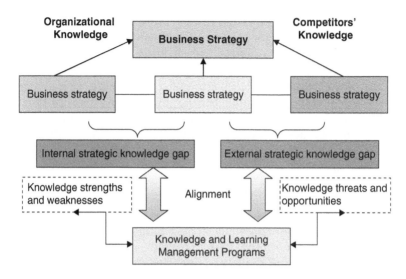

Figure 4.13 Identifying the strategic knowledge gaps
Source: Adapted from Zack et al. (1999).

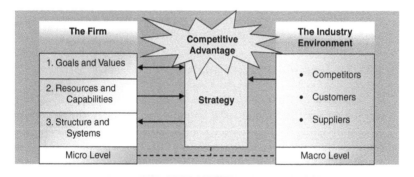

Figure 4.14 SWOT analysis
Source: Adapted from Grant (1998).

environment can be said to comprise its relationships with three groups: its customers; its competitors; and its suppliers.

Despite these advances, it is clear that the SWOT analysis framework has severe limitations in the new context in which the main features are the importance of knowledge as the main source of sustainable advantage, and worldwide hyper-competition. Without additional theories and models that can be used to identify and benchmark strengths, weaknesses, opportunities and threats, this framework does little more than provide a tool for organizing questions one should ask about a firm when choosing a strategy. The challenge is to move SWOT analysis away from generalities of 'strengths', 'weaknesses', 'opportunities', and 'threats' to more concrete factors and characteristics appropriate to the new realities. To accommodate the unpredictable characteristics that have emerged from an economy based on as fluid a resource as knowledge, it is proposed to extend the SWOT analysis, as described below. The extended SWOT analysis constitutes the basis for developing the ICBS framework.

4.2.6   Intellectual Capital Benchmarking System

The Intellectual Capital Benchmarking System (ICBS) is the most recent contribution to thinking about strategy formulation. The framework is thoroughly developed later in this chapter.

The extended SWOT analysis, described in the next section, offers the key factors to take into consideration when building strategies for entrepreneurial excellence. The main factors of the extended SWOT analysis also determine the information system required to measure and manage those factors. In other words, the main factors produce the ICBS that we have identified as a knowledge-based strategic management methodology and information system framework.

4.3   The extended SWOT analysis

As discussed in Chapter 2, the resource-based view and the activity-based view are the fundamental cornerstones that determine company competitiveness in the knowledge economy. Perspectives based on the resources, knowledge and capabilities of the firm (Barney, 1991; Grant, 1991, 1998; Teece *et al.*, 1997) stress that in turbulent times, and in times of rapid change in technology and in customer and industry needs, sustainable competitive advantages are mainly due to the intangibles of a company or, more specifically, to core competencies (which are, in practice, equivalent to core knowledge). But resources, *per se*, do not create value, and because the resource-based view focuses only on what the firm *has*, this view does not, in isolation, adequately explain *how* to deploy scarce resources to create superior value. To that end, the activity-based view (Porter, 1980, 1985, 1996) is a necessary complementary perspective which focuses on what the firm *does*, and takes into account that value creation results from the activities to which the resources are applied.

Sustainable advantage that comes from the application of core knowledge requires a combination of superior knowledge and superior learning. Building and improving core knowledge requires organizational learning capabilities, including the appropriate learning structures and information systems. These assumptions highlight the importance of benchmarking and evaluating the strengths, weaknesses, opportunities and threats of an organization's current knowledge platform and position.

In a hyper-competition world, strategic competitive benchmarking has become an essential learning tool. That valuable knowledge can be obtained only from systematic and frequent comparison with the world-class processes and core competencies of competitors in the same business segments. Organizations are now competing on the basis of core knowledge and core competencies, and opportunities and threats come mainly from competitors who offer the best in the same industry segment. Carpenter and Nakamoto (1989) suggest that consumer preferences are, at least in part, the outcome of competition.

As a result of the above discussion, the SWOT analysis framework moves from that shown in Figure 4.14 to that shown in Figure 4.15. In effect, there is a change from a simple SWOT analysis to an extended SWOT analysis. The extended SWOT analysis helps us to identify the strategic knowledge.

But how do we recognize the organization's strategic knowledge? If the application of some specific body of knowledge can be shown to

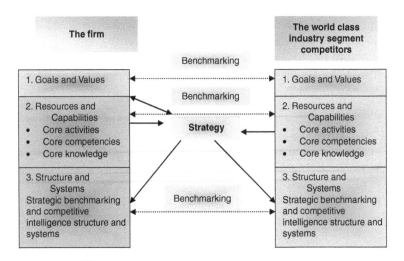

Figure 4.15   The extended SWOT analysis
Source: Viedma (2004).

create and sustain a competitive advantage by enabling an organization to formulate and execute its competitive strategy better, then that knowledge is a strategic resource. It is thus instructive to note that, in the knowledge-based competition, the essential ingredients for success in the knowledge acquisition are observation, learning and adaptation. Business intelligence process constitutes an operational process of continuous learning and adaptation to assist management with decision-making in the modern knowledge-based organization.

4.4 Business intelligence process

Most organizations operate in a reactive mode, focused on identifying events after they have happened rather than having a system of 'early warning' in place (Gilad and Herrings, 1996). To be competitive, organizations have to perform like a 'nervous system', capable of triggering the company's reflexes in reaction to or in anticipation of danger or need. Fuld (1995) argues that competitive intelligence must be a functional part of the strategic management system. It is therefore instructive that formulating a sound strategy demands a competitive or business intelligence process.

Business intelligence is the activity of monitoring the firm's external environment for the information that is relevant to the decision-making process in the company (Gilad and Gilad, 1988). The key point is to use strategic intelligence in the decision-making process. This means that the company has to make intelligence operative and capable of guiding decisions in organizations since if the intelligence gathered is not usable (or operative), then it is not intelligence.

According to Gilad and Herrings (1996), business intelligence mitigates a company's risk of losing business opportunities because it allows it:

- to build a portfolio of competitive advantages over competitors' sustainable advantage;
- to create a competitive surprise for incumbents;
- to change the rules in order to unseat a leader;
- to leverage resources through the use of partners;
- to defend against competitors who are attempting to achieve surprise, or create new advantages, or change the rules of engagement, or lure away partners.

Sometimes, the terms 'business intelligence' and 'competitive intelligence' are used interchangeably. While there are many interpretations for both terms, the Society of Competitive Intelligence Professionals – SCIP (www.scip.org) distinguishes these two concepts in terms of their scope of action. For SCIP, 'business intelligence' refers to any combination of data, information and knowledge concerning the business environment in which the company operates that, when acted upon, will confer a competitive advantage or enable sound decisions to be made. As a systematic and ethical process of gathering, analysing, and managing external information that can affect the company's plans, decisions, and operations, competitive intelligence focuses on scanning a company's competitive landscape for opportunities, threats, risks and advantages.

Competitive intelligence is, thus, both a process and a product. As a process, it refers to the action of gathering, analysing and applying information about products, markets, and competitors for the short-term and long-term planning needs of the organization. As a product, competitive intelligence is the useable output that has been identified in response to the needs of an organization (Kahaner, 1996).

Taking into account the relevance of competitive intelligence for making strategic decisions, Rothberg and Erickson (2002) purpose to add a fourth pillar to the intellectual capital concept. This fourth pillar is denominated 'competitive capital' a capital generated through activities in competitive intelligence systems.

In summary, competitive intelligence supports the strategic process in organizations, acting as a 'sensor' to indicate to top management whether the organization is still competitive. At the same time, company vision, mission and strategic objectives act as a constant guide to the competitive intelligence process.

4.5 Benchmarking

In today's highly competitive market, rapidly changing global economy organizations have been encouraged to consider, and in many situations adopt or implement, competitive analysis as a means of collecting data and measures about the markets, products, sales, production costs or budgets of their competitors (Dorsch and Yasin, 1998; Yasin, 2002).

In recent years, extensive research has been conducted in order to provide organizations with the means to collect and interpret information, share knowledge and support decision-making. Among these management tools, benchmarking is gaining great popularity as a process of acquiring knowledge and experience about others, stimulating new and fresh ideas.

However, while competitive analysis focuses on product comparison, benchmarking looks beyond products and services to the operating and management skills that produce the products and services, and usually requires the active participation of all an organization's members. Hence, benchmarking is more than an analytical process: it is a tool for the encouragement of change.

But what does benchmarking refer to in the context of business? Essentially, benchmarking is a continuous systematic process for understanding and evaluating the products, services, or the current position of a business or organization that is recognized as representing best practice for the purpose of organizational improvement (Camp, 1989). Well-formulated strategies and the application of a good business formula require a clear understanding of the requirements of competitors and customers.

Benchmarking has been given many different definitions by different organizations and authors (Table 4.2) even though each offers the same

Table 4.2 Benchmarking definitions

Authors	Definitions
Camp (1989)	The continuous process of measuring products, services and practices against the toughest competitors or those companies recognized as industry leaders.
Geber (1990)	A process of finding world class examples of a product, service or operational system and then adjusting own products, services, or systems to meet or beat those standards.
Watson (1993)	The continuous input of new information to an organization.
Kleine (1994)	An excellent tool to use in order to identify a performance goal for improvement, identify partners who have accomplished these goals and identify applicable practices to incorporate into a redesign effort.
Stevenson (1996)	The process of measuring the performance of one's company against the best in the same or another industry.
APQC[1] (1999)	The process of continuously comparing and measuring an organization against business leaders anywhere in the world to gain information that will help the organization take action to improve its performance.

[1] APQC stands for American Productivity and Quality Center.

conclusion: that the search for industry best practice leads to superior performance (Camp, 1989).

These various definitions of benchmarking include some common elements in the continuous measurement and improvement of an organization's performance against the best in industry, and in obtaining information about new working methods and practices in other organizations (Horvath and Herter, 1992; Cox *et al.*, 1997).

The objective of benchmarking is to find what best practices are, to understand and evaluate the current position of a business or organization in relation to those 'best practices' and then propose what performance should be in the future (Figure 4.16). Benchmarking involves learning about our own practices, learning about the practices of others, and then making the change for improvement that will enable a company to meet or beat the best in the world. This notion of organizational adaptation suggests that benchmarking should not be seen as a one-off solution. Instead, benchmarking is an intentional and systematic process for obtaining a measure of superior performance – a benchmark – and creating enablers of it. If benchmarks are the 'what', then, benchmarking is the 'how'.

This practice had its origin in Japan. The first western company to perform a benchmark analysis was Rank Xerox in 1979 when faced with fierce competition from the extremely low prices of Canon copier machines (Jackson, 2001). It originated in product quality management as a method of seeking best practices by comparing performances. Applications of benchmarking have often been associated with a variety of managerial activities ranging from quality control and process management to strategic planning. To understand the growth, usefulness and applicability of this technique better, Dattakumar and Jagadeesh (2003) offer a comprehensive review of literature on benchmarking.

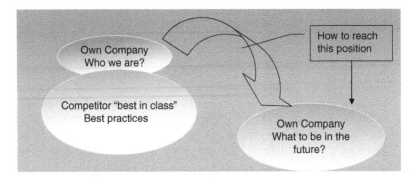

Figure 4.16 How to benchmark

4.5.1   Why benchmarking

Benchmarking is a widely recognized critical tool for decision-makers, who constantly look for techniques that enable them to improve the quality of their decisions. Drew (1997) notes that all the winners of the Baldrige award score highly on the use of benchmarking.

Boxwell (1994) identifies at least two reasons why benchmarking is becoming more common in industry:

* it is recognized as a more efficient way to make improvements;
* it speeds up an organization's ability to make improvements;
* it enables innovations (products or processes) to spread more rapidly through an industry and across industries where appropriate.

Benchmarking adds a new dimension to strategic thinking because it catalyses innovation and organizational changes in a way that exposes people to new approaches, systems and procedures, and fosters their creativity. It ensures that strategy formulation and strategy implementation is on track, constantly checking internal performance against 'best in the class'.

To be successful, it is crucial to have a full commitment to continuous improvement, an ability to learn from others, and a commitment to implement improvement. According to the literature, benchmarking produces the following set of benefits:

* it helps an organization to make better-informed decisions;
* it exposes an organization to innovation and breakthroughs;
* it allows an organization to see and think beyond its frontiers, and embrace change;
* it provides an organization with a methodology and a plan to implement and manage change;
* it forces an organization to investigate external industry best practices, incorporating those practices in its operations and strategies.

4.5.2   Selecting what to benchmark

In principle, we can benchmark everything that can be subject to observation and measuring. Initially, benchmarking was limited to products and services. Later on this technique was expanded to production and distribution processes and organizational support functions as well. More recently, benchmarking has been applied to more intangible aspects, such as strategic and cultural activity. Figure 4.17 demonstrates the evolution of benchmarking application over time.

Benchmark processes offers us a better understanding and more knowledge about the processes of design, R&D activities, production processes,

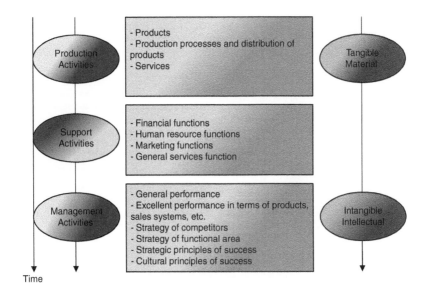

Figure 4.17 Benchmarking application over time

work methods and production technologies. The benchmarking of processes can be applied not only to the best competitors but also to the best businesses operating in similar fields or with similar problems.

The more difficult and intangible benchmarking application is that applied to the strategy of the best competitors. The objective is to search for how competitors achieve their sustainable competitive advantage through their production, support and management activities. The focus is not on the processes of doing things but on the strategic and cultural principles that stimulate the creation, maintenance and improvement of processes, methods and practices.

The nature and effectiveness of benchmarking is based on:

- what we benchmark;
- against whom we benchmark, that is, the benchmarking activities (strategic or operational) and the benchmarking context; and
- the extent to which learning is incorporated into the organization, because benchmarking is basically learning from others. It is using the knowledge and the experience of others to improve the organization.

Adam and Van de Water (1995: 25) suggest that a number of questions should be used to aid the decision (Figure 4.18).

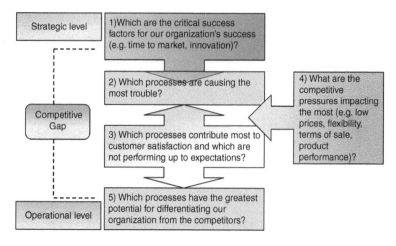

Figure 4.18 Questions influencing 'what to benchmark'
Source: Adapted from Adam and Van de Water (1995).

The answers to these questions help us to identify the competitive gap. This gap provides a measure of the improvement an organization would like to make.

A point to emphasize is that benchmarking studies are time sensitive. What is a standard of excellence today may be the expected performance of tomorrow. Moreover, there is no single 'best practice' because it varies from one person to another and every organization differs in terms of the mission, culture, environment and technological tools available. Best practice' should be seen as being among those practices producing superior outcomes and being judged as good examples within the area.

4.5.3 Describing how to benchmark

The benchmarking theory is built upon performance comparison, gap identification and changes in management process (Watson, 1993; Camp, 1989). As implied in various definitions, benchmarking is a continuous and systematic process. A typical benchmarking practice involves several steps, usually in a Plan, Do, Check and Act (PDCA) sequence. However, some authors purpose variants of the PDCA sequence as depicted in Figure 4.19.

The 'plan' phase includes the selection of functions/processes to benchmark, the identification of potential benchmarking partners and the type of benchmark on which to start. The stage of 'doing' consists of to characterize the selected processes using metrics and documenting business practices. Data (metrics and business practices) are

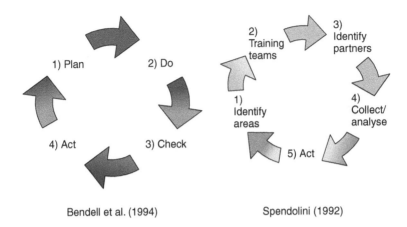

Figure 4.19 Benchmarking cycle

collected on the company that is the benchmarking partner. The 'check' phase involves the comparison of findings by means of a gap analysis to observe whether negative or positive gaps exist between the benchmarking company and the benchmarking partner. The 'act' phase refers to the launching of projects either to close negative gaps or maintain positive gaps. In addition, Spendolini (1992) adds a phase for training teams because benchmarking requires staff to be trained and guided in the process to ensure that maximum benefit is obtained.

Overall, the PDCA cycle is a 'trial and learning' framework whose essence lies in its ability to facilitate learning and foster organizational change.

Boxwell (1994) describes a benchmarking method in eight points (Figure 4.20)

(1) Which activities are to be benchmarked? To be effective and efficient, companies must focus only on those activities they do well (that is, on the core activities and core knowledge of the different business units)
(2) What critical success factors to measure? It is crucial to know which critical success factors should be evaluated for the activities selected in point 1
(3) Select 'best in class' companies, identifying the best practices of others and drawing comparisons – either competitors or companies operating in other sectors
(4) Measure the 'best in class' performance using the key success factors identified in point 2

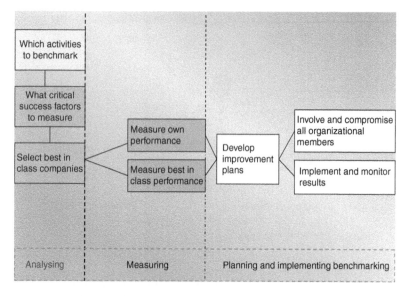

Figure 4.20   Benchmarking process
Source: Adapted from Boxwell (1994).

(5)   Measure and compare the own company performance with that of the best in class performance. This is a way to identify the competitive gap and to understand why it exists

(6)   Develop improvement plans

(7)   Involve all members of the organization in order to reach the goals in the programmes specified in point 6

(8)   Implement and monitor results.

The approach to the benchmarking process is determined by whether it is carried out internally, within a sector, with direct competitors, or with the 'best in class'.

4.5.4   Types of benchmarking

Benchmarking is a very versatile tool that can be applied in a variety of ways. The selection of benchmarking type depends on the processes being analysed, the availability of data, and the available expertise in the institution. Generically, benchmarking can be classified as two groups: internal and external benchmarking. Internal benchmarking covers comparisons made within an organization, and external benchmarking refers to comparisons with external organizations. The latter is divided into competitive, functional, and generic or 'best in class' (Camp, 1989; Zairi, 1992). The process is essentially the same for each category. The main differences are what to benchmark and with whom it will be benchmarked. Based on the goals to achieve, we can still consider three categories of benchmarking as depicted in Figure 4.21. They are: performance benchmarking; process benchmarking; and strategic benchmarking.

Internal benchmarking

Internal benchmarking can be conducted in large, decentralized institutions where there are several departments or units that conduct similar processes, or between organizations operating as part of a chain in different countries. If part of an organization has an excellent performance, others can learn how it can be achieved. All benchmarking processes should start by dealing with internal benchmarking because this requires an organization to examine itself, and it provides a baseline for comparison with others. An advantage to internal benchmarking is

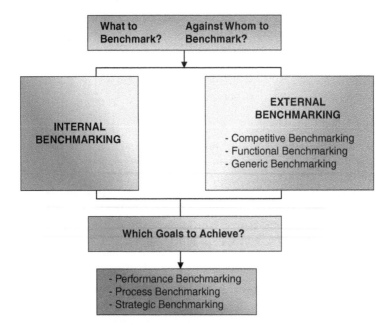

Figure 4.21 Types of Benchmarking

the ability to deal with partners who share a common language, culture and systems, having easy access to data.

External benchmarking

External benchmarking requires a comparison of work with external organizations in order to discover new ideas, methods, products and services (Cox and Thompson, 1998). The objective is to improve one's own performance continuously by measuring it, comparing it with that of others, and determining how they achieve their performance levels. This type of benchmarking allows one to learn from the best practices and experiences of others who are at the leading edge.

Competitive benchmarking

The more common competitive benchmarking analyses processes in peer institutions that are competing in similar markets. This type of benchmarking is very sensitive because it is very difficult to obtain healthy collaboration and cooperation from direct competitors. It may be difficult to obtain data from competitors and therefore to apply the lessons to be learnt from them. Further, Karlof and Ostblom (1993) specify another risk: there may be a tendency to focus on the factors that make competitors distinctive, instead of searching for factors contributing to excellent performance. Despite those risks, competitive benchmarking has several benefits. Among them, Vaziri (1992) includes the ability to create a culture that values continuous improvement to achieve excellence, increases responsiveness to changes in the external environment and shares best practices between partners.

Functional benchmarking

Functional benchmarking refers to comparative research and to attempts to seek world- class excellence by comparing business performance not only with competitors but also with the best businesses operating in similar fields and performing similar activities, but in a different industry. The objective is to identify the best practices in any type of organization that is considered excellent in what we want to benchmark (process, method, product and service).

Generic or best in class benchmarking

Generic benchmarking relates to comparisons of business functions that are the same regardless of business. It uses the broadest data collection from different industries to find the best operations practices available. This means that a school's accounting department would look at the accounting department of a manufacturing organization that has been identified as having the fastest operations. It is believed that it is easier to obtain data in such arrangements, as best in class organizations are more likely to share their experiences, than in competitive benchmarking.

As mentioned above, and depending on the goals to be achieved, we can still differentiate between performance benchmarking, process benchmarking and strategic benchmarking.

Performance benchmarking

This relates to the comparison of performance measures in order to know how well one's organization compares to another. Performance benchmarking focuses on assessing competitive positions through comparing the products and services of other competitors. When dealing with performance benchmarking, organizations seek to evaluate the quality of their product or services in relation to competitors, on the basis of elements such as reliability, quality, speed, and service characteristics.

Process benchmarking

This is about comparing a process in one's own organization with best practice in another business in order to improve one's own process. Process benchmarking focuses on the day to day operations of the organization. Its task is to improve the way processes are carried out every day.

Strategic benchmarking

Strategic benchmarking focuses on how companies compete. It deals with top management and long-term results. This form of benchmarking looks at the strategies organizations are using to make themselves successful.

Strategic benchmarking can be applied to competitors or to a 'best in class' company, regardless of the industry (Figure 4.22).

Zairi (1992) still refers to two approaches to benchmarking: one is driven by cost factors (Figure 4.23); the other aims to establish a performance gap that outlines competitive parameters to obtain superior performance (Figure 4.24).

A cost-driven approach will lead to short-term incremental improvements.

Whatever the perspective guiding the process of benchmarking, formulating successful strategies and taking decisions requires systematic and up-to-date information on the following subjects:

- the competitive environment of the company's specific business activity;

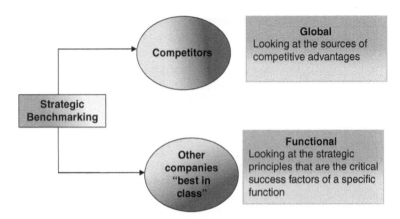

Figure 4.22   Strategic benchmarking

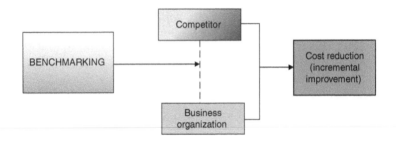

Figure 4.23   Cost-driven benchmarking.
Source: Adapted from Zairi (1992).

- the competitive gap between the company and the international market leaders; and
- knowledge of the causes of the competitive gap.

4.5.5   Strategic competitive benchmarking

Systematic and up-to-date information on the competitive environment of the company's business activity requires that organizations embark on strategic competitive benchmarking.

According to Spendolini (1992), competitive benchmarking involves identifying the products, services and work processes of the organization's direct competitors. The objective of competitive benchmarking is to identify specific information about a competitor's products, processes and business results and then make comparisons with those of the own

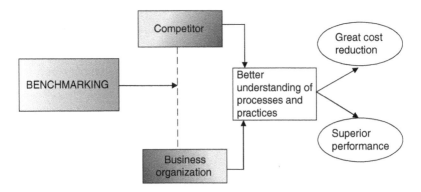

Figure 4.24 Process-driven benchmarking.
Source: Adapted from Zairi (1992).

organization. Competitive benchmarking is also useful in positioning the organization's products, services and processes relative to the marketplace. In many cases, the business practices of our competitors do not represent 'best in class' performance or best practices. However, this information is valuable because our competitors' practices affect the perceptions of our customers, suppliers, shareholders and potential customers, and all of them have a direct effect on our eventual business success.

When we move from competitive benchmarking to strategic competitive benchmarking (Watson, 1993) we mainly focus on core activities, core competences and, especially, core knowledge as depicted in Figure 4.25. Worldwide industry hyper-competition has ensured that strategic competitive benchmarking has become an essential learning tool.

Identifying and analysing core activities, core competencies and core knowledge are decisively important in a hyper-competitive environment, as organizations' success increasingly depends on a better understanding of the client's needs (actual and potential) and the competitor's strategies. Benchmarking is essentially a practice of identifying adaptive strategies to sustain competition.

Studies of market orientation demonstrate that, because competitors may adversely affect an organization, firms should focus on trying to understand their strengths, weaknesses and strategies, allowing the company to prepare for competitor activity and so minimize its adverse effects. Understanding the strengths and weaknesses of competitors might help organizations to know which product, market, or parts of those markets, to enter or avoid (Porter, 1979).

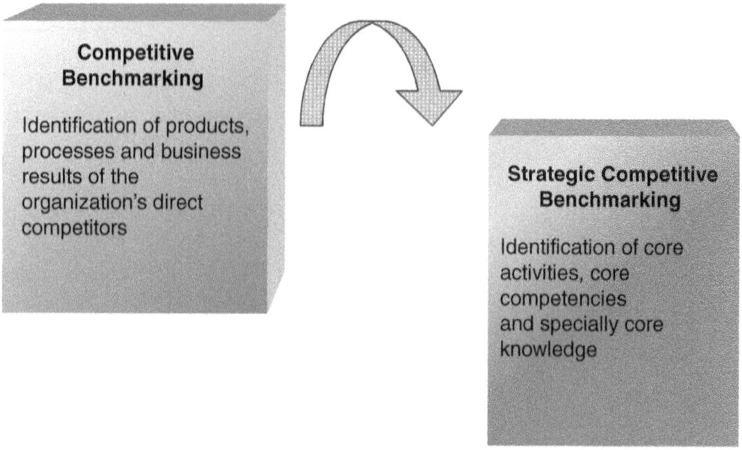

Figure 4.25   Moving from competitive benchmarking to strategic competitive benchmarking

4.5.6   The competitive gap

Knowing the causes of the competitive gap between a company and international market leaders in the same business activity is the key issue for increasing company competitiveness (Figure 4.26).

If core knowledge is the key strategic asset, improving existing core knowledge and building new core knowledge are fundamental tasks. This valuable knowledge can be obtained only from systematic and frequent comparison with world-class processes and the core competencies of competitors in the same business segments.

Each business activity has the specific relevant intellectual capital that explains the competitive gap. Having determined that intellectual capital, we use it as the basis of comparison in order to benchmark the 'world best' competitors in the same business activity.

In the context of the global knowledge economy, intellectual capital definitely represents the cause of any competitive gap. However, Marr (2004) argues that, to make benchmarking applicable to intellectual capital processes, some changes should be considered in the way benchmarking is carried out. Benchmarking intellectual capital on an operational level means that we have to benchmark knowledge processes, since knowledge management is the core activity for managing intellectual capital.

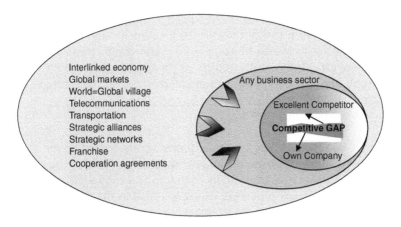

Figure 4.26 Knowing the causes that produce the competitive gap

Knowledge of successful processes is difficult to transfer so any attempt to benchmark intellectual capital management processes requires that we first understand whether the corporate context will allow such practices. Further, as knowledge is embedded in complex and dynamic contexts, it must be understood not only in terms of the corporate context but also in terms of corporate epistemology. In practice, we should first identify and understand the knowledge management processes that best match the corporate epistemology in order to benchmark intellectual capital processes, (Marr *et al.*, 2003, 2004).

4.6   The ICBS methodologies and frameworks: IICBS, OICBS, SCBS

Based on the theoretical principles developed earlier in this book, we are now in a position to build the Intellectual Capital Benchmarking System (ICBS) model. The ICBS is a knowledge-based strategic management information system framework that has been built drawing direct inspiration from the resource-based view and the activity-based view and tries to refine the classic strategic SWOT analysis, using benchmarking as a versatile learning tool.

The ICBS has a strategic view. The starting point for the ICBS is the firm's mission, strategy, and objectives. An element that differentiates ICBS from other intellectual capital models is the fact that 'the best in class' global competitor is also considered, thus allowing benchmarking to be undertaken in a systematic and permanent way.

The focus is defined in terms of core knowledge, core competencies or core capabilities, not products or services. Products or services are simply the manifestation of competencies and, in turn, competencies can be modulated into a variety of products.

Grant (1998:181) explains:

> ... in a world where customer preferences are volatile, the identity of customers is changing, and the technologies for serving customer requirements are continually evolving, an externally focused orientation does not provide a secure foundation for formulating long-term strategy. When the external is in a state of flux, the firm's own resources may be a much more stable basis on which to define its identity. Hence, a definition of a business in terms of what it is capable of doing may offer a more durable basis for strategy than a definition based upon the needs which the business seeks to satisfy.

Therefore, leveraging resources and capabilities across many markets and products, rather than targeting specific products for specific markets, becomes the strategic driver. While products and markets may come and go, resources and capabilities are more enduring. In this sense, competitive advantage based on resources and capabilities is potentially more sustainable than that based solely on product and market position.

All this reasoning leads to the fundamental role of resources and capabilities in strategy formulation – the basic assumption in building the ICBS frameworks.

The ICBS allows companies to compare their core competencies or intellectual capital with those of the best world competitors from the same activity segment. ICBS is grounded in certain factors that determine competitiveness in the global market environment (Figure 4.27).

Environment: This refers to the specific business unit environment. It includes Porter's competitive forces (customers, competitors, suppliers, entry barriers, and substitutive products), as well as demand evolution (past behaviour and foreseeable future), and the extent to which the activity in question is internationalized.

Outcomes: Expected economic and financial outcomes of the specified business unit.

Customer needs: Customer segment needs that the company expects to cover through the business unit activities.

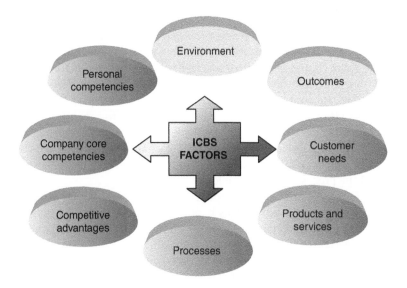

Figure 4.27   Factors of the ICBS model

Products and services: Products and services with their attributes, characteristics, functions, and embedded knowledge and technologies.

Processes: 'Value chain' activities, primary as well as secondary: those that are necessary to produce current products and services. These activities are made up of core business activities, outsourcing activities, and strategic alliances and cooperation agreement activities.

Competitive advantages. These are competitive advantages generated mainly in the different 'value chain' core business activities.

Company core competencies. Essential knowledge or core competencies that will produce competitive advantages.

Personal competencies. Professionals, managers, and support staff competencies and capabilities that will generate core competencies.

This eight-factor framework is flexible and allows identification and evaluation of the core competencies or essential knowledge within each particular factor. The framework explains how sustainable competitive advantages are achieved in final products and services.

Companies, if they want to be successful, need to produce competitive products and services. That is, they must focus on their core business activities, and outsource others. They must also work through carefully chosen cooperation agreements and strategic alliances with suppliers and other companies.

Nevertheless, competitive products and services are not easily achieved. Much work is needed to establish competitive advantages in each core business activity of the value chain. Core competencies in the value chain's core business activities produce products and services with competitive advantages and high knowledge or intellectual capital content. Innovation and research and development play fundamental roles in those core business activities. They allow the acquisition of new knowledge and new core competencies which, in turn, generates new products and services, intelligent products, new processes, new technologies, and so on – simultaneously improving both the present products and the processes and technologies that follow.

Finally, the acquisition of core competencies and the securing of all these competitive advantages is only possible through the actions of the people held to be crucial to the company in its technological and managerial scope. The personal competencies of these key people are responsible for the generation of core competencies, which, in turn, produce competitive advantages.

ICBS identifies the relevant factors and criteria for a specific activity segment. The systematic and continuous use of ICBS allows firms to generate intellectual capital balance sheets that complement the financial statements, and guides firms to improve, nurture and manage their intellectual capital.

Theoretically, the ICBS methodologies are based on the identification and evaluation of the core competencies of a company (company A) compared to that of its best world competitor (company B), as depicted in Figure 4.28. The suitable basis of comparison is the corresponding Business Units (BUs) of each company.

Within each business unit the value chain mechanism reveals the core competencies that explain the success of Company B's business unit (Figure 4.29). The core competencies that flow from the products and processes of the value chain are the items to benchmark in order to know the causes of the competitive gap.

As we have seen, the core competence (Prahalad and Hamel, 1990) and dynamic capabilities (Teece *et al.*, 1997) approaches put emphasis on the internal processes that a firm utilizes, as well as how they are deployed and how they will evolve. They have the benefit of indicating that competitive advantage is not just a function of how to compete; it is also a function of the assets one has to compete with, and how these assets can be deployed and redeployed in a changing market.

Some models have been developed in recent times in search of sustainable competitive advantages. These models, as we have seen, manage IC over the two 'value chains'; that is to say, the operations value chain and the innovation value chain.

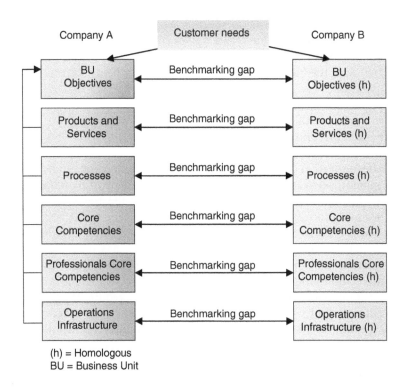

Figure 4.28 Intellectual Capital Benchmarking System (ICBS)

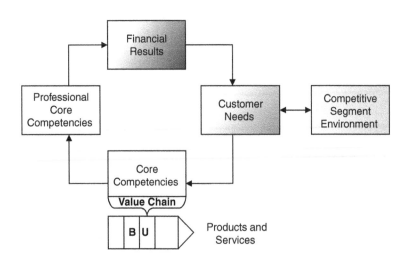

Figure 4.29 Core competencies in the value chain that explain the company's success

Nevertheless, to be more specific, we need to consider how value is created in each value chain (i.e. operation and innovation) of the internal business process value chain.

In fact, the business process value chain can be divided into major processes:

- the innovation process
- the operation process.

The innovation process is made up of product design and product development, whereas the operations process is made up of manufacturing, marketing, and post-sale service. Figure 4.30 illustrates the internal business process value chain perspective.

As previously noted, strategy formulation in dynamic environments, even those mainly based on core capabilities, has different features when dealing with the operations process than when dealing with the innovation process. Core capabilities can be very different in the two processes. Generally, innovation and creativity require the pooling of different and complementary resources, while the production process requires efficiency, and thus focus and similarities of knowledge. This corresponds to open vs. closed processes, which call for different structural configurations.

The operations process requires core capabilities and core competencies to produce competitive products and services. However, the nature of those core capabilities and competencies are, in nature, different from those required by the innovation process. In order to create desirable extended products and services that can compete in internationalized markets, firms need to exploit a wide range of skills beyond their traditional core competencies. Consumers are more demanding and more design aware. In addition, rapid changes in technology provide

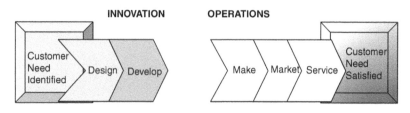

Figure 4.30   The internal business process value chain within a traditional perspective

Source: Adapted from Kaplan and Norton (1996:27).

new products and changes in existing ones, and the pressure to speed up the market introduction of new products also affects business. To integrate such requirements, complementary assets such as marketing, manufacturing and after sales service are often needed to ensure the successful commercialization of an innovation (Teece, 1986).

Thus, the ICBS considers the business process 'value chain' broken down into its two constituent parts. The general model of ICBS considers the innovation process value chain and the operations process value chain, providing specific methodologies and information systems for each of the constituent parts. Figure 4.31 illustrates this.

Thus, considering the particularities of each business process, the ICBS methodologies and frameworks can be divided into three partial models, as depicted in Figure 4.32. The first, the OICBS, refers to operations core activities and core knowledge, whereas the second, the IICBS, refers to innovation core activities and knowledge. The SCBS complements the two others intellectual capital models, focusing on social capital existing in a cluster location.

While the OICBS and the IICBS rely on the ability of a company to build sustainable competitive advantages from its internal intellectual capital, the SCBS emphasizes the role of the intellectual capital of other companies, organizations and institutions and specifically of those of the cluster, microcluster or territory where the company is located.

We have said that making good decisions depends on well-formulated strategies, anchored in good business formulas. The ICBS is a valuable

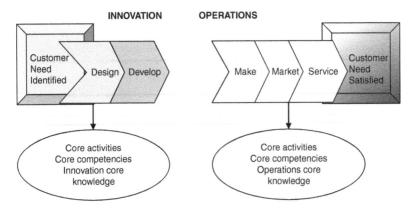

Figure 4.31 Business process value chain within the ICBS perspective

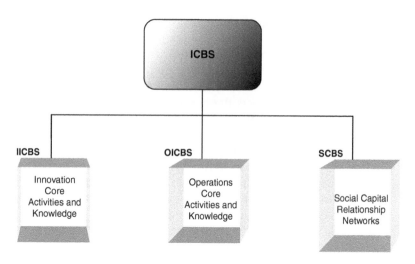

Figure 4.32   The ICBS frameworks

management information tool that helps organizations to achieve this purpose. On the other hand, well-implemented strategies are anchored in good business recipes. The Balanced Scorecard (BSC) and InCaS – Made in Europe provide the recipe that enables ingredients (i.e. tangible and intangible assets) already in existence in organizations to be combined and reconfigured for value creation.

To sum up, achieving excellence in the knowledge economy (our value proposition) depends on strategies that are well formulated and effectively implemented. We have developed, in this book, the theoretical principles that support two key important management tools that organizations should integrate into their overall business strategies. They are the ICBS for strategies formulation and BSC or InCaS – Made in Europe for strategies implementation (Figure 4.33).

4.7   Conclusion

This chapter focuses on the tools available for formulating business strategies. Traditional frameworks have had a lasting influence on strategic management but are now becoming the subject of critique because the assumptions they rely on cannot capture the dynamism and complexity of our environment.

In addition, the majority of intellectual capital representative models follow a strategic implementation approach. In fact, it is assumed that,

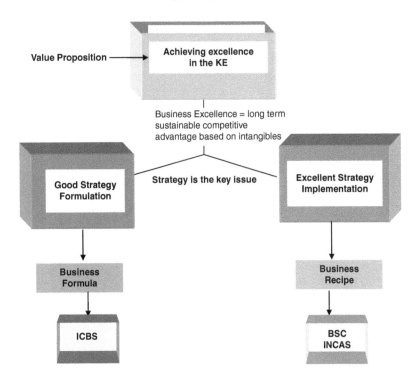

Figure 4.33   Formulating good strategies and implementing excellent strategies

in the company where the intellectual capital model will be applied, there is a strategy already formulated in clear and explicit terms. In this case, the intellectual capital model takes the strategic formula as given and concentrates on successful strategy implementation through managing intangibles in a systematic and continuous way. However, strategy researchers argue that success in business is always due to good strategy formulation (business formula) and excellent strategy implementation (business recipe).

ICBS fills this gap in the intellectual capital field by supporting the successful strategy formulation process in the knowledge economy context. ICBS is both a new management method and a new management tool that allows companies to benchmark their core innovation and operational capabilities against the world-class competitors in their sector. It is a framework built around the key factors and criteria that determine competitiveness in the context of global markets and it can be used to account for sustainable competitive advantages that might lead to superior performance and wealth creation. It identifies the specific competitiveness factors which are relevant in a given business sector, and audits and benchmarks the core capabilities or key intellectual capital that the company needs to develop to reach its future goals and successfully compete with 'best in class' competitors.

5
Operations Intellectual Capital Benchmarking System (OICBS)

5.1 Introduction

The operations process produces ordinary products and services through the systematic operations value chain. The systems, structures, and processes that the company already has in place serve as platforms for extending its knowledge and developing the new knowledge necessary for succeeding in the marketplace.

To be competitive, the operations process requires core competencies and core capabilities. Competitive products and services are not easily achieved. A lot of work is needed to build and sustain competitive advantages in the different core business activities of the value chain. Companies must focus on the areas where they do well (that is on the core activities and core knowledge of the different business units that make up the operations process) and subcontract (outsource) all others. They may establish cooperative agreements and strategic alliances with suppliers and other carefully selected companies. Core competencies can be built up within the individual company or in alliance with several companies.

The Operations Intellectual Capital Benchmarking System (OICBS) is a strategic information system that allows companies to benchmark against world-class competitors, in terms not only of core competencies but also of the processes, products and services produced by the operations of the company's business unit. In addition, it also benchmarks the operations infrastructure.

5.2   The OICBS framework

The OICBS theoretical framework is also based upon the resource-based and knowledge-based perspectives of the firm, and the activity-based view. An underlying proposition of the resource-based view and the knowledge-based view is that in addition to physical and financial resources, firms frequently need knowledge-based resources that are often tacit, implicit and non-codified, thereby creating knowledge barriers and making them difficult for competitors to imitate (Miller and Shamsie, 1996). Such knowledge may not be separable from the individuals or teams that configure, develop, and apply the resources to the firm's competitive position (Winter, 1987). Collective knowledge, the basis of most core competencies, is accumulated in employee skills and embedded in technical systems (for example, software and databases), organizational routines, values, and norms.

Based on such assumptions, the OICBS framework aims to discover the core knowledge and core activities that are the prime reason for sustainable competitive advantages (Viedma, 2004). For this purpose we use two important tools:

- the 'value chain' as a tool of analysis; and
- the benchmarking process.

The value chain analysis (see Figure 5.1) helps us to identify the core competencies of each business unit, and the benchmarking process (see Figure 5.2) allows us to identify the gaps, giving the necessary information for taking appropriate corrective action and for learning from past errors. The process of competitive benchmarking allows us to determine the specific competitiveness factors and criteria which are relevant for a given business activity.

The OICBS framework can be articulated in terms of eight competitiveness factors as defined in Figure 5.3.

These eight factors allow us to evaluate the core competencies or intellectual capital within each business unit

(1) *Customer needs.* The customer segment needs that the company expects to cover through the business unit activities
(2) *Business unit objectives.* Business unit activities lead to products and services through the corresponding processes using company and professional core capabilities and company operations infrastructure. The ultimate objectives of the business unit are the

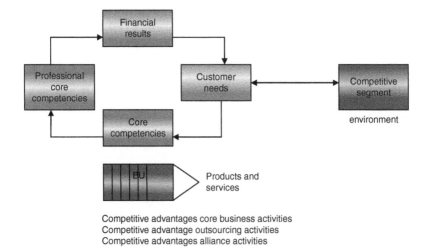

Figure 5.1 Value chain analysis of business units' core competencies
Source: Viedma (2004:43).

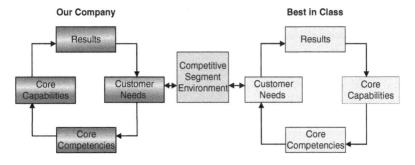

Figure 5.2 The process of benchmarking in OICBS
Source: Viedma (2004:44).

expected financial results through the satisfaction of customer needs

(3) *Products and services.* Products and services with their attributes, characteristics, functions, and embedded knowledge and technologies

(4) *Processes.* Operations 'value chain' activities that produce current products and services. These activities are made up of core business activities, outsourcing activities, and strategic alliances and

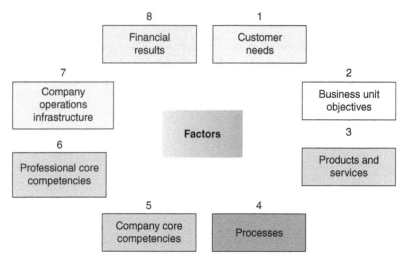

Figure 5.3   The eight-factor framework
Source: Viedma (2004:44).

cooperation agreement activities. Competitive advantages will be generated mainly in the different 'value chain' core business activities. Core competencies are mainly embodied in the core business activities of the value chain

(5) *Company core competencies.* Essential knowledge, or core competencies that will lead to competitive advantages, unique processes, and competitive products and services within the business unit.

(6) *Professional core competencies.* Professionals, managers, and support staff competencies and capabilities that will generate and perfect core capabilities and core competencies.

(7) *Company operations infrastructure.* Operations infrastructure (mainly intangible assets) that the company has for the use of different business units. The company operations infrastructure covers the following issues: knowledge management; information and telecommunications technology; company culture; information systems; organizational structure; human capital management; and leadership.

(8) *Financial results.* Expected economic and financial results from the business unit.

The eight-factor framework is flexible enough to allow changes in some of the factors, in the light of demands by the company and environment.

Summing up, Figure 5.4 complements and completes Figures 5.1, 5.2 and 5.3, and gives a full overview of the main elements that make up the OICBS framework.

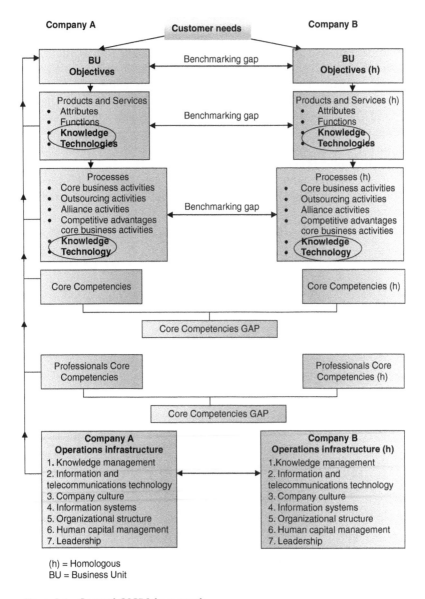

Figure 5.4 General OICBS framework

Source: Viedma (2004:45).

The General OICBS framework aims to show, in each of the flow chart steps or phases, the core knowledge and core technologies that are the prime reason for sustainable competitive advantages.

Keeping in mind the tree metaphor used in Chapter 2, we can also consider the company that performs current activities as a tree in which the visible part (the trunk, branches and fruits) corresponds to the tangible assets of a company. The invisible part of the tree (the roots of the tree below ground) corresponds to the intangible assets of the company. The two parts – tangible and intangible – are inseparable (see Figure 5.5). The roots of the tree send the sap through the trunk and the branches to the fruits. In a similar way, knowledge and its aggregates – competencies, capabilities and intellectual capital – make up the business sap that flows from the roots to the processes, and thus to the products and services.

To continue with the tree metaphor, each company business unit can be assimilated to a specific tree, and the whole company has

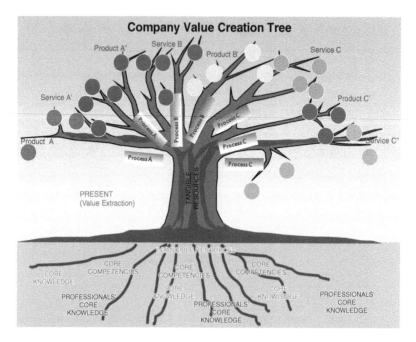

Figure 5.5 Operations tree
Source: Viedma (2004:42).

as many trees as it has business units. Each of these trees is fed with knowledge from its roots. In analysing each particular tree (that is, each individual business unit), we use the value chain as an analysis tool.

Furthermore, the company has at its disposal an intangible operations infrastructure that is shared by all the business units. This infrastructure corresponds to the fertile soil in which all the company trees are planted. This fertile soil nourishes the roots (core knowledge) of each individual company tree (see Figure 5.6).

The OICBS methodology draws inspiration from the tree metaphor. The flow chart in Figure 5.7 is a summary representation of the OICBS working scheme. The flow chart shows that within each company tree (business unit) an analysis can be made, successively, of the fruits (products and services), the branches (processes), and the roots (core competencies and professional core competencies). For this purpose *ad hoc* personalized questionnaires can be used. In addition, the overall soil fertility (operations infrastructure) can be analysed.

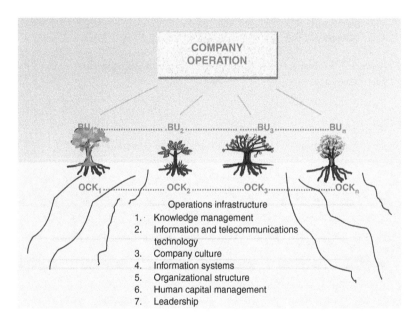

Figure 5.6 Company operations infrastructure
Source: Viedma (2004:42).

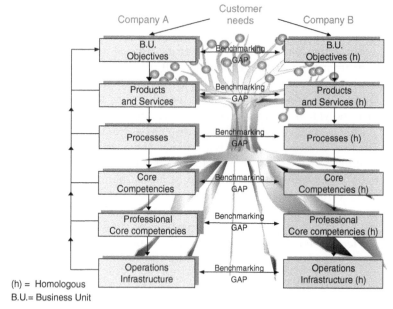

(h) = Homologous
B.U.= Business Unit

Figure 5.7 Operations intellectual capital benchmarking system
Source: Viedma (2004:43).

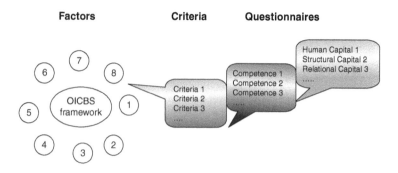

Figure 5.8 Specific OICBS framework
Source: Viedma (2004:46).

In the same way, the alternative explanation based on the tree metaphor makes it possible to compare each specific tree (business unit) with the homologous tree of the best of the competition, thus facilitating the benchmarking of fruits (products and services), branches (processes), roots (core competencies and professional core competencies) and soil fertility (operations infrastructure). The benchmarking gap provides the necessary information for taking appropriate corrective actions.

5.3   The OICBS implementation process

The OICBS general framework that we have described is a general framework that can be used to generate a specific OICBS framework suitable to a specific business context. We customize the OICBS general framework for a specific business context through questionnaires and by those criteria that best suit the specifications of a given business design. At the same time, we give appropriate weights to the criteria and questionnaires. Figure 5.8 illustrates the process described above.

Given that a large part of the information may not be known precisely, all questions in all the OICBS questionnaires have a 'response precision' box that indicates the accuracy of each particular answer. By integrating the results of the 'response precision' boxes, the OICBS framework permits the degree of reliability of the benchmarking and its constituent parts to be measured. Plans can then be established for systematically improving information acquisition and to set up an intelligence team in the company.

As explained above, the OICBS is a strategic information system built around a framework of eight factors (criteria) in the questionnaires, which fulfils the requirements of an extended SWOT analysis. OICBS is thus also a strategic information system that allows companies to benchmark against world-class competitors in terms not only of core competencies but also the processes, products, and services produced by the operations of the company's business units. It also benchmarks the operations infrastructure.

Finally, the processing of questionnaires corresponding to each of the company competitiveness factors provides us with useful management information, in particular the balance sheets, which can be obtained for the company as whole or for each competitiveness factor. Some examples of balances and results are given in Figure 5.9.

The OICBS implementation chart is presented below (Figure 5.9).

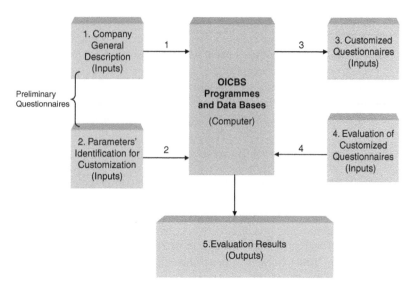

Figure 5.9   OICBS Implementation Chart

Step 1: Company General Description

Preliminary questionnaires have to be filled up to collect the company's data

- General description (brief company history)
- Company's activities and business units
- Objectives and global strategy
- Balance sheets and profit and loss accounts
- Team works
- Make up the assessment teams
- Sources of information

Step 2: Identification of Parameters for Customization

Once the preliminary questionnaires have been obtained, the second phase is to customize the evaluation. Identification of parameters will make it possible to customize the final questionnaires (to adapt final questionnaires to the company's characteristics)

- Identification of competitors
- Business Units of the company
- Competitive gap
- Products/services to be benchmarked
- Attributes or functions of products/services
- Value chain
- Team work groups and sources of information

Step 3: Customized Questionnaires

Based on information collected in the previous phases, the system generates customized questionnaires to be filled up by top management and professional people, including

- Product evaluation
- Core business competitive advantages
- Outsourcing competitive advantages
- Alliances and cooperation agreement competitive advantages
- Core competencies analysis
- Personal competencies
- Environment evaluation

Step 4: Evaluation of Customized Questionnaires

Once filled in, information collected through questionnaires will be processed by the computer.

Step 5: Evaluation Results

Final results comprise the following information:

1) Summary Results

- Competencies benchmarking
- Key success factors
- Intellectual Capital Balance Sheet
- Precision Indexes

2) Detail Results

- Products evaluation

- Evaluation of 'value chain' core business activities
- Evaluation of value chain outsourcing activities
- Evaluation of alliances and cooperation agreements
- Outsourcing level
- Evaluation of competitive environment

3) Core Competencies Results

- Core and personal competencies (summary)
- Core and personal competencies (detail)

The system has been tested and successfully implemented in more than 50 small and medium-sized European enterprises.

Some examples of balances and results are given below in Figures 5.10 and 5.11.

The system is very flexible and allows for different reporting formats. The next practical case is an actual example of moving from the former balance sheet to the web format report.

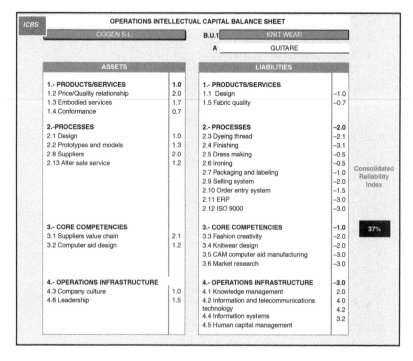

Figure 5.10   Operations intellectual capital balance sheet (summary)

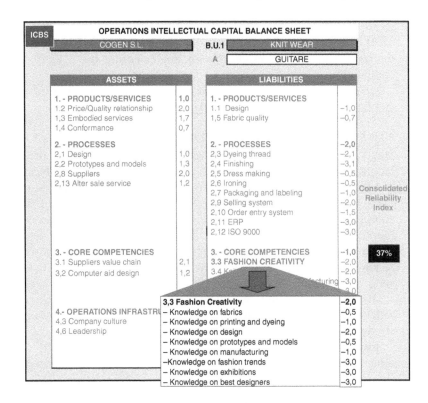

Figure 5.11 Operations intellectual capital balance sheet (detail)

5.4 Practical case

The purpose of the practical cases is to provide an overview of how ICBS works in order to understand the functionalities of the system. Obviously, a complete understanding of the system is only possible after carefully reading the user manual and using the software in practical applications.

In order to carry out the implementation chart, the company organizes different workshops that are tailored-made to the specific characteristics of each one of the different phases into which the implementation chart is divided. Top managers are the only participants in the workshops but other managers, expert in specific areas, could be invited in order to define strategic issues or provide some relevant information. The workshops need to be guided by a moderator who is an expert in ICBS methodology and systems software. As well as the moderator, the company should appoint an ICBS project manager who will be responsible for implementing the ICBS in the company.

For confidential reasons, we have not provided the name of the company that inspired the practical case that follows.

Step 1:   Company's General Description (1st Workshop)

Smart Fashion Ltd is a company dedicated to the design and manufacture of men's casual new clothes. Smart Fashion is an SME, located in the Barcelona region of Spain and it operates only in the Spanish market. Nevertheless, it is forced to compete with the world-class competitors that operate in Spain. It is a wholesaler with its own brands. The mission of the company is to dress the modern young man in smart designer clothes that break away conventional criteria. As a wholesaler, they only sell to exclusive retailers for each particular geographic area.

The company has only one business unit and it competes with very well known world-class competitors such as Adolfo Dominguez, Mango, Stradivarius, Maximo Dutti and Pull and Bear.

Information on balance sheets, P/L accounts, BUs profitability and other relevant financial and economic indicators were also collected in this workshop.

Step 2:   Identification of Parameters for Customization (2nd Workshop)

Relevant parameters for customization were indentified in the following areas:

- identification of competitors;
- customer needs satisfaction;
- products/services to be benchmarked;
- products/services attributes or functions;
- value chain activities.

Mango and Stradivarius were selected as the most suitable competitors to be benchmarked.

The parameters identified for customer needs satisfaction were:

- current needs: original design; fashion; quality and price; and for

- future needs: original design; fashion; quality; price; and fabric technology.

In this particular case there is only one product to be benchmarked, that is 'casual clothing for youngsters' and the main attributes identified for this product are the following: design; garment novelty; price fashion, avant-gardism; quality; quick service; brand; originality; and constant renewal.

The different activities of the value chain are listed sequentially, identifying which of them are 'core activities' and which 'non-core activities'. The 'non-core' activities may be outsourced.

Core activities included: fashion creation; prototypes; garment selection; purchasing garments and accessories; pattern making; finishing and labelling; wholesale; shipment management; post-selling services; computer systems; logistics; human resources; administration; and marketing.

'Non-core activities' included: trimming; dressmaking; ironing; general services; and distribution.

Step 3: Customized Questionnaires

The computer processed the information provided at Step 2, producing customized questionnaires to be filled in at Step 4.

Step 4: Evaluation of Customized Questionnaires
(3rd Workshop)

Customized questionnaires were now evaluated by the workshop participants. These questionnaires were the basis for the evaluation results of Step 5.

Step 5: Evaluation Results (4th Workshop)

The main outputs of OICBS are the evaluation results produced in this phase. The most meaningful results are shown in the following figures:

Smart Fashion Ltd has the following three core competencies: fashion creation; wholesaling; and dressmaking. Their particular evaluation is given below.

The system also provides detailed results on each of the core activities, outsourcing activities, alliance activities and core competencies. Detailed results also include personal staff assessments using the

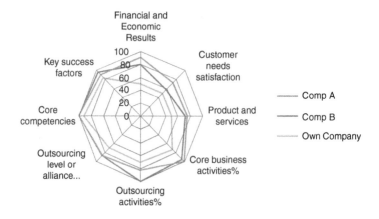

		OWN	Comp A	Comp B
1	Financial and Economic Results	50	90	80
2	Customer needs satisfaction	50	72.50	57.50
3	Products and services	50	75	71
4	Core business activities %	73	99	95
5	Outsourcing activities%	71	84	100
6	Outsourcing level or alliance activities%	70	86	86
7	Core competencies	91.58	98.33	98.33
8	Key success factors	84	90	96
	Media	67.45	86.85	85.48

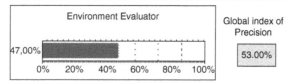

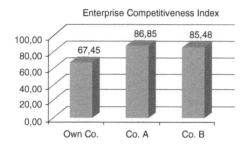

Figure 5.12   OICBS summary results

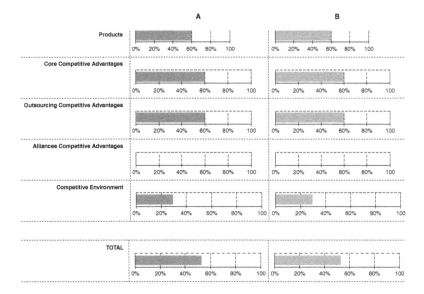

Figure 5.13 Precision index evaluation

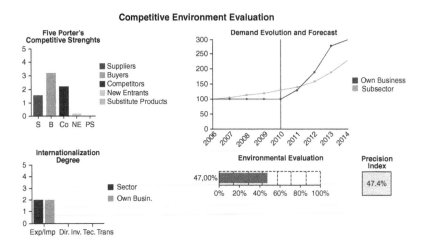

Figure 5.14 Competitive environment evaluation

		OWN	Comp A	Comp B
1	Financial and Economic Results	50	90	80
2	**Customer needs satisfaction**	50	72.50	57.50
3	Products and services	50	75	71
4	Core business activities %	73	99	95
5	Outsourcing activities %	71	84	100
6	Outsourcing level or alliance activities %	70	86	86
7	Core competencies	91.58	98.33	98.33
8	Key success factors	84	90	96

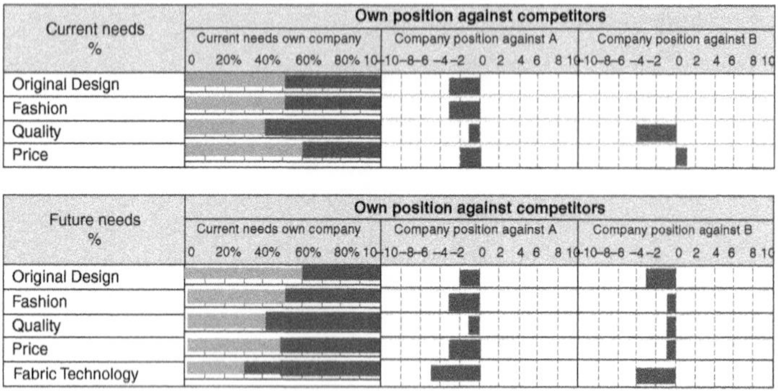

Figure 5.15   Customer needs satisfaction

		OWN	Comp A	Comp B
1	Financial and Economic Results	50	90	80
2	Customer needs satisfaction	50	72.50	57.50
3	**Products and services**	**50**	**75**	**71**
4	Core business activities %	73	99	95
5	Outsourcing activities%	71	84	100
6	Outsourcing level or alliance activities %	70	86	86
7	Core competencies	91.58	98.33	98.33
8	Key success factors	84	90	96

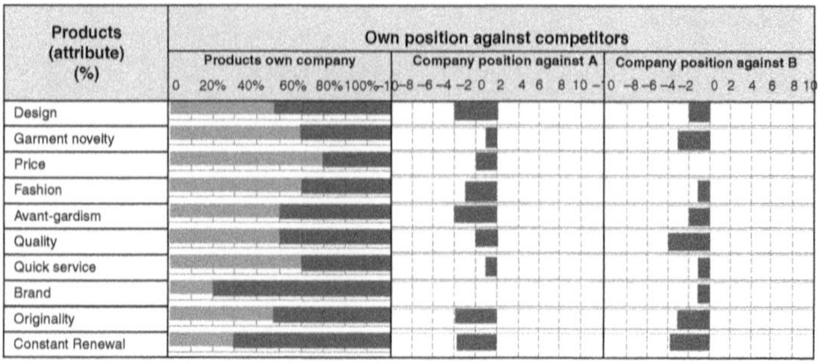

Figure 5.16   Products and services

		OWN	Comp A	Comp B
1	Financial and Economic Results	50	90	80
2	Customer needs satisfaction	50	72.50	57.50
3	Products and services	50	75	71
4	**Core business activities %**	**73**	**99**	**95**
5	Outsourcing activities%	71	84	100
6	Outsourcing level or alliance activities%	70	86	86
7	Core competencies	91.58	98.33	98.33
8	Key success factors	84	90	96

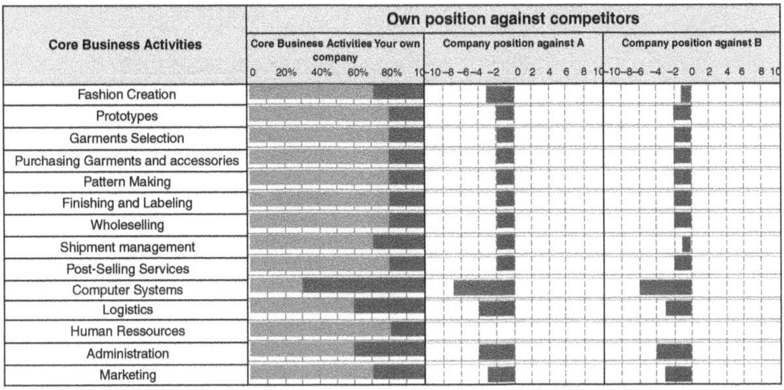

Figure 5.17 Core business activities

		OWN	Comp A	Comp B
1	Financial and Economic Results	50	90	80
2	Customer needs satisfaction	50	72.50	57.50
3	Products and services	50	75	71
4	Core business activities %	73	99	95
5	**Outsourcing activities%**	**71**	**84**	**100**
6	Outsourcing level or alliance activities%	70	86	86
7	Core competencies	91.58	98.33	98.33
8	Key success factors	84	90	96

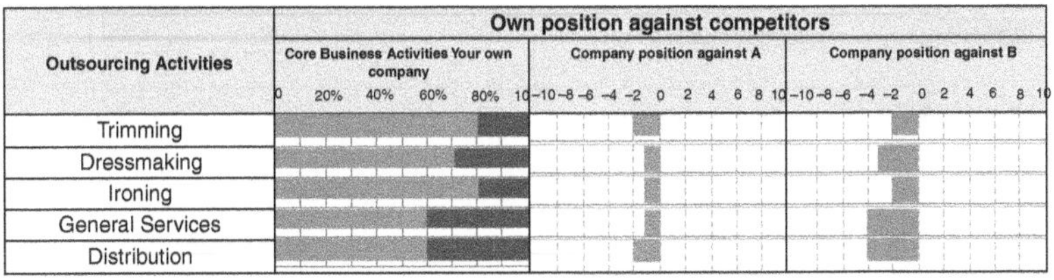

Figure 5.18 Outsourcing activities

		OWN	Comp A	Comp B
1	Financial and Economic Results	50	90	80
2	Customer needs satisfaction	50	72.50	57.50
3	Products and services	50	75	71
4	Core business activities %	73	99	95
5	Outsourcing activities%	71	84	100
6	**Outsourcing level or alliance activities%**	**70**	**86**	**86**
7	Core competencies	91.58	98.33	98.33
8	Key success factors	84	90	96

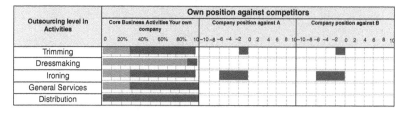

Figure 5.19 Outsourcing level

		OWN	Comp A	Comp B
1	Financial and Economic Results	50	90	80
2	Customer needs satisfaction	50	72.50	57.50
3	Products and services	50	75	71
4	Core business activities %	73	99	95
5	Outsourcing activities %	71	84	100
6	Outsourcing level or alliance activities %	70	86	86
7	**Core competencies**	**91.58**	**98.33**	**98.33**
8	Key success factors	84	90	96

Core Competencies	OWN	Company A	Company B
Fashion creation (8)	9.38	10	10
Wholesales (10)	9.10	9.50	9.50
Dressmaking (9)	9.00	10	10
TOTAL	9.16	9.83	9.83

Figure 5.20 Core competencies

Fashion creation

	OWN	Company A	Company B
Fashion creation (8)	9,38	10	10
Wholesales (10)	9.10	9.50	9.50
Dressmaking (9)	9.00	10	10

Core competence (Fashion creation)	Own position against competitors		
	Core competence own company	Company position against A	Company position against B
	0 20% 40% 60% 80% 10	-10-8-6 -4 -2 0 2 4 6 8 10	-10-8-6 -4 -2 0 2 4 6 8 10
Leading Designers			
Design			
Fashion Trend			
Cut and Pattern Making			
Printing and Colouring			
Fairs			
Dressmaking			
Garments			

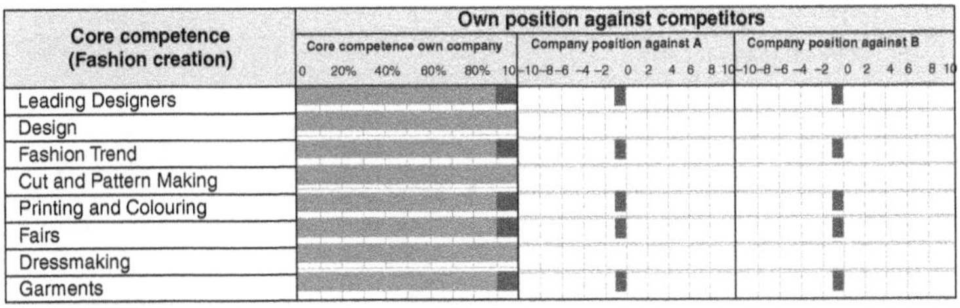

Wholesale

	OWN	Company A	Company B
Fashion creation (8)	9.38	10	10
Wholesales (10)	9.10	9.50	9.50
Dressmaking (9)	9,00	10	10

Core competence (Wholesales)	Own position against competitors		
	Core competence own company	Company position against A	Company position against B
	0 20% 40% 60% 80% 10	-10-8-6 -4 -2 0 2 4 6 8 10	-10-8-6 -4 -2 0 2 4 6 8 10
Kindless			
Orders Preparation			
Sold Garments			
Dealings and negotiations			
Getting information from Customers			
Factory Communications			
Information Systems			
Listening and understanding customer needs			
Trust			
Shipping Preparation			

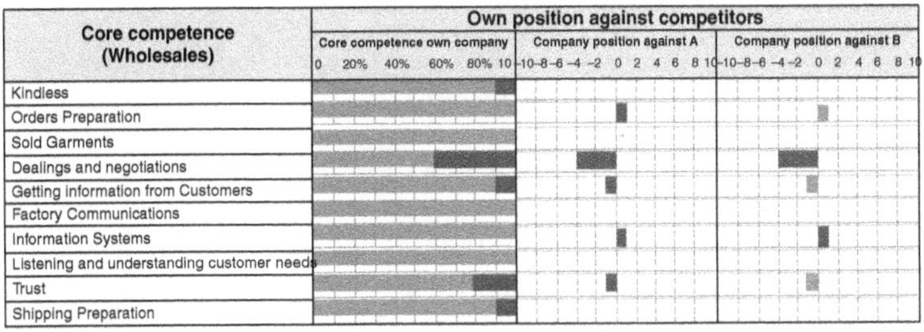

Dressmaking

	OWN	Company A	Company B
Fashio creation (8)	9 .38	10	10
Wholesales (10)	9.10	9.50	9.50
Dressmaking (9)	9.00	10	10

Core competence (Dressmaking)	Own position against competitors		
	Core competence own company	Company position against A	Company position against B
	0 20% 40% 60% 80% 10	-10-8-6 -4 -2 0 2 4 6 810	-10-8-6 -4 -2 0 2 4 6 8 10
Workshops			
Workshop Organization			
Outsourcing Experience			
Main Staff			
Prototypes and test System			
Workshops Choices			
Monitoring and Control			
Workshops Loyality			
Delivery and reception Logistics			

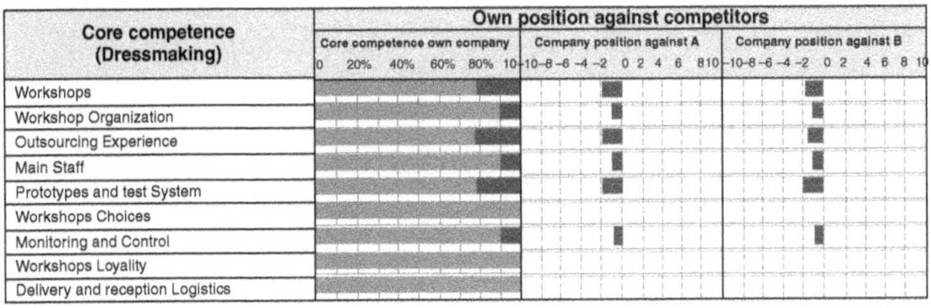

Figure 5.20 Continued

		OWN	Comp A	Comp B
1	Financial and Economic Results	50	90	80
2	Customer needs satisfaction	50	72.50	57.50
3	Products and services	50	75	71
4	Core business activities %	73	99	95
5	Outsourcing activities%	71	84	100
6	Outsourcing level or alliance activities%	70	86	86
7	Core competencies	91.58	98.33	98.33
8	**Key success factors**	**84**	**90**	**96**

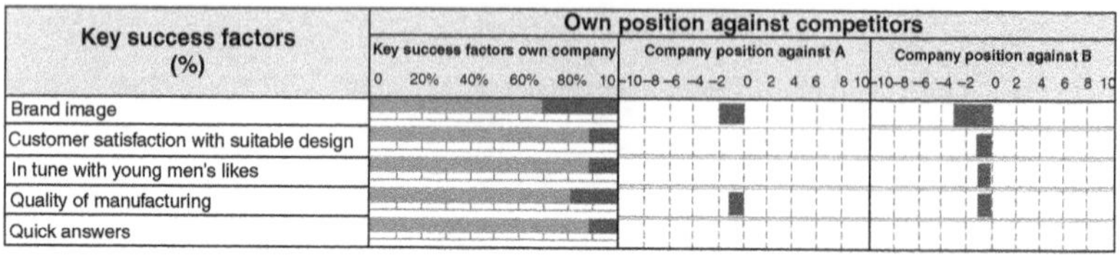

Figure 5.21   Key success factors

following factors: technological competence; management competence; experience; relationship; attitude; and intellectual agility.

5.5   Benefits from using OICBS

The main benefits from using OICBS are the following:

- Making a strategy check-up that allows companies to evaluate their existing business models and their competitive advantages.
- Learning from the best competitors that surpass one's own competitive operations capabilities.
- Identifying the specific operations capabilities factors and criteria which are relevant in a given business activity.
- Through the OICBS factors framework, enabling the identification, audit and benchmark of the operations core competencies that are the main sources of long term sustainable competitive advantages.
- When using OICBS in an orderly, systematic and reiterative way, we obtain operations capabilities balance sheets that are future-oriented. They complement and perfect the finance balance sheets, leading companies to leveraging operations IC.

- Selecting in a systematic and organized way the necessary information for evaluating relevant factors, core operations competencies, and operations IC.
- Giving to the SME's managers access to operations competencies and operations IC management in a systematic and organized way.
- Facilitating the work of the Benchmarking and Competitive Intelligence team.

6
Innovation Intellectual Capital Benchmarking System (IICBS)

6.1 Introduction

Innovation has become a major driver of business success and a prerequisite for sustainable development in a globalized world.

The only things that give an organization a sustainable edge are what it knows, how it uses what it knows, and how fast it can learn new things. Pressures to innovate (continuously and quickly) and to seek out new sources of differential advantage are now the essence of any strategy.

Confronted with increasing global competition, organizations can no longer survive on their own innovation efforts. Innovation activities are increasingly international and require more 'open' approaches.

However, although there is general agreement on the key role of knowledge as a source of competitive advantage, few in the industry know how to manage IC to produce value in an efficient way. This lack of expertise is especially relevant when dealing with the acquisition of new knowledge, which is one of the key drivers of the innovation process.

IICBS identifies, audits, and benchmarks the core capabilities or key IC that the company needs in order to develop and to reach its future goals and successfully compete with 'best in class' competitors.

Organizations that want to pursue innovation do not have to rely on internal competencies alone (Chesbrough, 2003). They can absorb and utilize knowledge from outside the company through different forms of collaboration with external partners such as customers, suppliers, and even with competitors. Under the paradigm of open innovation, firms can and should use external ideas as well as internal ideas, thus creating an open platform around their innovations so that customers, employees, and even competitors, can build upon an ongoing, evolving community of users, doers and creators.

6.2   The IICBS framework

Similar to the OICBS, the Innovation Intellectual Capital Benchmarking System (IICBS) is a framework that focuses on the innovation process. The innovation process represents the long wave of value creation, and it is the most powerful driver of future financial results. In that sense, competing successfully in the long run means innovating, and innovating entails building new competencies, new capabilities, and new knowledge. If resources provide the inputs, organizational capabilities represent the firm's capacity to coordinate them, put them to productive use, and shape them into innovative outputs (Collis, 1994).

To compete successfully in the future, companies need to innovate in a systematic way. The way to innovate is through projects that have the clear objective of satisfying the emerging needs of customers. Customer needs satisfaction is achieved through the project's new products and services. Nevertheless, competitive products and services are not easily achieved. A lot of work is needed in order gradually to establish competitive advantages in the different core activities of the value chain process. Core competencies and core capabilities in the core project activities of the 'value chain' produce new products and services with competitive advantages and a high knowledge or intellectual content. In addition, the company innovation infrastructure, that is, the company R&D department, must give the necessary support to the whole process.

Finally, the acquisitions of core capabilities, and the achievement of all those competitive advantages, is only possible through the actions of the different project leaders who decide on and carry out objectives and strategies, and who shape business culture with their ways and methods.

When companies compete for the future (Hamel and Prahalad, 1994), they compete on building and deploying their core competencies and capabilities in a consistent way. Consistency depends, first of all, on a strong consensus about which competencies to build and support and, secondly, on the stability of the management teams charged with competence development. Such consistency is unlikely unless senior managers agree on what competencies should be built. Without such a consensus, a company's competence-building efforts may well fragment, as various business units pursue their independent competence-building agenda, or the firm may simply fail to build new competencies.

Another important assumption of this framework is that companies do not compete with new products but, at a deeper level, they compete on their capacity to develop new products, or over their core competencies (Hamel and Prahalad, 1994). In their strategies, companies focus on product leadership but compete to establish core competencies. As argued by Prahalad and Hamel (1990), organizations would be well advised to avoid the risks associated with managing a set of unrelated businesses, and instead 'stick to the knitting' by relying on a set of core competencies.

Companies do not compete on products and services. They really compete on the underlying capabilities that make the products and services possible. To conceptualize firms as portfolios of competencies, rather than as portfolios of products or services, gives a better perspective on the firm's innovative abilities and renewal prospects (Wernerfelt, 1984; Danneels, 2002). Accordingly, competing for the future will be about competing for future capabilities (the source of new processes, products, and services) against the world-class future capabilities of the best future competitors.

Empirical studies of innovation demonstrate that, in general: (i) innovation begins with the creation of a new kind of knowledge within a firm; and (ii) the new knowledge is not 'product-centric' but 'process-centric', that is, it is about a new way of doing something.

An excellent company embraces innovation by constantly introducing change. Not change for the sake of change, and not change simply to follow the pack, but reinventing the way work gets done. Such innovations include:

- new work structures – teams, networks, and outsourcing;
- new work procedures – advanced technology, new manufacturing methods, information technology, quality management, and process cycle time;
- human resource management strategies to ensure strategic fit with business goals and inject flexibility – constant training, recruiting the best talent, and rewarding employees; and
- creating a work environment to spur innovation – encouraging risk-taking behaviours and valuing experimentation.

The paradigm of a competitive or excellent company, in the context of global markets, and especially the 'innovative company' paradigm,

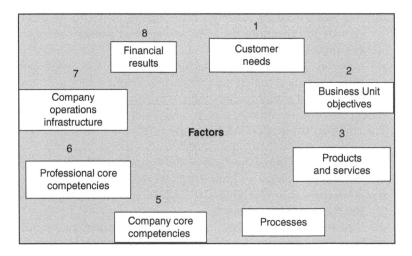

Figure 6.1   The eight factors framework

provide us with the basis for constructing the IICBS general framework. The merit of the IICBS framework is that it provides a systematic
approach to identifying the specific innovation and competitiveness
factors that are relevant to a given business sector.

The IICBS framework can be articulated as the eight factors depicted
in Figure 6.1.

(1) *Customer emerging needs.* Potential or emerging 'customer segment'
needs that the company expects to cover through the project.
(2) *Project objectives.* The project is the innovation business unit that
leads to new products and services through new processes, using
company and professional core competencies and company innovation infrastructure. The ultimate objectives of the project are the
expected financial results.
(3) *New products and services.* New products and services with their
attributes and characteristics and functions.
(4) *New processes.* Primary and support value chain activities that
produce the project's new products and services. These activities
are made up of core project activities, outsourcing activities, and
strategic alliances and cooperation agreement activities.
(5) *New company core capabilities.* Essential knowledge or core capabilities that will make possible and will lead to competitive advantages,
new processes, and new products and services within the project.

(6) *New professional core capabilities.* Professionals', managers', and support staff's capabilities that will generate and perfect core capabilities and core competencies.

(7) *Company innovation infrastructure.* Research and development infrastructure (tangible and intangible assets) that the company has and that is available to different projects.

The company innovation infrastructure covers the following issues:

(a) Is technology innovation part of the business strategy?
(b) What is the company's knowledge and technology standard?
(c) Is the research and development department working together with the other main departments?
(d) How well organized is the research and development department?
(e) How many resources are allocated to the innovation function?
(f) Are there any technologies information systems? How are they performing?
(g) How are they performing the technology management systems?

(8) *Financial results.* Expected economic and financial results from the project.

The eight factor framework is flexible enough to allow changes to some of their factors, in response to the company and environmental circumstances.

The IICBS framework evaluates or assesses innovation capabilities, using the value chain analysis as described in Figure 6.2, which makes possible the realization of new projects that will lead to new products and services through the appropriate processes. The IICBS also assesses the innovation infrastructure which supports all the new projects that the company has started or is going to start in the near future.

We can identify characteristics of the IICSB framework that are similar to those we have established in discussing the OICBS framework.

The ICSB methodology and frameworks draw inspiration from an alternative explanation (Viedma, 2001). Based on the metaphor of a tree, we can consider the company that performs innovation activities as a new tree in which the visible part (that is, the trunk, the branches, and the fruits) corresponds to the tangible assets of the innovative company (see Figure 6.3). The invisible part of the tree (that is, the roots of the tree below ground) corresponds to the intangible assets of innovative companies. The two parts – tangible and intangible – are

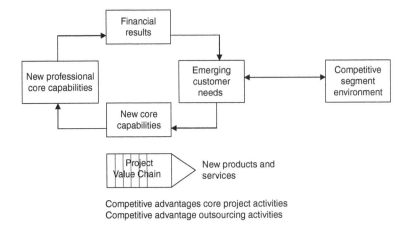

Figure 6.2   Innovation value chain as an analytical tool

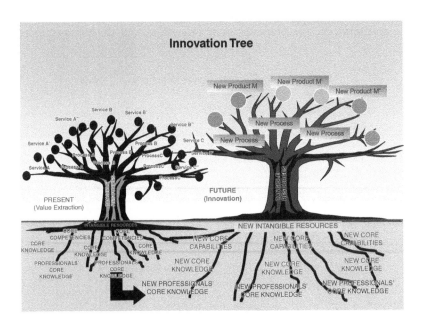

Figure 6.3   Innovation tree

Source: http://www.intellectualcapitalmanagementsystems.com.

inseparable. The roots of the tree send the sap through the trunk and the branches to the fruits. In a similar way, knowledge and its aggregates – competencies, capabilities, and intellectual capital – make up the flows from the roots to the new processes, and thus to the new products and services.

Continuing with the tree metaphor, each company project unit can be assimilated to a specific tree and the whole company has as many trees as it has project units. Each of these trees is fed with the knowledge of its roots. Furthermore, the company has at its disposal a common intangible innovation infrastructure that is shared by all the project units. This infrastructure corresponds to the fertile soil in which all the company trees are planted. This fertile soil nourishes the roots (core knowledge) of each individual innovation company tree (see Figure 6.4).

The assessment process is carried out in a two-fold fashion as depicted in the flow chart of Figure 6.5. On one side, we take as reference benchmarks the innovative project objectives and goals of Company A; on the other side, we take as a reference benchmark the equivalent innovative project of the best world competitor (Company B). The flow chart shows that, within each company innovation tree (project unit), an analysis can be made, successively, of the fruits (new products and services), the branches (new processes), and the roots (new core

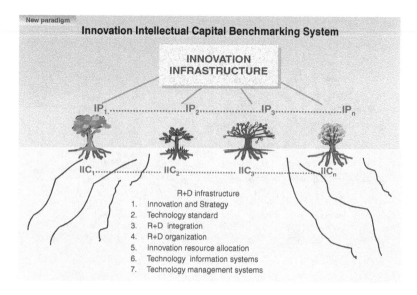

Figure 6.4   Innovation industry sector infrastructure
Source: http://www.intellectualcapitalmanagementsystems.com.

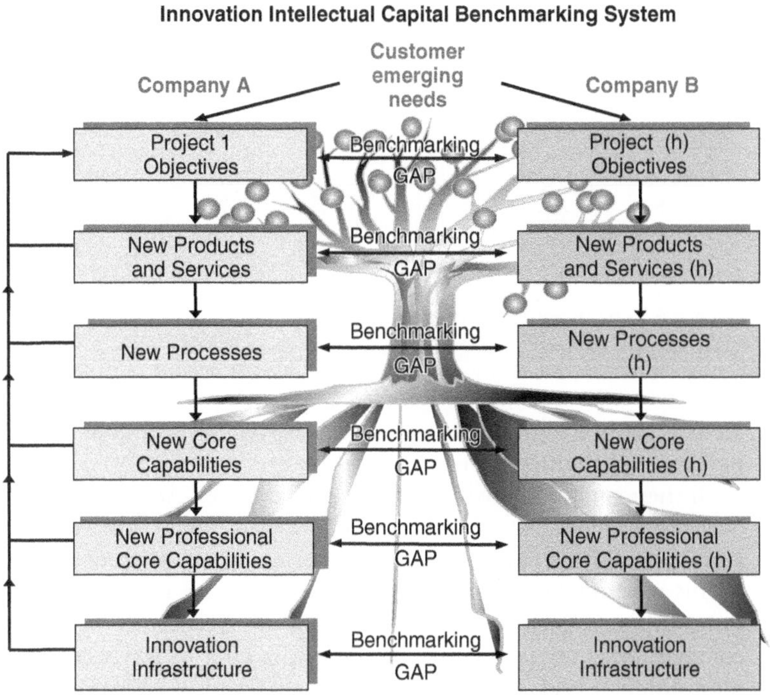

Innovation Intellectual Capital Benchmarking System

Figure 6.5 Innovation Intellectual Capital Benchmarking System (IICBS)
Source: http://www.intellectualcapitalmanagementsystems.com.

competencies and professional core competencies). For this purpose, *ad hoc* personalized questionnaires can be used. In addition, the overall soil fertility (innovation infrastructure) can be analysed.

As mentioned above, in analysing each particular tree (that is, each individual project unit), we use the innovation value chain as an analysis tool. We argue that it is a useful approach because it helps to identify the interrelationships between innovative products and innovation capabilities. If products with a closer fit to a firm's competencies tend to be more successful, the effect that new product projects have on a firm's competencies is a crucial issue to be observed in the trajectory of firm's renewal and development.

Prusak (1996) argued that the only thing that gives an organization a competitive edge, the only thing that is sustainable, is what it knows, how it uses what it knows, and how quickly it can know something new. In addition, Teece *et al.*, (1997) called attention to the need for the renewal of firms' competencies in changing environments. Thus, we

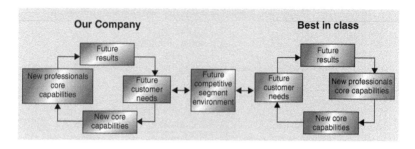

Figure 6.6 The process of benchmarking in IICBS

Source: http://www.intellectualcapitalmanagementsystems.com.

are now dealing with new essential knowledge, new core competencies, new core capabilities, or new IC.

All these analyses have the ultimate purpose of discovering, in each of the flow chart steps, the new core knowledge and new core technologies that are the prime reason for sustainable competitive advantages.

This methodology makes it possible to compare each specific tree (innovation project) with the corresponding tree of the best of the competition, thus facilitating the benchmarking of leaves and fruits (new products and services), branches (new processes), roots (new core competencies and new professional core competencies), and soil fertility (innovation infrastructure). The benchmarking process is shown in Figures 6.5 and 6.6. In these figures, the benchmarking gap provides the necessary information for taking appropriate corrective action and for learning from past errors.

6.3   The IICBS implementation process

The IICBS general framework described above can be used to generate the specific IICBS framework suitable to a specific business context.

The general framework with eight factors is used for moving from the general framework (general context) to the specific framework (specific business context), as depicted in Figure 6.7.

We customize the IICBS general framework for a specific business context by means of the criteria and questionnaires, as defined in Figure 6.8, or by choosing among the criteria and questionnaires the ones that best suit the specifications of a given business design. The process of competitive benchmarking allows us to determine the specific competitiveness factors and criteria that are relevant to a firm's

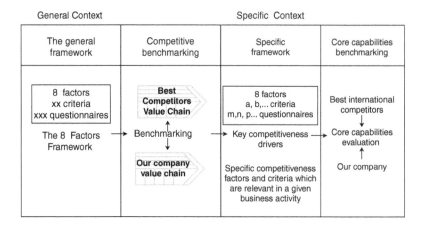

Figure 6.7   From a general to a specific context
Source: Viedma (2001:159).

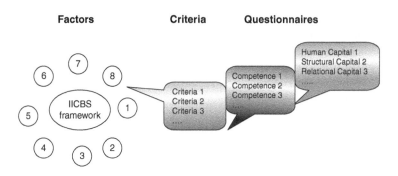

Figure 6.8   Specific IICBS framework
Source: Viedma (2001:158).

business activity. These factors and criteria may also be termed key competitiveness drivers.

The questionnaires that are directly derived from the criteria allow us to evaluate and benchmark core capabilities in the specific business context.

When filling out the questionnaires, the different benchmarking teams are able to define and evaluate the innovation core capabilities, and within the core capabilities, the three main types of IC (human capital, structural capital and relational capital).

Given that a large part of the information (above all, on the best in class competitor project) may not be known precisely, all the questions in all the IICBS questionnaires have a 'response precision' box.

By integrating the results of the response precision boxes, the IICBS method also permits us to evaluate the reliability of the benchmarking and its constituent parts in establishing plans for systematically improving information acquisition. It also supports the creation of a competitive intelligence team in the company.

The following elements are involved in putting the IICBS method in practice:

- A general database that contains all the possible criteria and questionnaires to be used. This means that each factor can be looked at in the greatest possible detail.
- A user-system interface that enables criteria and questionnaires to be adapted to the particularities of each business segment and business project.
- Successive responses to the personalized questionnaires, which are used to create the specific database for a given company and a given business project.
- Specific software that allows to process the information contained in the specific database and to obtain a series of outputs in the form of competitiveness figures, results, and balances.

The same procedure for implementation of the IICBS is used as when dealing with the OICBS (see Chapter 5). See the chart below (Figure 6.9).

Results for innovation infrastructure are obtained when we customize the innovation infrastructure to fit the industry sector. Based on information collected in the previous phases, the system generates customized questionnaires to be filled in by top management. Once filled in, information collected through questionnaires will be processed in the computer (see Figure 6.10).

The processing of questionnaires corresponding to each of the company competitiveness factors provides us with the innovation capabilities results and balance sheets. These results and balance sheets can be obtained for the project as a whole or for each competitiveness factor.

Some examples of balances and results are given below in Figures 6.11 and 6.12.

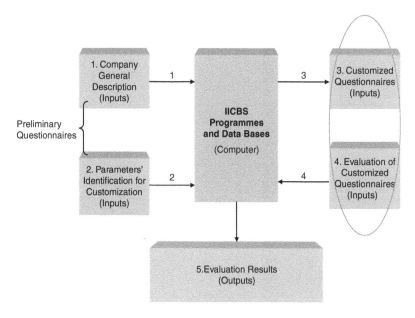

Figure 6.9   IICBS implementation chart for each project unit

6.4   Benefits from using IICBS

The main benefits from using IICBS are the following:

- Creating a strategy check-up that allows companies to evaluate their innovation projects and their innovation capabilities.
- Learning from the best competitors who surpass one's own competitive innovation capabilities.
- Identifying the specific innovation capabilities, factors, and criteria which are relevant to a given business activity.
- Enabling the identification, audit and benchmark, through the IICBS factors framework, of the innovation core capabilities or innovation IC that are the main sources of long-term sustainable competitive advantages.
- When using IICBS in an orderly, systematic, and reiterative way, we obtain innovation capabilities balance sheets that are future-oriented and complement and perfect finance balance sheets, enabling companies to leverage innovation IC.

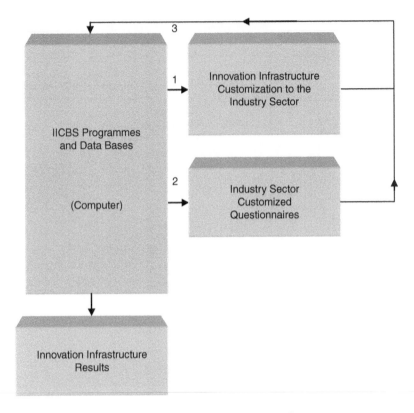

Figure 6.10   Innovation infrastructure implementation chart

- Allowing the selection, in a systematic and organized way, of the necessary information for evaluating relevant factors, core innovation capabilities, and innovation IC.
- Giving an SME's managers access to innovation capabilities and innovation IC management in a systematic and organized way.
- Facilitating the work of the Benchmarking and Competitive Intelligence team.

6.5   Integrating IICBS and OICBS

The IICBS and OICBS frameworks and information systems are similar and we can move from OICBS to IICBS considering the equivalent concepts and terms, as shown in Table 6.1.

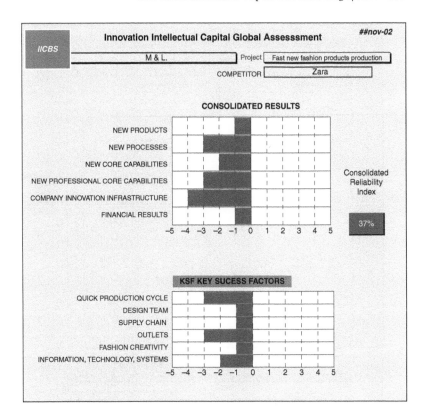

Figure 6.11 Innovation intellectual capital global assessment

The main differences between the two methodologies result from dealing with the differences between the operations process and the innovation process.

Senior managers effectively integrate the ICBS frameworks into the overall business strategy in a similar way to the integration of other strategy-focused models, such as the balanced scorecard (Kaplan and Norton, 1996) and the IAM (Sveiby, 1997). Nevertheless, in the particular case of ICBS, two new functions have to be performed for the *ad hoc* teams made up of junior and senior managers. These two functions are competitive benchmarking and competitive intelligence.

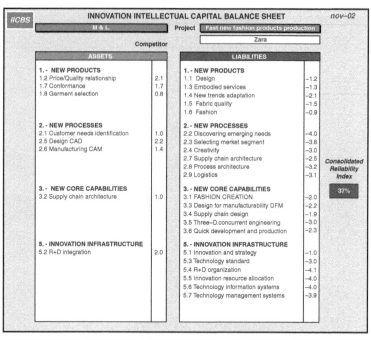

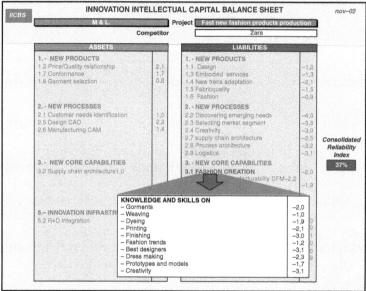

Figure 6.12 Innovation intellectual capital balance sheets

Table 6.1 OICBS and IICBS equivalent concepts and terms

OICBS	IICBS
Business unit	Project unit
Products and services	New products and services
Processes	New processes
Intangible resources	New intangible resources
Core competencies	New core competencies
Professional core competencies	New professional core competencies
Customer needs	New customer needs
Operations value chain	Innovation value chain
Results	Future results
Operations figures	Innovation figures
Operations infrastructure*	Innovation infrastructure

Note: This item is not developed as the company is aware of its operations infrastructure.
Source: Viedma (2004:48).

In summary, the overall benefits obtained from the systematic and continued use of ICBS methodology are:

- conducting a competitiveness strategy check-up in the knowledge economy context; and
- obtaining competencies, capabilities statements, and balance sheets that complement and complete financial balance sheets, and lead companies to leverage core knowledge.

7
Social Capital Benchmarking System (SCBS)

7.1 Introduction

In the knowledge economy, organizations build sustainable competitive advantages that rely not only on their internal IC, but also on the IC of other companies, organizations and institutions and, specifically, on that of the cluster (Porter, 1990), micro-cluster or territory where the company is located. This kind of IC, basically external, and of a relational nature, is one of the main constituents of networked organizations. From now on, it will be called social capital (Nahapiet and Goshal, 1998) because it is embedded in the social fabric (texture) of the nearby environment. Theoretical work in the field of social capital (Coleman, 1988; Burt, 1992; Putnam, 1993; Nahapiet and Goshal, 1998; Castiglione *et al.*, 2008) provides a solid foundation for examining how networked organizations can rely on their social capital to build competitive advantages.

At the same time, and more recently, a new school in strategic thinking has started to consider clusters, attaching a geographic dimension to the value-creating system. The 'ecosystem theory' not only attributes the success of firms to their presence in attractive markets or to the availability of superior resources for production, but also offers a new perspective, arguing that the entire value-creating system of a firm contributes to its success. This explicitly includes its network of business partners and its relationship towards them.

The present models of IC are focused on the internal IC value chain and do not take into account this social capital when building and managing networked organizations that intend to achieve sustainable competitive advantages. The Social Capital Benchmarking System

(SCBS) tries to fill up this gap, providing the foundation of a visible social capital model that complements the existing IC models.

SCBS is both a new management method and a new management tool, which identifies, audits, and benchmarks the resources and capabilities of social capital that exists in alternative cluster locations that are necessary to develop the specific network organization that each particular business model requires. SCBS has been successfully piloted in five European enterprises.

7.2   Building the SCBS framework: theoretical background

Intelligent enterprise (Quinn, 1992), which has been presented as a new paradigm for a new era to build sustainable competitive advantages, concentrates on building and exploring core activities and core competencies, and relying on the capabilities of external suppliers for other activities considered non-strategic and non-core.

But, at the same time, when building internal core competencies, an intelligent enterprise needs the cooperation of other companies', organizations' and institutions' resources and capabilities. More and more, firms must turn to partnering – often with their rivals – to secure the right resources and capabilities for pursuing new opportunities. As more companies realize the need to acquire outside knowledge, they are searching for partners to exchange knowledge, skills and technologies. The ability to survive in today's competitive environment requires skills that often do not exist within the organization (Farrell and Taylor, 1995). Even though few managers are accustomed to working with undefined boundaries between collaboration and competition, the need to take advantage of the unfamiliar skills and capabilities that can come from interdependent networks of alliances and cooperation agreements is a *sine qua non* condition for building proprietary core capabilities that can lead to sustainable competitive advantages (Doz and Hamel, 1998).

In the context of KE, networking and cooperation within and between organizations becomes a typical way to organize operations and to conduct business (Hastings, 1995), emerging as an alternative and arguably superior organizational form to that of markets and hierarchies. The networking idea has been especially attractive as a means by which SMEs can collaborate to compete more effectively in the global marketplace. The premise is that clustering and networking among smaller firms provides them with the potential to achieve collectively more than they could individually, in assessing and competing in world markets. By building networks, companies look for benefits, such as 'time-to-market', cost-reduction, and the availability of resources and materials, competitiveness and, mostly, an increase in, and broadening of their competencies (Ranta, 1998; Järvenpää and Mäki, 2002).

Empirical research shows that networks have numerous advantages for the participating firms. Organizations can produce more with lower costs because of decreasing transaction costs. The closeness to knowledge infrastructures (university and R&D centres) and improved communication networks (transport, telecommunications, energy) fosters the spill-over of the R&D results and the transfer of knowledge useful to firms for solving real-life problems. Learning is interactive, involving creators, producers and users in experimentation and exchange of information.

An important and distinctive feature of networked-based organizational forms is the capacity to put together complementary, autonomous actors in an adaptive way. Thanks to their inherent flexibility, networks can search for innovative combinations of complementary competencies and activities more quickly and do so at less cost than hierarchical organizational forms. It is these complementarities between actors and competencies that give networks distinctive competitive advantages in unstable environments. By networking, companies can concentrate on their own competencies and, at the same time, utilize the knowledge and competencies of other companies, organizations and institutions in the network. This kind of IC is basically the bulk of the relationship or relational capital held by the enterprise, easily forming profitable alliances and partnerships.

The arguments above lead to Figure 7.1 where the intelligent enterprise network is presented.

7.2.1   Cluster resources and capabilities

The idea of geographic clustering among firms that collaborate and cooperate for economic advantage is not new. While Porter's (1990) concept has gained prominence since the early 1990s as a potential vehicle for industrial and regional economic policy, the presence of this phenomenon can be traced back in history as far as the eleventh century to the medieval guilds and craft associations, with enduring cultural traditions in northern Italy (Putnam, 1993), France, and Germany.

There is extensive literature on the clustering of competitive industries but there is, at the same time, a common denominator in that

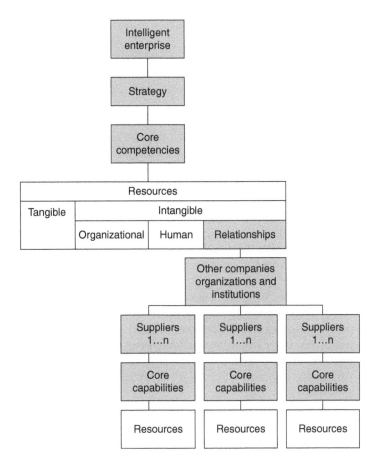

Figure 7.1 Intelligent enterprise network
Source: Viedma (2004:430).

literature (Piore and Sabel, 1984; Porter, 1990; Harrison, 1994; Porter and Stern, 1999). These common features become evident from the following excerpts:

> In healthy regions, competitiveness and innovation are concentrated in clusters, or interrelated industries, in which the regions specialize. Even with other favourable circumstances for innovation, innovation is made more difficult if firms are isolated or if innovative capability is absent in related fields. Innovation tends to be facilitated by the presence of a cluster, particularly where the

cluster is concentrated geographically. Firms within a cluster are often able to more clearly and rapidly perceive new buyer needs than can isolate competitors. Silicon Valley and Austin-based computer companies, for example, plug into customer needs and trends quickly and effectively, with an ease nearly impossible to match elsewhere (Porter and Stern, 1999:19).

A distinction has to be drawn between those parts of corporate activity where spatial proximity is important and those where it is not. The view of writers ... who have studied this is that commercial (sales, strategic, or financial) and basic scientific networks can work well at a long distance. However, dealing with practical, production-related issues, such as designing software or making product adjustments or applications, tend to be geographically a clustering phenomenon. Trust is built between lower managers, and the networks that they build are kept going for long as possible until they are destroyed by mergers and acquisitions (Cooke and Morgan, 1993:75).

Competitors in many internationally successful industries and often entire clusters of industries are frequently located in a single town within a nation. The vast majority of Italy's woollen textile producers, for example, are located in two towns. While geographic concentration of Italian industries is widely recognized however, what is less understood is how prevalent the phenomenon is (Porter, 1990:154–5).

Concentrations of domestic rivals are frequently surrounded by suppliers, and located in areas with concentrations of particularly sophisticated and significant customers. The city or region becomes a unique environment for competing in the industry. The information flow, visibility and mutual reinforcement within such a local give meaning to Alfred Marshall's insightful observation that in some places, an industry is in the air (Porter, 1990:155–6).

Silicon Valley is [now] best viewed as an American variant of the industrial districts of Europe´s technologically dynamic regional economies in which networks of specialist producers both compete and cooperate in response to fast changing global markets. In these districts, technical skill and competence are widely diffused, small and medium sized firms achieve external economies through complex supplier and subcontracting relations, and the region (not the firm) is the locus of production. The result is a decentralized system which is more flexible than the traditional, vertically-integrated corporation.

While these firms serve global markets and collaborate extensively with foreign suppliers, their key relationships tend to be local
(Harrison, 1994:108–9).

From these excerpts it is possible to conclude that location matters
when a competitive enterprise builds a set of different relationships
in a world where vertical integration is practically disappearing, and
location matters because first-class competitors in an industry segment
are always clustered in cities and regions together with other competitors, suppliers, customers, and other related industries and institutions.
In addition, clustering facilitates, through personal contacts, the access
to tacit knowledge that is the key ingredient of other companies' organizations' and institutions' core capabilities, and the one that guarantees
long-term sustainable competitive advantages. Nevertheless, relationships can be divided into two groups. In the first are the ones that
are inside the cluster and in the second are the ones that are outside
the cluster. The proportion between the two groups varies depending
on the industry segment and the specific strategies of the different
companies, but the main bulk of relationships, is always inside the cluster. All that has been said is shown in Figure 7.2.

7.2.2 Social capital as an important constituent of network organization

There is a common understanding that the KE relies on embedded
social structures, social relations and social activities (Manning, 2010).
Social activities are a set of critical resources that 'enable the creation of
essential competencies' (Bueno and Salmador, 2004:557) and increase
the capacities for the creation, sharing and management of knowledge
that generates sustainable competitive advantages (Lesser and Cothrel,
2001). In the knowledge era, firms are becoming embedded within a
complex web of interconnections that span markets, governments and
communities. As mentioned above, companies and organizations in the
KE build sustainable competitive advantages, not only by relying on
their own IC, but also on the IC of other companies, organizations and
institutions; namely, on those of the cluster, micro-cluster or territory
where the company is located. This kind of IC, basically external and of
a relational nature, is one of the main constituents of networked organizations, which we call social capital.

The concept of networked organizations has several meanings
(Nhoria and Eccles, 1996). It may include different and new organizational options, much informal communication (inside and outside

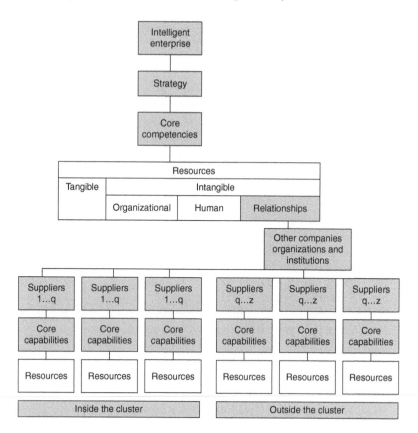

Figure 7.2   Network structure: Inside and outside the cluster
Source: Viedma (2004:432).

the organization), and rigorous concepts about interrelationships and interaction. The source of competitive advantage lies into the richness of the organization's relationships. A networked organization is 'communication-rich' (Nhoria and Eccles, 1996) and 'relational embedded' (Granovetter, 1992).

Harrison (1994) distinguishes four types of production networks: the craft-type industries; the small firm-led industrial districts; the geographically clustered big firm-led production systems; and, the strategic alliances production networks. We will not focus on the particularities of these types of networks, and on those of other types of networks, such as starburst, federal or spider web forms. For the purpose of our work, a network organization is one that, in order to build internal core competencies (IC), extensively uses, through cooperation agreements, other companies', organizations', and institutions' core competencies (IC).

Such interdependencies provide the stimulus for developing many organizationally embedded forms of social capital. Anderson *et al.* (2007:249) define social capital as 'a social relations artefact, produced in interactions but that resides within a network'. Nahapiet and Goshal (1998) note that networks and networks structures represent facets of social capital that influence the range of information available and provide access to resources, creating opportunities to combine and exchange knowledge. In addition, Burt (1992), describing 'structural holes' as those areas of the network not well connected, provides strong evidence for the positive impact of social networks on organizational performance. According to the author, one of the benefits of high levels of social capital is the limiting of structural holes within the network

Social capital as a concept has its roots in the field of sociology and was first used in community studies. Both social capital and IC are new disciplines and their research was developed independently until the late 1990s, when Nahapiet and Goshal (1998) published their seminal work on *Social Capita, Intellectual Capital and Organizational Advantage*. In this work, they proposed that a firm's capacity to create social capital provides an encouraging environment for IC creation. They posit that firms are better placed to create social capital than markets, with consequent organizational advantages. Such advantages derive from the importance of networks of strong, cross-cutting personal relationships developed over time which provide the basis for trust, cooperation, and collective action (Nahapiet and Goshal, 1998). In the same vein, Cohen and Prusak (2001:4) define social capital as 'the stock of active connections among people: the trust, mutual understanding and shared values and behaviours that bind the members of human networks and communities and make co-operative action possible'.

In fact, the concept of social capital has many definitions but for the purpose of our work we will use that of Nahapiet and Goshal (1998:243). They define social capital as 'the sum of the actual and potential resources embedded within, available through, and derived from the network of relationships possessed by an individual or social unit. Social capital thus comprises both the network and the assets that may be mobilized through that network'. The authors focus on the creation of IC as a social artefact arising from the interaction of individuals. Their definition of IC stresses the socially and contextually embedded forms of knowledge and knowing as a source of value. IC is seen as being created through the combination and exchange of knowledge among individuals. In turn, social capital provides the mechanism that maximizes knowledge combination and exchange.

In a simpler fashion, we say that social capital is the sum of resources and capabilities that belong to the network of organizations, which has been built by the intelligent enterprise in order to compete successfully (Viedma, 2004).

7.2.3   Social capital as the main source of cluster sustainable competitive advantage

The literature suggests that the presence of social capital enhances knowledge creation (Hoffman *et al.*, 2005), facilitates the development of IC (Nahapiet and Goshal, 1998; Bueno and Salmador, 2004) and core competencies (Kogut and Zander, 1996), encourages cooperative behaviour (Coleman, 1988), and facilitates access to resources through network ties (Burt, 1992). Other authors such as Hoffman *et al.* (2005) and Manning (2010), also suggest that organizations with high levels of social capital have more knowledge management capabilities than organizations with low levels of social capital.

Across geographical contexts, social capital plays an important role not only in the economic performance of firms (Baker, 1990) but in the prosperity of geographic regions (Putnam, 1993; Ketels and Memedovic, 2008) and nations (Fukuyama, 1995).

However, a network does not itself promote knowledge sharing nor is social capital a natural phenomenon that emerges from networking. The existence of both – networks and social capital – represent the product of an endless effort on both the individual level and between firms. The formal and informal networks between people in a common location are the product of long-term interaction and form part of social capital (Putnam, 1993). This social capital, in turn, represents the value of human connections based on confidence and personal networks with a community vocation (Cohen and Prusak, 2001).

Social capital has a multi-dimensional nature (Koka and Prescott, 2002). Hoffman *et al.* (2005) describe social capital as a construct comprising five dimensions. They are: information channels; social norms; identity; obligations and expectations; and moral infrastructure. Information channels consist of personal relationships that people develop with each other through a history of interaction. Social norms are a common belief system that contains shared knowledge and history, shared strategic visions, systems of meanings, and normative value orientations (Nahapiet and Goshal, 1998), which allow participants to communicate their ideas and make sense of common experiences. Identity occurs when individuals see themselves as at one with another person or group of people (Nahapiet and Goshal, 1998), enhancing concern for collective goals. Obligations and expectations are viewed as the positive interactions (namely, trust and reciprocity) that occur between individuals in networks. Moral infrastructure is the structure that allows network actors to encourage norms of conduct within the network's scope of influence.

Clusters are part of a broader competitiveness framework and the literature supports the positive impact of cluster presence on prosperity (Porter *et al.*, 2007; Schiele, 2008). The prosperity of a location, and the opportunities for its companies and clusters to reach high levels of productivity, depends on the general business environment, not just the macroeconomic, social, political and legal context, geography, and other institutional aspects. The local cluster thus offers an environment for the evolution of a common language, social bonds, norms, values and institutions, that is, a social capital (Putnam, 1993), giving rise to institutional arrangements that become increasingly specialized, trusted and unique, facilitating the fluidity of knowledge exchange. Within a network, obligations and expectations lead to collective trust (Kramer *et al.*, 1996). In turn, collective trust, when it has emerged from a process of learning, strengthens obligations and expectations (Sabel, 1993).

Although some argue that the role of the nation or region is diminishing in an era of rapid globalization, others insist that the local environment plays a continued, or possibly, increasingly important role, because firms may enjoy insider access to specialized inputs such as skills, applied technology, tailored infrastructure and a core of advanced customers and suppliers with which the firm can interact and create new knowledge (Porter and Sölvell, 1999). This argument is supported by the erosion of the traditional basis of competitive advantage, which is rapidly shifting from static advantages of scale and low input prices to relentless innovation and upgrading of competitive advantage. Whereas some of the knowledge embedded in products, components and machinery can travel the world through trade or investment, knowledge embedded in social capital does not, as it involves a large number of actors within a local cluster and is path-dependent due to local circumstances, accumulated routines, and unique relationships.

As noted earlier, when dealing with clusters, resources, and capabilities, relationships with customers, organizations and institutions that belong to the cluster, are privileged relationships because they are the only ones capable of transmitting the social tacit knowledge or the 'collective knowledge' (Spender, 1996). This 'collective knowledge' represents the knowledge embedded in the core competencies and core capabilities, which may remain relatively hidden from individual actors – in the forms of social and institutional practices – but may be accessible and sustained through their interaction (Spender, 1996; Prahalad and Ramaswamy, 2000). It is this type of knowledge that distinguishes the performance of firms. Hence, the importance of clusters located in a specific city, region or territory.

Relationships with other companies and organizations outside the cluster location usually transmit only explicit knowledge or 'objectified knowledge' (Spender, 1996). This shared corpus of knowledge is less relevant to the process of gaining and sustaining competitive advantages. In that sense, social capital belonging to the cluster's outside network will be rated lower than the social capital inside the network.

7.2.4 Profiting from social capital when building networked organizations: The need to benchmark

When the intelligent enterprise is focusing on core competencies (IC) and core activities, and strongly specializes in those core competencies and activities, all the other activities, and the development of other competencies, are left to the companies of the network and, especially, to the ones inside the 'cluster-city', the 'cluster-region' or the 'cluster-territory'. In that context, it is crucial to choose the right cluster among the different possible cluster options, because the cluster will be the foundation of the network construction.

Smedlund and Pöyhönen, (2005) demonstrate that a regional cluster's knowledge-based competitive advantages relies on three types of network: i) production networks; ii) development networks; and iii) innovation networks. At the production network level, the innovations invented in the innovation network are converted into profitable business. Innovation can be new products, new methods or processes of production. The development network assures the intermediary relationships between the production and innovation networks. The innovation network follows its strategic goal of inventing new knowledge, products, production methods, or processes. These value networks (Allee, 2000) make the creation, transferring and implementing of knowledge effective within the cluster.

When members of a cluster are located in close proximity, they can capture synergies that increase productivity, innovative capacity, and new business formation. Clusters innovate faster because they draw on local networks that link technology, resources, information, and talent. Information flows freely, and innovation spreads rapidly through the relationships between customers and suppliers. Furthermore, a dynamic cluster also offers stimulating rivalry, with important informational and incentive benefits.

Hence, an accurate evaluation of different cluster options, starts with the evaluation of the strategy, the business model and industry segment of the intelligent enterprise. Figure 7.3 presents this process.

Once the business model and, especially, the industry segment is well defined, it is essential to focus on the best cluster location in the world, where the most competitive and excellent companies of the industry segment are located. The best cluster in the world will be the reference model and any optional alternative cluster location will need to be benchmarked against the best cluster in the world. In consequence, benchmarking in a systematic way is an unavoidable

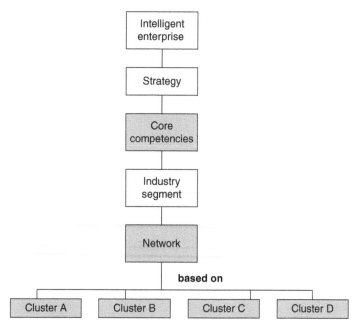

Figure 7.3 Choosing the best cluster
Source: Viedma (2004:434).

practice if profiting from existing social capital becomes a strategy priority of the intelligent enterprise.

7.3 Building the SCBS general framework

SCBS is a framework built around the key factors and criteria that determinate a cluster's competitiveness in the context of global market. It draws inspiration from Michael Porter's determinants of national advantage (Porter, 1990). The factors considered are:

(a) resources and capabilities;
(b) demand;
(c) suppliers and other related industries;
(d) firms strategy, culture and structure;
(e) competitors; and
(f) government

SCBS identifies the relevant factors and criteria that allow the best networked construction for a specific business activity. Figure 7.4 illustrates the key factors that support the SCBS framework and Figure 7.5 describes the general SCBS framework.

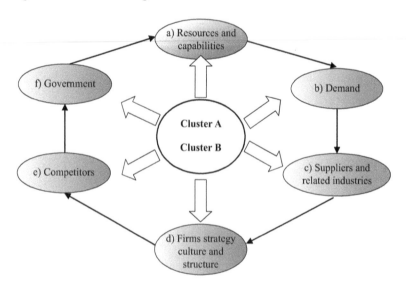

Figure 7.4 Factors of SCBS framework
Source: Viedma (2004:435).

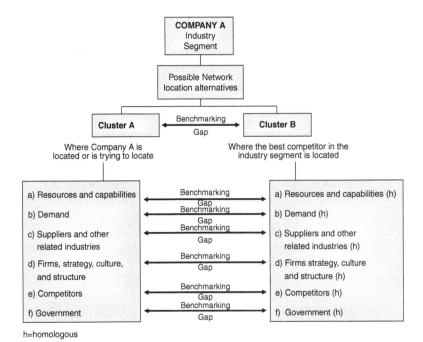

Figure 7.5 SCBS general framework
Source: Viedma (2004:435).

The definition and the content of each particular factor are given below.

Resources and capabilities. This refers to the cluster position with respect to different resources and capabilities such as: physical resources (land, water, mineral, timber deposits, fishing grounds, hydroelectric power, climate, location); human resources (quantity, skills and costs of personnel); financial resources (amount and cost of capital available in the different forms); knowledge resources (scientific and technical knowledge that resides in universities, research institutes, private research facilities. business and scientific literature, etc.); and infrastructure (type, quality and user cost of available infrastructure such as transportation system, mail and parcel delivery, communications systems, telecommunications system, health care, housing stock, cultural institutions, and so on). A firm's competitive advantage is the result of the productive combination and use of all its resources, whether physical, financial, human or organizational. The underlying knowledge that managers use when combining and integrating the firm's resources is arguably the most important resource for the firm (Conner and Prahalad, 1996).

Demand. This refers to home demand for the products and services of the industry segment. The three main attributes of home demand are: the nature and composition of buyer needs; the size and pattern of the growth of home demand; and the quality and sophistication of home demand when compared to international standards. The importance of demanding customers as a source of innovation has been verified in several studies (Håkansson, 1989). Demanding customers drive domestic commercialization activities toward 'best in the world' technologies and create a strong market pull for innovation.

Suppliers and other related industries. This refers to suppliers and other related industries that are internationally competitive. Home-based first-class suppliers are crucial to the process of outsourcing but especially for the process of improving, upgrading and innovation. The presence in the cluster of competitive related industries gives a cluster's firms the opportunity to share value chain activities in technology development, manufacturing, distribution, marketing and service. All this improves a firm's core competencies and creates new ones.

Firm strategy, culture and structure. This refers to the conditions in the cluster, and specifically in the industry segment, which determine how companies are created, organized and managed. This factor also includes the cultural context in which firms develop their activities.

Competitors refers to domestic rivalry within the cluster. There is a close association between vigorous domestic rivalry and the creation of sustainable competitive advantages in an industry segment. Having world-class competitors at home fosters imagination, creativity and innovation. It is a challenging situation that encourages the process of learning in order to surpass the best in class competitors.

Government influences the five other determinants of the cluster's competitive advantages that have been describe above. In this case, we refer not only to national government but also to local government. The influence on the other factors can be direct or indirect and, what it is more important, they can be either positive or negative. On the role of government, Porter (1990:71) asserts:

Factor conditions are affected through subsidies, policies towards the capital markets, policies toward education, and the like. The Government's role in shaping local demand conditions is often more subtle. Government bodies establish local product standards or regulations that mandate or influence buyer needs. Government is also often a mayor buyer of many products in a nation.... Government shapes the circumstances of related and supporting industries in countless other ways ... Government policy also influences firm strategy, structure and rivalry, through such devices as capital market, regulations, tax policy and antitrust laws (Porter, 1990:127).

Diverse groups (rival firms, government, universities, suppliers and other related industries, research institutes, and so forth) contribute to cluster strength. They are self-reinforcing and act as a system. Domestic rivalry, for example, stimulates the development of unique pools of specialized skills and the formation or attraction of specialized suppliers. Active local rivalry also upgrades the demand of home customers, which presses firms to improve and offer insights into existing and future customer needs.

At the same time each one of the six factors is broken down into a set of different criteria and each criterion is evaluated through questionnaires.

The operating system is the following: Company A, which belongs to a specific industry segment, once defined its core competencies needs to assess which cluster location is the best for building its networked organization. If the company were located in Cluster A, or were trying to locate in Cluster A, Cluster B, where the best competitors within the industry segment are located, might be a better cluster location. Evaluation of the two possible locations is carried out through the factors of the SCBS model.

This model assesses social, physical and financial capital because the three types of capital always go together and because access to physical and financial capital is always secured through social capital. The assessment process is done through the extensive use of factors, criteria and questionnaires.

The six factors of the SCBS model, individually and as a system, create the context in which firms are born and compete. Firms gain competitive advantages in industries when their home base affords better ongoing information and insight into product and process needs. Firms gain competitive advantage when the goals of owners, managers and employers support intense commitment and sustained investment. Ultimately, territories succeed in particular industries because their home environment is the most dynamic and the most challenging, and stimulates and prods firms to upgrade and widen their advantages over time (Porter, 1990; Schiele, 2008).

7.3.1   From the general to the specific SCBS framework

The SCBS general framework, which we have already described, is one that can be used to generate the specific framework suitable to a specific firm strategy, to a specific business model and to a specific industry segment.

The SCBS methodology is about selecting which cluster location is the best for a company building its networked organization. For that, as in Figure 7.6, the company analyses other clusters where the best competitors within the industry segment are located.

The SCBS general framework consists of six factors, each with an array of criteria and, for each criterion, one or several questionnaires aiming at evaluating the criteria. We customize the SCBS general framework to a specific industry segment by choosing and weighing up, among criteria and questionnaires, the ones that best suit the specifications of a given industry segment. Figure 7.7 illustrates this process.

The questionnaire's administration aims are:

(1)   to collect general data about the company (for example, a company's historical data, business activities, core competencies, organizational structure, projects, and so on);
(2)   to select the clusters to be benchmarked from the geographical location of competitors considered excellent;

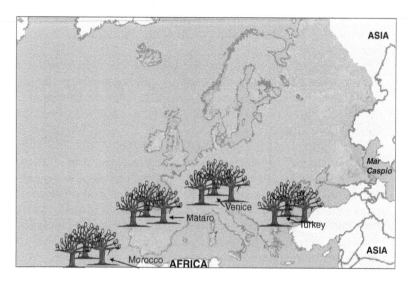

Figure 7.6   Optional location knitwear industry segment

Factors   Criteria   Questionnaires

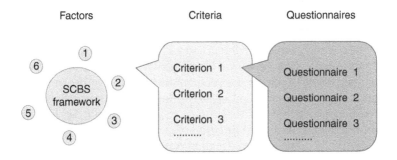

Figure 7.7 Specific SCBS framework
Source: Viedma (2004:437).

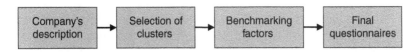

Figure 7.8 Sequential phases in the questionnaires administration

(3) to identify the key factors of the clusters benchmarking to the company's activity;

(4) to build final customized questionnaires for each specific company.

Figure 7.8 illustrates these sequential phases that lead to the choice of a social capital alternative cluster location that is the source of sustainable relational competitive advantages.

When filling in the questionnaires, the benchmarking teams are able to evaluate the relevant criteria of an industry segment cluster and, among them, the relevant criteria that make up the cluster social capital.

Given that a large part of the information (above all, in the cluster of the best competitor) may not be known precisely, all questions in all the SCBS questionnaires have a 'response precision' box that indicates the accuracy of each particular answer. Integrating the results of the response precision boxes of the SCBS framework permits us to measure the degree of reliability of the benchmarking and its constituent parts in order to establish plans for systematically improving information acquisition and to set up an intelligence team in the company.

7.3.2   The key role of social capital benchmarking in the framework construction

SCBS is a new management method and a new management tool which enables a specific company to benchmark the resources and capabilities of the cluster in which the company is located, against the resources and capabilities of the best cluster in the world to successfully develop the business activity of that company. At the same time, because the tool supplies relevant information on a cluster's social capital, the tool may also be used as an information system or, even better, as a decision support system. Moreover, SCBS not only benchmarks core capabilities, but also the resources underlying them and make such capabilities possible. In other words, SCBS benchmarks social, physical and financial capital as well.

The six factors framework is used for moving from the general framework (general context) to the specific framework (specific industry segment). We customize the general framework through two types of variables: the criteria and the questionnaires; and through a benchmarking process that covers the activities of two clusters: the one where our company is located, or is trying to locate; and the one where the best competitor in the industry segment is located.

The process of cluster benchmarking allows us to determine the specific competitiveness factors and criteria, which are relevant to a cluster industry segment. These factors and criteria may also be called key cluster competitiveness drivers. The questionnaires that are directly derived from the criteria allow us to evaluate and benchmark the alternative cluster location for a company in a specific industry segment, in order to build the best possible network. For better comprehension of the above, Figure 7.9 depicts the construction process.

7.4   The SCBS implementation

The following elements are involved in putting the SCBS method into practice:

(1) A general database that contains all the possible criteria and questionnaires to be used. This means that each factor can be looked at in the greatest detail. In Figure 7.10 we see an example of a company operating in the knitwear clothing industry segment choosing the best location.

(2) A user-system interface that enables criteria and questionnaires to be adapted to the particularities of each company industry segment.

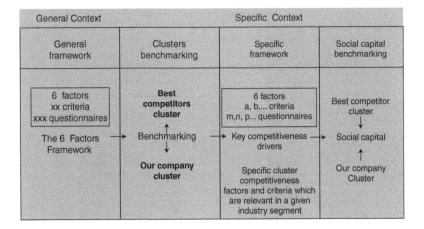

Figure 7.9 The role of social capital benchmarking in the framework construction
Source: Viedma (2004:438).

(3) The successive responses to the personalized questionnaires are used to create the specific database that contains all the information on the alternative cluster locations for a given industry segment.

(4) Specific software, which incorporates the factors, criteria, questionnaires, and the theory and principles set out in the theoretical background, enables us to process the information contained in the database and to obtain a series of outputs in the form of social capital assessment results and balance sheets.

The processing of questionnaires corresponding to each of the cluster factors and criteria provides us with the social capital results and balance sheets. These results and balance sheets can be obtained for the whole social capital or for each particular factor. Some examples of balances and results are given below (Figures 7.11 and 7.12). Assets items are those sub-factors where Cluster A has the advantage, while the liabilities items represent those sub-factors where Cluster B outperforms Cluster A.

From the results above we can conclude that, in terms of the 'resources and capabilities' benchmarking factor, Cluster B has advantages over Cluster A, having a consolidated reliability index greater than 80 per cent. Similar analysis should be developed for the remaining five cluster competitiveness drivers.

Industry Segment: Knitwear clothing industry			
Cluster A		**Cluster B**	
Cluster A points (minus) Cluster B points		**Cluster B points (minus) Cluster A points**	
A) Resources and capabilities		0.33	A) Resources and capabilities
Natural resources			Natural resources
Industrial real estate			Industrial real estate
Climate			Climate
Unskilled personnel			Unskilled personal
Capital		0.65	Capital
Skilled personnel		1.16	Skilled personnel
Educational and research centers		1.10	Educational and research centers
Alternative energy			Alternative energy
Telecommunications			Telecommunications
Science and technology		0.82	Science and technology
Conventional energy	0.07		Conventional energy
Transportation infrastructure		0.14	Transportation infrastructure
Infrastructure to live		0.50	Infrastructure to live
Related resources provision			Related resources provision
B) Demand		0.80	D) Demand
Demand segmentation		0.70	Demand segmentation
End user refinement		0.75	End user refinement
Pressure for innovation and upgrading		1.05	Pressure for innovation and upgrading
Demand internationalization		0.50	Demand internationalization
C) Suppliers and other related industries		0.75	C) Suppliers and other related industries
Suppliers internationalization		1.50	Suppliers internationalization
Suppliers purchasing power			Suppliers purchasing power
Support sectors		0.50	Support sectors
Related industries outsourcing		0.32	Related industries outsourcing
Strategic networks		0.50	Strategic networks
D) Firms strategy culture and structure		0.71	D) Firms strategy culture and structure
Strategic objectives		0.50	Strategic objectives
Culture		0.31	Culture
Industry segment prestige		1.02	Industry segment prestige
Firm structure	0.02		Firm structure
Managers and workers		0.50	Managers and workers
E) Competitors		0.50	E) Competitors
F1) Government (direct intervention)		0.34	F1) Government (direct intervention)
F2) Government (indirect intervention)	0.35		F2) Government (indirect intervention)
Influence on resources and capabilities	0.02		Influence on resources and capabilities
Influence on demand	0.50		Influence on demand
Influence on related sectors			Influence on related sectors
Influence on strategy			Influence on strategy
Influence on competitors			Influence on competitors
Political factors	0.50		Political factors
Labour law	0.05		Labour law
Tax and commercial law	0.50		Tax and commercial law

Figure 7.10 Cluster competitiveness drivers in benchmarking questionnaire

7.5 Benefits from using SCBS

SCBS identifies, audits and benchmarks the resources and capabilities or the social capital that is present in an alternative cluster location and which is necessary in order to develop the specific network organization that each particular business model or industry segment requires. As a result, the, benefits of using SCBS are the following:

(1) Identifying the 'world best' cluster location, where the intelligent enterprise is able to establish the necessary relationships that

Industry segment: Knitwear clothing industry

CLUSTER A : Mataró   CLUSTER B : Treviso

Cluster A points - Cluster B points		Cluster B points - Cluster A points
Assets		**Liabilities**
A) RESOURCES AND CAPABILITIES	0.33	A) RESOURCES AND CAPABILITIES
Capital	0.65	Capital
Skilled personnel	1.16	Skilled personnel
Educational and research centers	1.10	Educational and research centers
Science and technology	0.82	Science and technology
Conventional energy 0.07		Conventional energy
Transportation infrastructure	0.14	Transportation infrastructure
Infrastructure to live	0.50	Infrastructure to live
B) DEMAND	0.80	B) DEMAND
Demand segmentation	0.70	Demand segmentation
End user refinement	0.75	End user refinement
Pressure for innovation and upgrading	1.05	Pressure for innovation and up grading
Demand internationalization	0.50	Demand internationalization
C) SUPPLIERS&OTHER RELATED INDUSTRIES	0.75	C) SUPPLIERS&OTHER RELATED INDUSTRIES
Suppliers internationalization	1.50	Suppliers internationalization
Support sectors	0.50	Support sectors
Related industries outsourcing	0.32	Related industries outsourcing
Strategic networks	0.50	Strategic networks
D) FIRMS STRATEGY CULTURE& STRUCTURE	0.71	D) FIRMS STRATEGY CULTURE&STRUCTURE
Strategy objectives	0.50	Strategy objectives
Culture	0.31	Culture
Industry segment prestige	1.02	Industry segment prestige
Firms structure 0.02		Firms structure
Managers and workers	0.50	Managers and workers
E) COMPETITORS	0.50	E) COMPETITORS
F1) GOVERNMENT (direct intervention)	0.34	F1) GOVERNMENT (direct intervention)
F2) GOVERNMENT (indirect intervention) 0.35		F2) GOVERNMENT (indirect intervention)
Influence on resources and capabilities 0.02		Influence on resources and capabilities
Influence on demand 0.50		Influence on demand
Political factors 0.50		Political factors
Labour law 0.05		Labour law
Tax and commercial law 0.50		Tax and commercial law

Figure 7.11   Social Capital global assessment: Balance sheet

each specific business model requires in order to build its network organization.

(2) Identifying the specific external social capital factors and criteria which are relevant in a given business model or industry segment.

(3) Through the SCBS factors framework, enabling the identification, audit, and benchmark of the social capital alternative cluster location that is the source of sustainable relational competitive advantages.

(4) When using SCBS in an orderly, systematic and repetitive way, we obtain social capital balance sheets that are future-oriented and

CLUSTER A : Mataró			CLUSTER B:	Treviso	
RESOURCES AND CAPABILITIES	**WEIGHTING**		**QUESTIONNAIRES RESULTS**		
	0–5	%	**Cluster A**	**Cluster B**	
Natural resources	0	0.0	0.00	0.00	
Industrial real estate	3	7.9	3.50	3.50	
Climate	0	0.0	0.00	0.00	
Unskilled personnel	0	0.0	0.00	0.00	
Capital	3	7.9	3.00	3.65	
Skilled personnel	5	13.2	3.19	4.35	
Educational and research centers	4	10.5	3.10	4.20	
Alternative energy	0	0.0	0.00	0.00	
Telecommunications	5	13.2	3.27	3.27	
Science and technology	4	10.5	3.23	4.05	
Conventional energy	5	13.2	3.00	2.93	
Transportation infrastructure	5	13.2	3.86	4.00	
Infrastructure to live	4	10.5	3.50	4.00	
Related resources provision	0	0.0	0.00	0.00	

Resources and capabilities weighted average (0–5)		
Cluster A	Cluster B	
2.19	2.52	

Consolidated reliability index	>80%

Figure 7.12 Partial assessment of social capital resources and capabilities.

which complement and perfect finance and intellectual capital balance sheets, leading companies to be able to leverage social capital.

(5) The selection in a systematic and organized way of the necessary information for evaluating relevant social capital factors and criteria.

(6) The identification of the key areas in which in-depth benchmarking can be carried out in the future.

(7) Promoting organizational learning through benchmarking teams, assessment teams, project teams and strategic teams.

(8) Introducing a common language for company managers when dealing with social capital or external resources and capabilities.

(9) Measuring the reliability of the relevant information and progress in acquiring this information.

(10) Facilitating the work of the benchmarking and competitive intelligence teams.

(11) Facilitating the work of the knowledge and intellectual capital managers.

(12) Giving to managers of small and medium enterprises access to social capital management in a systematic and organized way.

8
Conclusions

At the end of the journey, we would like to conclude by summarizing the essential content of the book, and by highlighting the main contributions of ICBS methodologies and frameworks to achieving entrepreneurial excellence in the knowledge economy context.

The advent of the knowledge economy has fundamentally changed the basis of wealth creation in modern social communities. Knowledge and other human-based intangibles have become the fundamental resources for wealth creation.

The theoretical foundations of wealth creation in the knowledge economy are mainly found at the micro level in the modern discipline of strategic management and, more specifically, in the following three well-known perspectives: the resource-based view; the dynamic capabilities based view; and, more recently, the knowledge-based view.

Nevertheless, these theoretical foundations at the micro level have to be complemented at the macro level by the recent developments in what is called 'strategic management of intangibles' in cities, regions and nations. These recent developments are based on a complex body of principles and theories, such as institutional and evolutionary economics, cultural and social economics, systems theory, systems and innovation, triple helix, regional science and more recently knowledge-based development.

Other approaches at the macro level perspective come from the competitiveness literature. In that sense, Stéphane Garelli (2002) argues that:

> Nations themselves do not compete, rather, their enterprises do. There is no doubt that competitive enterprises are the main engines of a country's competitiveness. Competition among nations can be

seen in the areas of education and know-how. In a modern economy, nations do not rely only on products and services, they also compete with brains. The ability of a nation to develop an excellent education system and to improve knowledge in the labor force through training is vital to competitiveness.

Same way Michel Porter (2005) considers that:

> Wealth is actually created in the microeconomic level of the economy. Wealth can only be created by firms. The capacity for wealth creation is rooted in the sophistication of the operating practices and strategies of companies, as well as in the quality of the microeconomic business environment in which a nation's companies compete. More than 80 percent of the variation of GDP per capita across countries is accounted for by microeconomic fundamentals. Unless microeconomic capabilities improve, macroeconomic, political, legal, and social reforms will not bear full fruit.

Based on these theoretical foundations, some basic principles on wealth creation in the knowledge economy context have been constructed. They are the following:

(1) The wealth or poverty of a nation is strongly dependant on the number of competitive or excellent companies that it has.
(2) Government does not create wealth but contributes to facilitating or hindering wealth creation.
(3) An excellent or competitive company is one that achieves long-term extraordinary profits due to the fact that it has a business model with sustainable competitive advantages.
(4) In the knowledge economy, sustainable competitive advantages are mainly based on intangibles. Consequently, strategic management of intangibles or intellectual capital becomes a fundamental task.
(5) The strategy perspective is the key to business excellence.
(6) Business excellence is always the result of good strategy formulation and superior strategy implementation.
(7) Good strategy formulation and superior strategy implementation is always a human task and strongly depends on the quality and leadership of the top management team and key professional people.
(8) In a continuously changing environment, business models quickly become out of date and, as a consequence of that, innovation in business models becomes an urgent need.

(9) In any company, the essential activity is always innovation in the business model so it can be converted in an excellent or competitive business model.

(10) Companies alone do not create wealth. They need the collaboration of other companies, universities and research institutes, financial institutions, government and other organizations and institutions and, especially, the existing ones in the cluster, region or nation where the company is located. In other words, they need to be an active part of a territorial open innovation system and of what some authors like to call knowledge-based ecologies.

Following the criteria of the above principles, this book has dealt with wealth creation at the firm level in the knowledge economy context but has not considered the territorial innovation systems or knowledge-based ecologies that have been mentioned in Principle 10.

This book has been about achieving entrepreneurial excellence in the knowledge economy context through the systematic use of ICBS.

ICBS is the output of long-term research carried out by Dr. Viedma and his team in the field of intangibles or intellectual capital, the main sources of sustainable competitive advantages in the context of the knowledge economy.

After a carefully review of the theoretical foundations of entrepreneurial excellence, we concluded, as we have stated before, that business excellence is always due to good strategy formulation and superior strategy implementation. The analysis of the practical models and methodologies that contribute to the development of entrepreneurial excellence leads to the realization that the majority of them focus on the process of strategy implementation. This means that strategy formulation is totally left in the hands of the very well known SWOT analysis.

ICBS is a methodology and a framework for successful strategy formulation in the knowledge economy or, in other words, 'the competitiveness strategy check up for organizations in the knowledge economy'. It tries to improve SWOT analysis substantially and to fill in the existing gap in strategy formulation models and methodologies, allowing enterprises to evaluate their business models and their competitive advantages using as a reference for evaluation the world 'best in class' competitors. For that specific purpose, ICBS relies on competitive benchmarking and competitive intelligence techniques. When using ICBS in a systematic and reiterative way, we obtain ICBS scorecards and balance sheets that lead enterprises to better decision-making, helping them to determine future goals, to innovate in their business models, and to gain and sustain competitive advantages.

In order to establish the relevance of ICBS for achieving entrepreneurial excellence in the knowledge economy context we rely again on Peter Drucker (1977), whose thoughts can be summarized in the following statement: *Efficiency is doing things right, effectiveness is doing the right things. Doing the right thing is more important than doing the things right.*

Consequently, effectiveness is more important and relevant than efficiency. The process of strategy formulation is mainly about choosing the right things to do or, in other words, it deals mainly with effectiveness.

ICBS is fundamentally concerned with effectiveness because of its focus on intellectual capital (intangibles) and strategy formulation. This makes ICBS more relevant than any other equivalent model or methodology.

References

Foreword by John S. Edwards

Granovetter, M. S. (1973), 'Strength through weak ties', *American Journal of Sociology*, 78, 6, pp. 1360–1380.

Introduction

Drucker, Peter (1977). *An abridged and revised version of management: Tasks, responsibilities, practices.* Great Britain: Pan Books Ltd. in association with Heinemann. pp. 44–45.

1   The Knowledge Economy

Adams, M. and Oleksak, M. (2010). *Intangible capital*. California: Praeger.

Andriessen, D. and Tissen, R. (2000). *Weightless wealth: Find your real value in a future of intangible assets*. London: Financial Times Prentice-Hall.

Arthur, W.B. (1996). 'Increasing returns and the new world of business'. *Harvard Business Review*, 74, 4, 100–9.

Augier, M. and Teece, D.J. (2005). 'An economics perspective on intellectual capital'. In Marr, B. (ed.), *Perspectives on intellectual capital – multidisciplinary insights into management, measurement, and reporting*. Oxford: Butterworth-Heinemann, 3–27.

Bang, A., Cleemann, C.M. and Bramming P. (2010). 'How to create business value in the knowledge economy. Accelerating thoughts of Peter F. Drucker'. *Management Decision*, 48, 4, 616–27.

Barney, J.B. (1991). 'Firm resources and sustained competitive advantage'. *Journal of Management,* 17, 99–120.

Bertels, T. and Savage, C.M. (1998). 'Tough questions on knowledge management'. In Von Krogh, G., Roos, J. and Klein, D. (eds.), *Knowing in firms – understanding, managing, and measuring knowledge*. London: Sage Publications Inc., 7–25.

Bounfour, A. and Edvinsson, L. (2005). *Intellectual capital for communities*. Oxford: Butterworth-Heinemann.

Burton-Jones, A. (2000). *Knowledge capitalism*. Oxford: Oxford University Press.

Cappelli, P. (1999). 'Career jobs are dead'. *California Management Review*, 42, 1, 146–67.

Clarke, T. (2001). 'The knowledge economy'. *Education and Training*, 43, 4/5, 189–96.

Cooke, P., Gomez Uranga, M. and Etxebarria, G. (1997). 'Regional innovation systems: Institutional and organisational dimensions'. *Research Policy*, 26, 475–91.

Crocitto, M. and Youssef, M. (2003). 'The human side of organisational agility'. *Industrial Management & Data Systems*, 103/6, 388–97.

Daft, R. (1983). *Organisation theory and design*. New York: West.

D'Avini, R. (1994). *Hypercompetition: Managing the dynamics of strategic manoeuvring.* New York, NY: New York.

Davenport, T.H. and Prusak, L. (1998). *Working knowledge – how organizations manage what they know.* Boston, Massachusetts: Harvard Business School Press.

David, P.A. and Foray, D. (2003). Economic fundamentals of the knowledge society. *Policy Futures in Education,* 1, 1, 20–47.

DeVol, R.C. (1999). *America's high-tech economy: Growth, development and risks for metropolitan areas.* Santa Monica: Milken Institute.

Drucker, P. (1969). *The age of discontinuity: Guidelines to our changing society.* London: Heinemann.

Drucker, P. (1993). *Post-capitalist Society.* Oxford: Butterworth-Heinemann Ltd.

Edvinsson, L. (2000). Some perspectives on intangibles and intellectual capital. *Journal of Intellectual Capital,* 1, 1, 12–16.

Galvin, R. (1996). 'Managing knowledge towards wisdom'. *European Management Journal,* 14, 4, 374–8.

Grant, R. (1996). 'Towards a knowledge-based theory of the firm'. *Strategic Management Journal,* 17, 109–22.

Gratton, L. and Ghoshal, S. (2003). 'Managing personal human capital: New ethos for the "volunteer" employee'. *European Management Journal,* 21, 1, 1–10.

Hamel, G. (2000). *Leading the revolution.* Boston, MA: Harvard Business School Press.

Handy, C. (1989). *The age of unreason.* London: Arrow.

Handy, C. (2001). 'Tocqueville revisited: The meaning of American prosperity'. *Harvard Business Review,* 79, 1, 57–63.

Hearn, G. and Rooney, D. (2002). 'The future role of government in knowledge-based economies'. *Foresight,* 4, 6, 23–33.

Hitt, M.A., Ireland, R.D., and Camp, S.M. (2001). Guest editor's introduction to the special issue: 'Strategic entrepreneurship: Entrepreneurial strategies for wealth creation'. *Strategic Management Journal,* 22, 479–91.

Johannessen, J-A, Olaisen, J. and Bjørn, O. (1999). 'Managing and organizing innovation in the knowledge economy'. *European Journal of Innovation Management,* 2, 3, 116–28.

Johnston, R. and Blumentritt, R. (1998). 'Knowledge moves to centre stage'. *Science Communication,* 20, 1, 99–105.

Ketels, C.H.M. and Memedovic O. (2008). 'From clusters to cluster-based economic development'. *International Journal of Technological Learning, Innovation and Development,* 1, 3, 375–92.

Kogut, B. and Zander, U. (1993). 'Knowledge of the firm, combinative capabilities, and the replication of technology', *Organization Science,* 3, 3, 383–97.

Lagendijk, A. (2000). 'Regional Paths of Institutional Anchoring in the Global Economy. The Case of the North-East of England and Aragón'. In J. Groenewegenen and W. Elsner (Eds.), *An Industrial Policy Agenda 2000 and Beyond - New Challenges to Industrial Policy.* Dordrecht: Kluwer Academic, 184–222.

Leonard-Barton, D. (1995). *Wellsprings of knowledge: Building and sustaining the sources of innovation.* Boston, MA: Harvard Business School Press.

Liebeskind, J.P. (1996). 'Knowledge, strategy and the theory of the firm'. *Strategic Management Journal,* 17 (special winter issue), 93–107.

Lundvall, B-Å and Forey, D. (1996). 'The knowledge-based economy: from the economics of knowledge to the learning economy'. In OECD *Employment and growth in knowledge-based economy.* Paris: OECD.

Lundvall, B.-Å and Johnson, B. (1994). 'The learning economy'. *Journal of Industry Studies*, 1, 2, 23–42.

Machlup, F. (1980). *Knowledge: Its creation, distribution, and economic significance.* Princeton, New Jersey: Princeton University Press.

Man, T.W.Y., Lau, T. and Chan, K.F. (2002). "The Competitiveness of Small and Medium Enterprises. A Conceptualisation with Focus on Entrepreneurial Competencies". *Journal of Business Venturing*, Vol. 17, pp. 123–142.

Marshall, A. (1890). *Principles of Economics. 1965 edition*, London: Palgrave Macmillan.

Marr, B. (2005). 'The evolution and convergence of intellectual capital as a theme'. In Marr, B. (ed.), *Perspectives on intellectual capital – multidisciplinary insights into management, measurement, and reporting.* Oxford: Butterworth-Heinemann.

Marr, B., Gupta, O., Pike, S. and Roos, G. (2003). 'Intellectual capital and knowledge management effectiveness'. *Management Decision*, 42, 8, 771–81.

Martins, B. and Viedma, J.M. (2006a). Innovating through the lens of social entrepreneurship to tackle poverty reduction. Paper presented to GLOBal network for Economics of Learning, Innovation and Competence building Systems (GLOBELICS) Conference. Trivandrum, Kerala, India, 4–7 October.

Martins, B. and Viedma, J.M. (2006b). 'The region's intellectual capital benchmarking system: Enabling economic growth through evaluation'. *Journal of Knowledge Management*, 10, 5, 41–54.

Maskell, P. and Malmberg, A. (1999). 'The competitiveness of firms and regions: 'ubiquitification' and the importance of localised learning'. *European Urban and Regional Studies*, 6, 1, 9–26.

Maturana, H. and Varela, F. (1980). *Autopoiesis and cognition: The realization of the living.* London: Reidl, D.

Nonaka, I. (1994). 'A dynamic theory of organizational knowledge creation'. *Organization Science*, 5, 1, 14–37.

Nonaka, I. and Takeuchi, H. (1995). *The knowledge creating company: How Japanese companies manage the dynamics of innovation.* Oxford: Oxford University Press.

Nonaka, I. and Konno, N. (1999). 'The concept of ba: Building a foundation for knowledge creation'. In Cortada, J.W. and Woods, J.A. (eds), *The knowledge management yearbook 1999–2000.* Boston: Butterworth-Heinemann, 37–51.

Nonaka, I., Toyama, R. and Konno, N. (2000). 'SECI, Ba and leadership: A unified model of dynamic knowledge creation'. *Long Range Planning*, 33, 5–34.

Organisation for Economic Co-Operation and Development (OECD) (1996). 'The knowledge-based economy'. In *1996 Science, technology and industry outlook.* Paris: OECD.

Organisation for Economic Co-Operation and Development (OECD) (2001). *Science, technology, and industry – Scoreboard 2001: Towards a knowledge-based economy.* Paris: OECD.

Organisation for Economic Co-Operation and Development (OECD) (2006). *Creating value from intellectual assets.* Meeting of the OECD council at Ministerial level.

Penrose, E.T. (1959). *The theory of the growth of the firm.* New York: John Wiley.

Pérez-Bustamante, G. (1999). 'Knowledge management in agile innovative organisations'. *Journal of Knowledge Management*, 3, 1, 6–17.

Peteraf, M.A. (1993). 'The cornerstones of competitive advantage: A resource-based view'. *Strategic Management Journal*, 14: 179–91.

Piore, M.J. and Sabel, C.F. (1984). *The second industrial divide: Possibilities for prosperity.* New York: Basic Books.

Pöyhönen, A. and Blomqvist, K. (2006). 'Knowledge-based view of the firm – foundations, focal concepts and emerging research issues'. In *Proceedings of the 7th European Conference on Knowledge Management*, Corvinus University of Budapest, Hungary, 4–5 September.

Prahalad, C.K. and Hamel, G. (1994). 'Strategy as a field of study: Why search for a new paradigm?' *Strategic Management Journal*, 15, 5–16.

Quinn, J.B. (1992). *Intelligent enterprise: A new paradigm for a new era*. New York: The Free Press.

Rijn, S. and Tissen, R. (2007). 'Building creative cities: Towards 'industry-based' knowledge management in urban vision development processes'. In *Proceedings of the 8th European Conference on Knowledge Management*, Spain, Barcelona, 6–7 September.

Romer, P.M. (1986). 'Increasing returns and long run growth'. *Journal of Political Economy*, 94, 1002–37.

Romer, P.M. (1996). 'Why indeed in America? Theory, history and the origins of modern economic growth'. *American Economic Review*, 86, 202–6.

Roos, G. (2005). 'An epistemology perspective on intellectual capital'. In Marr, B. (ed.), *Perspectives on intellectual capital – multidisciplinary insights into management, measurement, and reporting*. Oxford: Butterworth-Heinemann, 196–209.

Rumelt, R. P. (1984). 'Towards a strategic theory of the firm'. In Lamb, R.B. (ed.), *Competitive Strategic Management*. Engelwood Cliffs, NJ: Prentice-Hall, 566–70.

Schalk, R. and Rousseau, D.M. (2001). 'Psychological contracts in employment'. In Anderson, N., Ones, D.S., Kepir Sinangil, H. and Viswesvaran (eds), *Handbook of industrial work & organizational psychology*. Thousand Oaks: Sage, 133–42.

Schumpeter, J. (1934). *The theory of economic development*. Cambridge, MA: Harvard University Press.

Scott, A.J. and Storper, M. (2003). 'Regions, globalization, development'. *Regional Studies*, 37, 6–7, 549–78.

Sheehan, P. (1999). 'The global knowledge economy: Challenges for China's development'. *Working Paper 5*, Centre for Strategic Economic Studies, Victoria University of Melbourne, Australia.

Smedlund, A. and Pöyhönen, A. (2005). 'Intellectual capital creation: A knowledge system approach. In Bounfour, A. and Edvinsson, L. (ed.), *Intellectual capital for communities*. Oxford: Butterworth-Heinemann, 227–52.

Smith, A. (1776). *An inquiry into the nature and causes of the wealth of nations. 1910* edition, London: J.M Dent. First published 1776.

Smith, K. (2002). 'What is the "knowledge economy"? Knowledge intensity and distributed knowledge bases'. *UNU/INTECH Discussion paper*. United Nations University, Institute for New Technologies.

Solow, R. (1970). *Growth theory: An exposition*. London: Oxford University Press.

Sotorauta, M. (2003). 'Dynamic capacities in promotion of economic development of city-regions'. Paper presented at the 43rd European Congress of the Regional Science Association. Jyväskylä, Finland, [online] http://www-sre.wu-wien.ac.at/ersa/ersaconfs/ersa03/cdrom/papers/427.pdf

Spender, J-C. (1996a). 'Organizational knowledge, learning and memory: Three concepts in search of a theory'. *Journal of Organizational Change*, 9, 1, 63–78.

Spender, J-C. (1996b). 'Making knowledge the basis of a dynamic theory of the firm'. *Strategic Management Journal*, 17 (special winter issue), 45–62.

Spender, J-C. and Grant, R. M. (1996). 'Knowledge and the firm: Overview'. *Strategic Management Journal,* 17 (Special Winter Issue), 5–9.

Stewart, T.A. (1997). *Intellectual capital: The new wealth of nations.* New York: Doubleday.

Sveiby, K.E. (1997). *The new organizational wealth: Managing and measuring knowledge-based assets.* New York: Berrett-Koehler.

Sveiby, K.E. (2001). 'A knowledge-based theory of the firm to guide strategy formulation'. *Journal of Intellectual Capital,* 2, 4, 344–58.

Sylvester, E. and Klotz, L. (1983). *The gene age.* New York: Scribner's.

Toffler, A. (1980). *The third wave.* London: Collins.

Venzin, M., von Krogh, G. and Roos, J. (1998). 'Future research into knowledge management'. In Von Krogh, G., Roos, J. and Klein, D. (eds), *Knowing in firms – understanding, managing and measuring knowledge.* London: Sage Publications Inc., 26–66.

Viedma, J.M. (2005). 'Cities' Intellectual Capital Benchmarking System (CICBS): A methodology and a framework for measuring and managing intellectual capital of cities: A practical application in the city of Mataró'. In Bounfour, A. and Edvinsson, L. (eds), *Intellectual Capital for Communities.* Burlington, MA: Butterworth-Heinemann, 317–35.

Viedma, J.M. and Enache, C.M. (2007). 'Managing personal human capital for professional excellence: An attempt to design a practical methodology'. Paper presented at the 28th McMaster World Congress on Intellectual Capital & Innovation, Hamilton, Ontario, Canada, 24–26 January.

Vogt, E. (1995). 'The nature of work'. *Telecommunications,* 29, 21–7.

von Krogh, G. and Roos, J. (1995). *Organizational epistemology.* New York: Macmillan and St. Martin's Press.

Wernerfelt, B. (1984). 'A resource-based view of the firm'. *Strategic Management Journal,* 5, 2, 171–80.

Wiig, K.M. (1997). 'Knowledge management: An introduction and perspective'. *Journal of Knowledge Management,* 1, 1, 6–14.

The World Bank Group (2005). *World Development Indicators* [online] http://devdata.worldbank.org/wdi2005/Toc.htm

World Bank, (2003). 'Implementing knowledge economy strategies. Innovation, lifelong learning, partnerships, networks and inclusion'. *Knowledge Economy Forum II.* Helsinki, 25–28 March.

Yigitcanlar, T. (2009). 'Planning for knowledge-based urban development: global perspectives'. *Journal of Knowledge Management,* 13, 5, 228–42.

2   Entrepreneurial Excellence in the Knowledge Economy Context: The Theoretical Foundations

Abeysekera, I. (2006). 'The project of intellectual capital disclosure: Researching the research'. *Journal of Intellectual Capital,* 7, 1, 61–77.

Abeysekera, I. and Guthrie, J. (2004). 'How is intellectual capital being reported in a developing nation?' *Research in Accounting in Emerging Economies,* Supplement 2: Accounting and Accountability in Emerging and Transition Economies, 149–69.

Adams, M. and Olesak, M. (2010). *Intangible capital: Putting knowledge to work in the 21st century organization.* California: Praeger.

Allee, V. (2000). 'Reconfiguring the value network'. *Journal of Business Strategy,* 21, 4.

Alvarez, S.A. and Barney, J. (2007). 'Discovery and creation: alternative theories of entrepreneurial action'. *Strategic Entrepreneurship Journal,* 1, 11, 11–26.

Andriessen, D. (2001). 'Weightless Wealth'. Paper for the 4th World Congress on the Management of Intellectual Capital. McMaster University. January 17–19. Hamilton, Ontario, Canada, 1–10.

Andriessen, D. (2004). *Making sense of intellectual capital: Designing a method for the valuation of intangibles.* Burlington, UK: Butterworth-Heinemann.

Ansoff, H.I (1965). *Corporate strategy: An analytic approach to business policy for growth and expansion.* New York, USA: McGraw-Hill.

Barney, J.B. (1986). 'Strategic factor markets: Expectations, luck and business strategy'. *Management Science,* 31, 1231–41.

Barney, J.B. (1991). 'Firm resources and sustained competitive advantage'. *Journal of Management,* 17, 99–120.

Beattie, R. (1999). 'The creative entrepreneur: A study of the entrepreneur's creative processes'. http://www.babson.edu/entrep/fer/papers99/III/III_B/IIIB.html.

Black, J. and Boal, K. (1994). 'Strategic resources: Traits, configurations and paths to sustainable competitive advantage'. *Strategic Management Journal,* 15, 131–48.

Blair, M.M. and Wallman S.M.H. (2001). *Unseen wealth: Report of the brookings task force on intangibles.* Washington D.C: Brookings Institution Press.

Bounfour, A. (2003). 'The IC-dVAL approach'. *Journal of Intellectual Capital,* 4, 3, 396–412.

Bonn, I. (2005). 'Improving strategic thinking: A multilevel approach'. *Leadership and Organization Development Journal,* 26, 5, 336–54.

Bontis, N. (1998). 'Intellectual capital: An exploratory study that develops measures and models'. *Management Decision,* 36, 2, 63–76.

Bracker, J. (1980). 'The historical development of the strategic management concept'. *Academy of Management Review,* 5, 2, 219–24.

Brooking, A. (1996). *Intellectual capital: Core asset for the third millennium enterprise.* London: International Thomson Business Press.

Burnes, B. (1992). *Managing change. A strategic approach to organisational development and renewal.* London: Pitman Publishing.

Cabrita, M.R. (2009). 'Intellectual Capital: A phenomenon of interrelationships'. *International Journal of Business and Systems Research,* 3, 2, 229–56.

Cabrita, M.R. and Bontis, N. (2008). 'Intellectual Capital and Business Performance in Portuguese Banking Industry'. *International Journal of Technology Management,* 43, 1–3, 212–37.

Cabrita, M.R. and Vaz, J.L. (2006). 'Intellectual capital and value creation: Evidencing in the Portuguese banking industry', *Electronic Journal on Knowledge Management,* 4, 1, 11–19.

Caddy, I. (2000). 'Intellectual capital: Recognizing both assets and liabilities'. *Journal of Intellectual Capital,* 1, 2, 129–46.

Cannon, J.T. (1968). *Business strategy and policy.* New York: Harcourt, Brace and World.

Carlucci, D., Marr, B. and Schiuma, G. (2004). 'The knowledge value chain: How intellectual capital impacts on business performance'. *International Journal of Technology Management*, 27, 6/7, 575–90.

Chaminade, C. and Johanson, U. (2003). 'Can guidelines for intellectual capital management and reporting be considered without addressing cultural differences?'. *Journal of Intellectual Capital*, 4, 4, 524–38.

Chandler, A. (1962). *Strategy and structure: Chapters in the history of American industrial enterprise*. Cambridge Mass: MIT Press.

Coff, R.W. (1997). 'Human assets and management dilemmas: Coping with hazards on the road to resource-based theory'. *Academy of Management Review*, 22, 374–402.

Collis, D.J. (1994). 'Research note: How valuable are organizational capabilities?' *Strategic Management Journal*, special winter issue, 15, 8, 143–52.

Coyne, K.P. (1986). 'Sustainable competitive advantage – what it is and what it isn't'. *Business Horizons*, 29 (Jan-Feb), 54–61.

Coyne, K.P., Hall, S.J.D. and Clifford, G. (1997). 'Is your core competence a mirage?' *The Mckinsey Quarterly*, 1.

Danish Agency for Trade & Industry (DATI) (1998). *Intellectual capital accounts – reporting and measuring intellectual capital*. Copenhagen: DTI.

Day, G.S. and Wensley, R. (1988). 'Assessing advantage: A framework for diagnosing competitive superiority'. *Journal of Marketing*, 52, 2, 1–20.

Dierickx, I and Cool, K. (1989). 'Asset stock accumulation and sustainability of competitive advantage'. *Management Science*, 35, 12, 1504–13.

Douglas, E.J. and Shepherd, D.A. (2000). 'Entrepreneurship as a utility maximizing process', *Journal of Business Venturing*, 15, 3, 231–51.

Drucker, P. (1954). *The practice of management*. New York: Harper and Brothers.

Dzinkowski, R. (2000). 'The measurement and management of intellectual capital: An introduction'. *Management Accounting (UK)*, 78, 2, 32–6.

Edvinsson, L. (2000). 'Some perspectives on intangibles and intellectual capital 2000'. *Journal of Intellectual Capital*, 1, 1, 12–16.

Edvinsson, L., Hofman-Bang, P. and Jacobsen, K. (2005). 'Intellectual capital in waiting – A strategic IC challenge'. *Handbook of Business Strategy*, 133–40.

Edvinsson, L. and Malone, M. (1997). *Intellectual capital: Realising your company's true value by finding its hidden brainpower*. New York: Harper and Collins.

Edvinsson, L. and Sullivan, P. (1996). 'Developing a model for managing intellectual capital'. *European Management Journal*, 14, 4, 356–64.

Elkington, J. (1997). *Cannibals with forks: The triple bottom line of 21st century business*. Oxford: Capstone.

Enders, A., König, A., Hungenberg, H. and Engelbertz, T. (2009). 'Towards an integrated perspective of strategy: The value-process framework'. *Journal of Strategy and Management*, 2, 1, 76–96.

Erikson, T. (2002). 'Entrepreneurial capital: The emerging venture's most important asset and competitive advantage'. *Journal of Business Venturing*, 17, 275–90.

European Commission. (1995). *Teaching and learning: Towards the learning society*. Luxembourg: Office for Official Publications of the European Communities.

European Commission (2003). 'The measurement of intangible assets and associated reporting practices', prepared for the Commission of the European Communities, Enterprise Directorate General, April, http://ec.europa.eu/internal_market/services/docs/brs/competitiveness/2003-study-intangassets-full_en.pdf

Eustace, C.G. (2000). 'Intellectual property and the capital markets'. *CUBS Working Paper*, July. London: City University Business School.

Eustace, C.G. (2003). 'A new perspective on the knowledge value chain'. *Journal of Intellectual Capital*, 4, 4, 588–96.

Fox, J.M. (1975). 'Strategic planning: A case study'. *Managerial Planning*, 23, May/June, 32–8.

Gartner, W.B. and Carter, N.M. (2003). 'The language of opportunity'. In Steyaert, C. and Hjorth, D. (eds), *New movements in entrepreneurship*. London: Edward Elgar, 121–53.

Gibbert, M. Leibold, M. and Voelpel, S. (2001). 'Rejuvenating corporate intellectual capital by co-opting customer competence'. *Journal of Intellectual Capital*, 2, 2, 109–26.

Grant, R.M. (1991). 'The resource-based theory of competitive advantage: Implications for strategy formulation'. *California Management Review*, 33, 3, 114–35.

Grant, R. M. (1996). 'Toward a knowledge-based theory of the firm'. *Strategic Management Journal*, 17 (special winter issue), 108–22.

Grant, R.M. (1998). *Contemporary strategy analysis*. Oxford: Blackwell Publishers Ltd.

Gubman, E.L. (1998). *The talent solution. Aligning strategy and people to achieve extraordinary results*. McGraw-Hill.

Gupta, O. and Roos, G. (2001). 'Mergers and acquisitions: Through an intellectual capital perspective'. *Journal of Intellectual Capital*, 2, 3, 297–309.

Hall, R. (1989). 'The management of intellectual assets: A new corporate perspective'. *Journal of General Management*, 15, Autumn, 53–6.

Hall, R. (1992). 'The strategic analysis of intangible resources'. *Strategic Management Journal*, 13, 2, 135–44.

Hamel, G. and Prahalad, C.K. (1994). *Competing for the future*. Boston, MA: Harvard Business School Press.

Haanes, K. and Fjeldstad, Ø. (2000). 'Linking intangible resources and competition'. *European Management Journal*, 18, 1, 52–62.

Harvey, M.G. and Lusch, R.F. (1999). 'Balancing the intellectual capital books: Intangible liabilities'. *European Management Journal*, 17, 1, 85–92.

Hofer, C.W. and Schendel, D. (1978). *Strategy formulation: Analytical concept*. Minnesota: West Publishing Company.

Hofsted, G. (1991). *Cultures and organizations: Software of the mind*. New York: MacGraw-Hill.

Holloway, M. (2009). 'How tangible is your strategy? How design thinking can turn your strategy into reality'. *Journal of Business Strategy*, 30, 2/3, 50–6.

Hood, J.N. and Young, J.E. (1993). 'Entrepreneurship's requisite areas of development: A survey of top executives in successful entrepreneurial firms'. *Journal of Business Venturing*, 8, 115–35.

Hope, J. and Hope, T. (1998). *Competing in the third wave: The ten key management issues of the information age*. Boston: Harvard Business School.

Huang Y-C and Wu Y-C (2010). Intellectual Capital and Knowledge Productivity: The Taiwan Biotech Industry. *Journal of Management Decision*, 48(4), 580–599.

Hudson, W. (1993). *Intellectual capital: How to build it, enhance it, use it*. New York: John Wiley & Sons.

Hussi, T. and Ahonen, G. (2002). 'Managing intangible assets – a question of integration and delicate balance'. *Journal of Intellectual Capital*, 3, 3, 277–86.

Ihrig, M., Knyphausen-Aufseß, D., and O'Gorman, C. (2006). 'The knowledge-based approach to entrepreneurship: Linking the entrepreneurial process to the dynamic evolution of knowledge'. *International Journal of Knowledge Management Studies*, 1, 1/2, 38–58.

Intellectual Capital Statements. The New Guideline, (2003). Danish Ministry of Science, Technology and Innovation. Available at http://www.weightlesswealth. com/downloads/Intellectual_Capital_Statements_-_The_New_Guideline.pdf

International Accounting Standards Board (IASB) (1998). *International Accounting Standard (IAS) 38, Intangible assets*. London: International Accounting Standards Board.

International Federation of Accountants (IFAC) (1998). *The measurement and management of intellectual capital: An introduction study*, Vol. 7, New York, NY: International Federation of Accountants.

Itami, H. (1987). *Mobilizing Invisible Assets*. Cambridge, MA: Harvard University Press.

Jericó, P. (2001). *Gestión del Talento*. Essex, England: Prentice Hall/Financial Times.

Johnson, G. and Scholes, K. (2002). *Exploring corporate strategy. Text and cases.* 6th Edition. Essex; England: Prentice Hall/Financial Times.

Kantabutra, S. and Avery, G.C. (2010). 'The power of vision: Statements that resonate'. *Journal of Business Strategy*, 31, 1, 37–45.

Kaplan, R.S. and Norton, D.P. (1996a). 'Using the balanced scorecard as a strategic management system'. *Harvard Business Review*, 74, 1, 75–85.

Kaplan, R. S. and Norton, D. P. (1996b). *The balanced scorecard – Translating strategy into action*. Boston, MA: Harvard Business School Press.

Kaplan, R.S. and Norton, D.P. (2004). 'Measuring the strategic readiness of intangible assets'. *Harvard Business Review*, 82, 1, 52–63.

Kay, J. (1993). *Foundations of corporate success: How business strategies add value.* Oxford: Oxford University Press.

Kirzner, I.M. (1973). *Competition and entrepreneurship.* Chicago, IL: University of Chicago Press.

Klein, D.A., and Prusak, L. (1994). *Characterizing Intellectual Capital*, Cambridge, MA: Center for Business Innovation, Ernst & Young LLP.

Knight, D.J. (1999). 'Performance measures for increasing intellectual capital'. *Planning Review*, 27, 2, 22–7.

Koller, T. (1994). 'What is value-based management?' *The McKinsey Quarterly*, 3, 87–101.

Learned, E.P., Christensen, C.R., Andrews, K.R. and Guth, W.D. (1965). *Business Policy: Text and Cases.* Homewood: Richard D. Irwin.

Leonard-Barton, D. (1992). Core capabilities and core rigidities: A paradox in managing new product development. *Strategic Management Journal*, 3, 111–25.

Leonard-Barton, D. (1995). *Wellsprings of knowledge: Building and sustaining the sources of innovation.* Boston, MA: Harvard Business School Press.

Lev, B. (2001). *Intangibles: Management, measurement, and reporting.* Washington DC: The Brookings Institution.

Lippman, S.A. and Rumelt, R.P. (1982). 'Uncertain imitability: An analysis of interfirm differences in efficiency under competition'. *Bell Journal of Economics*, 13 (Autumn), 418–38.

Mahoney, J.T. and Pandian, J.R. (1992). 'The resource-based view of the firm within the conversation of strategic management'. *Strategic Management Journal*, 13, 5, 363–80.

Man, T.W.Y., Lau, T. and Chan, K.F. (2002). 'The competitiveness of small and medium enterprises. A conceptualisation with focus on entrepreneurial competencies'. *Journal of Business Venturing*, 17, 123–42.

Marr, B. (2005). *Perspectives on intellectual capital – multidisciplinary insights into management, measurement, and reporting*. Oxford: Butterworth-Heinemann.

Marr, B. and Chatzkel, J. (2004). 'Intellectual capital at the crossroads – managing, measuring, and reporting of IC'. *Journal of Intellectual Capital*, 5, 2, 224–30.

Marr, B., Gray, D., Neely, A. (2003). 'Why do firms measure Intellectual Capital'. *Journal of Intellectual Capital*, 4, 4, 441–64.

Marr, B. and Moustaghfir, K. (2005). 'Defining intellectual capital: A three-dimensional approach'. *Management Decision*, 43, 9, 1114–28.

Marr, B., Schiuma, G. and Neely, A. (2004). 'The dynamics of value creation: Mapping your intellectual performance drivers'. *Journal of Intellectual Capital*, 5, 2, 312–25.

Martin, W.J. (2004). 'Demonstrating knowledge value: a broader perspective on metrics'. *Journal of Intellectual Capital*, 5, 1, 77–91.

Martins, B. (2006). 'InCaS – State of the art in measuring and reporting intellectual capital'. Paper prepared to support the InCaS project, to be published.

Mayo, A. (2001). *The human value of the enterprise: Valuing people as assets – Monitoring, measuring, managing*. UK: Nicholas Brealey Publishing.

'MEasuRing Intangibles To Understand and improve innovation Management (MERITUM, 2002). Final report. http://www.pnbukh.com/files/pdf_filer/FINAL_REPORT_MERITUM.pdf

Miller, D. and Shamsie, J. (1996). 'The resource-based view of the firm in two environments: The Hollywood film studios from 1936 to 1965'. *Academy of Management Journal*, 39, 3, 519–43.

Mintzberg, H. (1987). 'Crafting strategy'. *Harvard Business Review*, 19, 2, 66–75.

Mintzberg, H. (1979). *The structuring of organizations*. Englewood Cliffs, N.J: Prentice-Hall.

Mintzberg, H. (1995). 'Strategic thinking as "seeing"'. In Garratt, B. (ed.) *Developing strategic thought*. San Francisco, CA: McGraw Hill.

Mintzberg, H. Ahlstrand, B. and Lampel, J. (1998). *Strategy safari. A guided tour through the wilds of strategic management*. New York, NY: The Free Press.

Murphy, P.J. (2009). 'Entrepreneurship theory and the poverty of historicism'. *Journal of Management History*, 15, 2, 109–33.

Nahapiet, J. and Ghoshal, S. (1998). 'Social capital, intellectual capital and the organizational advantage'. *Academy of Management Review*, 23, 2, 242–66.

Narayanan, V.K. (2001). *Managing technology and innovation for competitive advantage*. Englewood Cliffs, NJ: Prentice Hall.

Nelson R. and Winter, S. (1982). *An evolutionary theory of economic change*. Cambridge, MA: Harvard University Press.

O'Donnell, D., O'Regan, P., Coates, B., Kennedy, T., Keary, B. and Berkery, G. (2003). 'Human interaction: The critical source of intangible value'. *Journal of Intellectual Capital*, 4, 1, 82–99.

Organisation for Economic Co-Operation and Development (OECD) (1996). *Measuring What People Know: Human Capital Accounting for the Knowledge Economy*. Paris.

Organisation for Economic Co-Operation and Development (OECD) (1998). *Technology, Productivity and Job Creation. Best Policy Practices*, DSTI/IND/STP/ICCP (98)2/PART2.

Organisation for Economic Co-Operation and Development (OECD) (1999). *Measuring and Reporting Intellectual Capital: Experience, Issues and Prospects*. Amsterdam, June. http://www.oecd.org/document/1/0,3746,en_2649_34173_1932737_1_1_1_1,00.html

Ortiz, M.A. (2009). 'Analysis and valuation of intellectual capital according to its context'. *Journal of Intellectual Capital,* 10, 3, 451–88.

Oxford English Dictionary (2004). http://dictionary.oed.com/

Penrose, E.T. (1959). *The theory of the growth of the firm.* New York: John Wiley.

Peteraf, M.A. (1993). 'The cornerstone of competitive advantage: A resource-based view'. *Strategic Management Journal,* 14 (March), 179–91.

Peters, T.J. and Waterman, R.H. (1982). *In the search of excellence: Lessons from America's best-run companies.* New York: Harper and Row.

Pike, S. and Roos, G. (2004). 'Measurement issues in intellectual Capital – A review'. Paper presented at the 2004 International Forum of Intellectual Capital in Taiwan.

Polanyi, M. (1983). *The tacit dimension.* Gloucester, Mass: Peter Smith.

Porter, M.E. (1985). *Competitive advantage.* New York, NY: Free Press.

Porter, M.E. (1996). 'What is strategy?' *Harvard Business Review,* 7, 6, 61–78.

Powell, T. C. (2001). 'Competitive Advantage: Logical and philosophical considerations'. *Strategic Management Journal.* 22, 875–88.

Prahalad, C.K. and Hamel, G. (1990). 'The core competence of the corporation'. *Harvard Business Review,* May-June, 79–91.

Prahalad, C.K. and Ramaswamy, V. (2000). 'Co-opting customer competence'. *Harvard Business Review,* Jan-Feb, 79–87.

Quinn, J.B. (1992). *Intelligent enterprise: A new paradigm for a new era.* New York: Free Press.

Reed, R. and DeFillippi, R. J. (1990). 'Causal ambiguity, barriers to imitation and sustainable competitive advantage'. *Academy of Management Review,* 15 (January), 88–102.

Rindova, V.P. and Fombrun, C.J. (2001). 'Entrepreneurial action in the creation of the speciality coffee niche'. In Schoonhoven, C.B. and Romanelli, E. (eds), *The entrepreneurship dynamic.* California: Stanford University Press, 236–61.

Roos, G. (2005). 'Intellectual capital and strategy: A primer for today's manager'. *Handbook of Business Strategy,* 123–32.

Roos, G., Pike, S. and Fernström, L. (2006). *Managing intellectual capital in practice.* New York: Butterworth-Heinemann.

Roos, G. and Roos, J. (1997). 'Measuring your company's intellectual performance'. *Long Range Planning,* 30, 3, 413–26.

Roos, J., Roos, G., Dragonetti N.C. and Edvinsson, L. (1997). *Intellectual Capital: Navigating the new business landscape.* London: Macmillan Press.

Rothberg, H.N. and Erickson, G.S. (2002). 'Competitive capital: A fourth pillar of intellectual capital?' In Bontis, N. (ed.), *World Congress on Intellectual Capital Readings.* Boston, MA: Butterworth-Heinemann, 13–56.

Rumelt, R.P., Schendel, D.E. and Teece, D.J. (1994). *Fundamental issues in strategy.* Harvard Business School Press.

Saint-Onge, H. and Wallace, D. (2003). *Leveraging communities of practice for strategic advantage.* Burlington, MA: Butterworth-Heinemann.

Schendel, D.E. and Hofer, C.W. (1979). *Strategic management: A new view of business policy and planning.* Boston: Little, Brown.

Schwarz, M. and Nandhakumar, J. (1999). 'The evolution of strategy in a newly transformed organization: The interplay between strategy development and corporate culture'. In Hitt, Clifford, Nixon and Coyne (eds) *Dynamic resources – Development, diffusion and integration.* Chichester: John Willey & Sons, Ltd.

Securities and Exchange Commission-Inspired Task Force (SECITF) (2001). *Strengthening financial markets: Do investors have the information they need?* Report of an SEC-Inspired Task Force.

Shane, S. and Venkataraman, S. (2001). 'Entrepreneurship as a field of research: A response to Zahra and Dess, Singh and Erikson'. *Academy of Management Review,* 26, 1, 13–16.

Spender, J. C. (1996). 'Making knowledge the basis of a dynamic theory of the firm'. *Strategic Management Journal,* 17 (special winter issue), 45–62.

Stalk. G., Evans, P. and Schulman, L.E. (1993). 'Competing on capabilities: The new rules of corporate strategy'. In Howard, R. (ed.) *The learning imperative: Managing people for continuous innovation.* Cambridge: Harvard Business Review, 19–40.

Stewart, T.A. (1997). *Intellectual capital: The wealth of new organizations.* London: Nicholas Brealey Publishing Ltd.

Sullivan, P. J. (2000). *Value-driven intellectual capital: How to convert intangible corporate assets into market value.* New York, NY: John Wiley & Sons.

Sveiby, K.E. (1997). *The new organizational wealth: Managing and measuring knowledge-based assets.* San Francisco: Berrett-Koeheler Publishers, Inc.

Sveiby, K.E. (2001). 'A knowledge-based theory of the firm to guide strategy formulation'. *Journal of Intellectual Capital,* 2, 4, 344–58.

Sworder, C. (1995). 'Hearing the baby's cry: It's all in the thinking'. In Garratt, B. (ed.), *Developing strategic thought,* San Francisco, CA: McGraw Hill.

Teece, D.J. (1986). 'Firm boundaries, technological innovation and strategic management'. In Thomas, L.G. (ed.), *The economics of strategic planning,* Lexington, MA: Lexington Books, 187–99.

Teece, D.J., Pisano, G. and Shuen, A. (1990). 'Firm capabilities, resources, and the concept of strategy'. *Economic Analysis and Policy Working Paper,* EAP-38. Berkeley: University of California.

Teece, D.J., Pisano, G. and Shuen, A. (1997). 'Dynamic capabilities and strategic management'. *Strategic Management Journal,* 18, 7, 509–33.

Torvstiga, G. and Birchall, D.W. (2002). 'Strategic knowledge, sourcing, integration, and assimilation: A capabilities-portfolio perspective'. In Bontis, N. (Ed.), *World congress on intellectual capital readings,* 104–118.

Ulrich, D. (1998). 'Intellectual capital – competence x commitment'. *Sloan Management Review,* 39, 4, 15–27.

Ulrich, D. Zenger, J. and Smallwood, N. (1999). *Results-based leadership.* Boston: Harvard Business School Press.

Venkataraman, S. (1997). 'The distinctive domain of entrepreneurship research: An editor's perspective'. In Katz, J. and Brockhaus, R. (eds), *Advances in entrepreneurship, firm emergence, and growth,* Vol 3, Greenwich, CT: JAI Press, 119–38.

Viedma, J.M. (2003a). 'In search of an intellectual capital general theory'. *Electronic Journal of Knowledge Management,* 1, 2, 213–26.

Viedma, J.M. (2003b). 'OICBS: Operations Intellectual Capital Benchmarking System. An operations intellectual capital strategic management methodology'. http://icbsmonitor.com/Files/Viedma_CabritaICBS.pdf-19k

Viedma, J.M. (2003c). 'IICBS: Innovation Intellectual Capital Benchmarking System. An innovation intellectual capital strategic management methodology'. http://intellectualcapitalmanagementsystems.com/

Viedma, J.M. (2004a). 'Strategic knowledge benchmarking system (SKBS): A knowledge-based strategic management information system for firms'. *Journal of Knowledge Management*, 8, 6, 31–49.

Viedma, J.M. (2004b). 'Social capital benchmarking system: Profiting from social capital when building network organizations'. *Journal of Intellectual Capital*, 5, 3, 426–42.

Weick, K.E. (1995). *Sensemaking in organizations*. Thousand Oaks, CA: Sage.

Wernerfelt, B. (1984). 'A resource-based view of the firm'. *Strategic Management Journal*, 5, 2, 171–80.

Wernerfelt, B. (1989). 'From critical resources to corporate strategy'. *Journal of General Management*, 14, (Spring), 4–12.

Williamson, O. E. (1975). '*Markets and hierarchies*'. New York: Free Press.

3   The Practice of Entrepreneurial Excellence in the Knowledge Economy Context

Andriessen, D. (2001). 'Weightless wealth'. Paper for the 4th World Congress on the Management of Intellectual Capital. McMaster University. Hamilton, Ontario, Canada, 17–19 January.

Andriessen, D., Frijlink, M., Van Gisbergen, I. and Blom, J. (1999). 'A core competency approach to valuing intangible assets'. Paper presented to the International Symposium, Measuring and reporting intellectual capital: Experiences, issues and prospects, Amsterdam, 9–10 June.

Baldrige Performance Excellence Program. 2011–12 Criteria for performance excellence. [Online] http://www.nist.gov/baldrige/publications/upload/2011_2012_Business_Nonprofit_Criteria.pdf

Bontis, N. (2004). 'National intellectual capital index: A United Nations initiative for the Arab Region. *Journal of Intellectual Capital*, 5, 1, 13–39.

Brignall, S. and Modell, S. (2000). 'An institutional perspective on performance measurement and management in the "new public sector"'. *Management Accounting Research*, 11, 3, 281–306.

Brooking, A. (1996). *Intellectual capital: Core assets for the third millennium enterprise*. London: Thompson Business Press.

Chen, J., Zhu, Z. and Xie, H.Y. (2004). 'Measuring intellectual capital: A new model and empirical study'. *Journal of Intellectual Capital*, 5, 1, 195–212.

Danish Agency for Trade and Industry (DATI) (1998). *Intellectual capital accounts: New tools for companies*. Copenhagen: DTI Council.

Danish Agency for Trade and Industry (DATI) (2001). *A Guideline for Intellectual Capital Statements*, Danish Agency for Development of Trade and Industry, Copenhagen, Demark.

Drucker, P. (1993). *Post-capitalist Society*. Oxford: Butterworth-Heinemann Ltd.

Edvinsson, L. (1997). 'Developing intellectual capital at Skandia'. *Long Range Planning*, 30, 3, 366–73.

Edvinsson, L. and Malone, M. (1997). *Intellectual capital: Realising your company's true value by finding its hidden brainpower*. New York: Harper and Collins.

Gupta, O. and Roos, G. (2001). 'Mergers and acquisitions: Through an intellectual capital perspective'. *Journal of Intellectual Capital*, 2, 3, 297–309.

Hansson, J. (1998). 'Intellectual capital – the latest trick to make management scientific?' *Working paper*. The Management School, Lancaster University, UK.

Hussi, T. and Ahonen, G. (2002). 'Managing intangible assets – a question of integration and delicate balance'. *Journal of Intellectual Capital*, 3, 3, 277–86.

Johanson, U. (2003). 'Why are capital market actors ambivalent to information about certain indicators on intellectual capital?' *Accounting, Auditing & Accountability Journal*, 16, 1, 31–8.

Johanson, U. and Nilson, M. (1996). 'The usefulness of human resource costing and accounting'. *Journal of Human Resource Costing and Accounting*, 1, 1, 17–138.

Kaplan, R.S. and Norton, D. (1992). 'The balanced scorecard – measures that drive performance'. *Harvard Business Review*, 70, 1, 71–9.

Kaplan, R.S. and Norton, D. (1996). *The Balanced Scorecard: Translating strategy into action*. Boston, MA: Harvard Business School Press.

Kaplan, R.S. and Norton, D. (2001) *The strategy focused organization*. Boston, MA: Harvard Business School Press.

Kaplan, R.S. and Norton, D. (2004) *Strategy maps: Converting intangible assets into tangible outcomes*. Boston, MA: Harvard Business School Press.

Kloot, L. and Martin, J. (2000). 'Strategic performance management: A balanced approach to performance issues in local government'. *Management Accounting Research*, 11, 2, 231–51.

Koch, G.R, Leitner, K-H. and Bornemann, M. (2000). 'Measuring and reporting intangible assets and results in a European contract research organization'. Paper prepared for the Joint German-OECD Conference, Benchmarking Industry-Science Relationships, Berlin, Germany, at http://www.oecd.org/dataoecd/56/16/35322785.pdf

Lank, E. (1997). 'Leveraging human assets: The human factor'. *Long Range Planning*, 30, 3, 406–12.

Marr, B. and Adams, C. (2004). 'The balanced scorecard and intangible assets: Similar ideas, unaligned concepts'. *Measuring Business Excellence*, 8, 3, 18–27.

Marr, B., Gray, D. Neely, A. (2003). 'Why do firms measure intellectual capital'. *Journal of Intellectual Capital*, 4, 4, 441–64.

Marr, B., Schiuma, G. and Neely, A. (2004). 'Intellectual capital – defining key performance indicators for organizational knowledge assets'. *Business Process Management Journal*, 10, 5, 551–69.

Martins, B. (2006). 'InCaS – State of the art in measuring and reporting intellectual capital'. Paper prepared to support the InCaS project, to be published.

MEasuRing InTangibles to Understand and improve innovation Management (MERITUM). (2001). 'MEasuRing InTangibles to Understand and improve innovation Management – Final Report'. Project funded by the European Community under the Targeted Socio-Economic Research (TSER).

Mouritsen, J., Larson, H.T. and Bukh, P.N. (2005). 'Dealing with the knowledge economy: intellectual capital versus balanced scorecard'. *Journal of Intellectual Capital*, 6, 1, 8–27.

Neely, A., Adams, C. and Kennerley, M. (2002). *The performance prism: The scorecard for measuring and managing business success*. London: Financial Times Prentice Hall.

Niven, P.R. (2006). *Balanced Scorecard step by step: Maximizing performance and maintaining results*. Second edition, Hoboken, New Jersey: John Wiley & Sons, Inc.

O'Dell, C. and Grayson, C.J. (1998). *If only we knew what we knew: The transfer of internal knowledge and best practice*. New York: The Free Press.

Olve, N.G., Roy, J. and Wetter, M. (1998). *Performance drivers. A practical guide to using the balanced scorecard.* Hoboken, New Jersey: John Wiley and Sons.

Pasher, E. and Shachar, S. (2005). 'The intellectual capital of the state of Israel'. In Bounfour, A. Edvinsson, L. (eds), *Intellectual capital for communities: Nations, regions, and cities.* Oxford: Butterworth-Heinemann, 139–49.

Pike, S. and Roos, G. (2000). 'Intellectual capital measurement and holistic value approach (HVA)'. See http://www.intcap.com/downloads/ICS_Article_2000_IC_Measurement_HVA.pdf

Pike, S. and Roos, G. (2004a). 'Measurement issues in intellectual capital – A review'. Paper presented to the 2004 International Forum of Intellectual Capital in Taiwan.

Pike, S. and Roos, G. (2004b). 'Mathematics and modern business management'. Paper presented to the 25th McMaster World Congress Managing Intellectual Capital. Hamilton, Canada, January.

Prahalad, C.K. and Hamel, G. (1990). 'The core competence of the corporation'. *Harvard Business Review,* May–June, 79–91.

Pulic, A. (1998). 'Measuring the performance of intellectual potential in knowledge economy'. *http://www.measuringip.at/Opapers/Pulic/Vaictxt.vaictxt.html*

Roos, G. and Roos, J. (1997). 'Measuring your company's intellectual performance'. *Long Range Planning,* 30, 3, 413–26.

Roos, J., Roos, G., Dragonetti N.C. and Edvinsson, L. (1997). *Intellectual Capital: Navigating the new business landscape.* London: Macmillan Press.

Sackmann, S., Flamholz, E. and Bullen, M. (1989). 'Human resource accounting: A state of the art review'. *Journal of Accounting Literature,* 8, 235–64.

Skyrme, J.D. (2003). 'Measuring intellectual capital: A plethora of methods': *http://www.skyrme.com/insights/24kmeas.html*

Sveiby, K.E. (1997). *The new organizational wealth. Managing and measuring knowledge-based assets.* San Francisco: Berrett-Koeheler Publishers, Inc.

Sveiby, K-E. (2004). 'Methods for measuring intangible assets': *http://www.sveiby.com/articles/intangiblemethods.html*

The Nordic Industrial Fund (2003). 'How to develop and monitor your company's intellectual capital'. The Nordic Industrial Fund – Centre for Innovation and Commercial Development, Oslo, Norway, April.

Van den Berg, H.A. (2005). 'Models of Intellectual Capital Valuation: A Comparative Evaluation'. In Kambhammettu, S.S. (ed.), *Business Performance Measurement: Intellectual Capital – Valuation Models.* Hyderabad, India: Le Magnus University Press, 121–58.

Van der Meer-Kooistra, J. and Vosselman, G.J. (2000). 'Management control of interfirm transactional relationships: the case of industrial renovation and maintenance'. *Accounting, Organization and Society,* 25, 1, 51–77.

Viedma, J.M. (2004). 'Strategic Knowledge Benchmarking System (SKBS): A knowledge-based strategic management information system for firms'. *Journal of Knowledge Management,* 8, 6, 31–49.

4 Building an Integrative Methodology and Framework for Strategy Formulation

Acnur, N. and Englyst, L. (2006). 'Assessment of strategy formulation: How to ensure quality in process and outcome'. *International Journal of Operations and Production Management,* 26, 1, 69–91.

Adam, P. and Van de Water, R. (1995). 'Benchmarking and the bottom line: Translating business re-engineering into bottom-line results'. *Industrial Engineering*, 27, 2, 24.

American Productivity and Quality Center. (1999). What is best practice? Available at http://www.apqc.org, retrieved on April 2010.

Amit, R. and Schoemaker, P. (1993). 'Strategic assets and organizational rent'. *Strategic Management Journal*, 4, 1, 33–46.

Andrews, K.R. (1971). *The concept of corporate strategy*. Homewood, IL: Dow-Jones Irwin.

Andriessen, D. (2004a). 'Reconciling the rigor-relevance dilemma in intellectual capital research'. *The Learning Organization*, 11, 4/5, 393–401.

Andriessen, D. (2004b). *Making sense of intellectual capital*. Boston, MA: Elsevier Butterworth-Heinemann.

Ansoff, I. (1987). *Corporate strategy*. London: Penguin Books.

Ansoff, I.H. and McDonnell, E.J. (1990). *Implanting strategic management*. 2nd edition, Cambridge, Great Britain: Prentice Hall International (UK) Ltd.

Barney, J.B. (1991). 'Firm resources and sustained competitive advantage'. *Journal of Management*, 17, 1, 99–120.

Barney, J.B. (2002). *Gaining and sustaining competitive advantage*. 2nd edition, Upper Saddle River, New Jersey: Prentice Hall.

Bendell, T., Boulter, L. and Kelly, J. (1993). *Benchmarking for competitive advantage*. London, UK: Financial Times Pitman Publishing.

Boxwell, R. (1994). *Benchmarking for a competitive advantage*. New York: McGraw Hill.

Camp, R.C. (1989). *Benchmarking: The search for industry best practices that lead to superior performance*. New York, NY: Quality Press and Quality Resources.

Carpenter, G.S. and Nakamoto, K. (1989). 'Consumer preference formation and pioneering advantage'. *Journal of Marketing Research*, August, 285–98.

Cox, A. and Thompson, I. (1998). 'On the appropriateness of benchmarking'. *Journal of General Management*, 23, 3, 1–20.

Cox, J.R.W., Mann, L. and Samson, D. (1997). 'Benchmarking as a mixed metaphor: Disentangling assumptions of competition and collaboration'. *Journal of Management Studies*, 34, 2, 285–314.

Coyne, K.P. and Subramaniam, S. (1996). 'Bringing discipline to strategy'. *The Mckinsey Quarterly*, 4.

Dattakumar, R. and Jagadeesh, R. (2003). 'A review of literature on benchmarking'. *Benchmarking: An International Journal*, 10, 3, 176–209.

Dorsch, J.J. and Yasin, M.M. (1998). 'A framework for benchmarking in the public sector: Literature review and directions for future research'. *International Journal of Public Sector Management*, 11, 2/3, 91–115.

Drew, S.W. (1997). 'From knowledge to action: The impact of benchmarking on organizational performance'. *Long Range Planning*, 30, 3, 427–42.

Fuld, L.M. (1995). *New competitor intelligence: New business directions*. New York, USA: John Wiley & Sons, Inc.

Geber, B. (1990). 'Benchmarking: Measuring yourself against the best'. *Training*, November, 36, 44.

Gilad, B. and Gilad, T. (1988). *The business intelligence system: A new tool for competitive advantage*, New York: AMACOM.

Gilad, B. and Herrings, J.P. (1996). *The art and science of business intelligence analysis*. London: Jai Press Inc.

Grant, M.F. (1991). 'The Resource-based theory of competitive advantage: Implications for strategy formulation'. *California Management Review*, 33, 114–35.

Grant, Robert (1998). *Contemporary strategy analysis: Concepts, techniques, applications*. 3rd edition. Cambridge, UK: Blackwell Business.

Helms, M.M. and Nixon, J. (2010). 'Exploring SWOT analysis – where are we now? A review of academic research from the last decade'. *Journal of Strategy and Management*, 3, 3, 215–51.

Horvath, P. and Herter, N.R. (1992). 'Benchmarking: Comparison with the best of the best'. *Controlling*, 4, 1, 4–11.

Jackson, N. (2001). 'Benchmarking in UK HE: An overview'. *Quality Assurance in Education*, 9, 4, 218–35.

Johnson, G., Scholes, K. and Sexty, R.W. (1998). *Exploring strategic management*. Scarborough, Ontario: Prentice Hill.

Johnson, G. and Scholes, K. (2002). *Exploring corporate strategy. Text and cases*. 6th edition. Essex; England: Prentice Hall/Financial Times.

Kahaner, L. (1996). *Competitive intelligence*. New York: Simon and Schuster.

Kaplan, R.S. and Norton, D. (1996). *The Balanced Scorecard: Translating strategy into action*. Boston, MA: Harvard Business School Press.

Karlof, B. and Ostblom, S. (1993). *Benchmarking: A signpost of excellence in quality and productivity*. Chichester: John Willey & Sons.

Kempner, D.E. (1993). 'The Pilot Years: The growth of the NACUBO Benchmarking Project'. *NACUBO Business Officer*, 27(6), 21–31.

Kleine, B. (1994). 'Benchmarking for continuous performance improvement: Tactics for success'. *Total Quality Environmental Management*, Spring, 283–95.

Kogut, B. and Kulatilaka, N. (1994). 'Options thinking and platform investments: Investing in opportunity'. *California Management Review*, Winter, 52–71.

Lee, S.F. and Sai On Ko, A. (2000). 'Building balanced scorecard with SWOT analysis and implementing "Sun Tzu's the art of business management strategies" on QFD methodology'. *Managerial Auditing Journal*, 15, 1–2.

Marr, B. (2004). 'Measuring and benchmarking intellectual capital'. *Benchmarking: An International Journal*, 11, 6, 559–70.

Marr, B., Gray, D. and Neely, A. (2003). 'Why do firms measure intellectual capital'. *Journal of Intellectual Capital*, 4, 4, 441–64.

Marr, B., Schiuma, G. and Neely, A. (2004). 'Intellectual capital – defining key performance indicators for organizational knowledge assets'. *Business Process Management Journal*, 10, 5, 551–69.

Nickols, F. and Ledgerwood, R. (2006). 'The goals grid as a tool for strategic planning'. *Consulting to Management*, 17, 1, 36–8.

Porter, M. (1979). 'How competitive forces shape strategy'. *Harvard Business Review*, 57, 2, 5–8.

Porter, M. (1980). *Competitive strategy: Techniques for analysing industries and competitors*. New York: The Free Press.

Porter, M. (1985). *Competitive advantage*. New York, NY: The Free Press.

Porter, M. (1996). 'What is strategy?' *Harvard Business Review*, November–December, 61–78.

Prahalad, C.K. and Hamel, G. (1990). 'The core competence of the corporation'. *Harvard Business Review*, May–June, 79–91.

Roos, G. (2005). 'Intellectual capital and strategy: A primer for today's manager'. *Handbook of Business Strategy*, 123–32.

Rothberg, H.N. and Erickson, G.S. (2002). 'Competitive capital: A fourth pillar of intellectual capital?' In Bontis, N. (ed.), *World Congress on Intellectual Capital Readings*. Boston, MA: Butterworth-Heinemann, 13–56.

Sai On Ko, A. and Lee, S.F. (2000). 'Implementing the strategic formulation framework for the banking industry of Hong Kong'. *Managerial Auditing Journal*, 15, 9.

Spendolini, M.J. (1992). 'The benchmarking book'. AMACOM, a division of American Management Association. New York. 18–22.

Stevenson, W. (1996). *Productions/Operations Management*. 5th edition. Boston, MA.: Irwin Publishing Company.

Sveiby, K-E. (2001). 'A knowledge-based theory of the firm to guide strategy formulation'. *Journal of Intellectual Capital*, 2, 4, 344–58.

Teece, D.J. (1984). 'Economic analysis and strategic management'. *California Management Review*, 26, 3, 87–110.

Teece, D.J. (1986). 'Profiting from technological innovation: Implications for integration, collaboration, licensing and public policy'. *Research Policy*, 15, 285–305.

Teece, D.J., Pisano, G. and Shuen, A. (1997). 'Dynamic capabilities and strategic management'. *Strategic Management Journal*, 18, 7, 509–33.

Thompson, I. and Cox, A. (1997). 'Don't imitate, innovate'. *Supply Management*, 40–43.

Van Aken, J.E. (2004). 'Management research based on the paradigm of the design sciences: The quest for field-tested and grounded technological rules'. *Journal of Management Studies*, 41, 2, 219–46.

Vaziri, K. (1992). 'Using competitive benchmarking to set goals'. *Quality Progress*, October, 81, 5.

Viedma, J.M. (2004). 'Strategic knowledge benchmarking system (SKBS): A knowledge-based strategic management information system for firms'. *Journal of Knowledge Management*, 8, 6, 31–49.

Warren, K. (2002). *Competitive Strategy Dynamics*. New York, NY: Wiley

Watson, G. (1993). *Strategic benchmarking: How to rate your company's performance against the world's best*. Canada: John Wiley & Sons.

Yasin, M.M. (2002). 'The theory and practice of benchmarking: Then and now'. *Benchmarking: An International Journal*, 9, 3, 217–43.

Zack, M.H., Smith, D.E. and Slusher, J.A. (1999). *Knowledge and strategy*. Williamsburg, VA: Institute for Knowledge Management.

Zack, M.H. (2002). A strategic pretext for knowledge management, Proceedings of The Third European Conference on Organizational Knowledge, Learning and Capabilities, Athens, Greece, April 5, Available at http://www.alba.edu.gr/OKLC2002/Proceedings/

Zairi, M. (1992). 'The art of benchmarking: Using customer feedback to establish a performance gap'. *Total Quality Management*, 3, 2, 177–88.

5 Operations Intellectual Capital Benchmarking System (OICBS)

Miller, D. and Shamsie, J. (1996). 'The resource-based view of the firm in two environments. The Hollywood film studios from 1936 to 1965'. *Academy of Management Journal*, 39, 3, 519–543.

Viedma, J.M. (2004). 'Strategic knowledge benchmarking system (SKBS): A knowledge-based strategic management information system for firms'. *Journal of Knowledge Management*, 8, 6, 31–49.

Winter, S. (1987). 'Knowledge and competence as strategic assets'. In Teece, D. (ed.), *The competitive challenge: Strategies for industrial innovation and renewal.* New York: Harper and Row, 159–184.

6   Innovation Intellectual Capital Benchmarking System (IICBS)

Chesbrough, H.W. (2003). *Open innovation: The new imperative for creating and profiting from technology.* Cambridge, MA: Harvard Business School Press.
Collis, D. (1994). 'How valuable are organizational capabilities?'. *Strategic Management Journal,* 15, 143–152.
Danneels, E. (2002). 'The dynamics of product innovation and firm competences'. *Strategic Management Journal,* 23, 1095–1121.
Hamel, G. and Prahalad, C.K. (1994). *Competing for the future.* Boston, MA: Harvard Business School Press.
Kaplan, R.S. and Norton, D. (1996). *The Balanced Scorecard – translating strategy into action.* Boston, MA: Harvard Business School Press
Prahalad, C.K. and Hamel, G. (1990). 'The core competence of the corporation'. *Harvard Business Review,* May-June, 79–91.
Prusak, L. (1996). 'The knowledge advantage'. *Strategy and Leadership,* March-April.
Sveiby, K.E. (1997). *The new organizational wealth.* San Francisco CA: Berrett-Koehler.
Teece, D.J., Pisano, G. and Shuen, A. (1997). 'Dynamic capabilities and strategic management. *Strategic Management Journal,* 18, 7, 509–533.
Viedma, J.M. (2001). 'ICBS Intellectual Capital Benchmarking System'. *Journal of Intellectual Capital,* 2, 2, 148–164.
Viedma, J.M. (2004). 'SKBS. Strategic Knowledge Benchmarking System: a knowledge-based strategic management information system for firms'. *Journal of Knowledge Management,* 8, 6, 31–49.
Wernerfelt, B. (1984). 'A resource-based view of the firm'. *Strategic Management Journal,* 5, 2, 171–180.

7   Social Capital Benchmarking System (SCBS)

Allee, V. (2000). 'Reconfiguring the value network'. *Journal of Business Strategy,* 21, 4.
Anderson, A., Park, J. and Jack, S. (2007). 'Entrepreneurial social capital: Conceptualizing social capital in new high-tech firms'. *International Small Business Journal,* 25, 3, 245–272.
Baker, W. (1990). 'Market networks and corporate behaviour'. *American Journal of Sociology,* 96, 589–625.
Bueno, E. and Salmador, M.P. (2004). 'The role of social capital in today's economy: Empirical evidence and proposal of a new model of intellectual capital'. *Journal of Intellectual Capital,* 5, 4, 556–574.
Burt, R.S. (1992). *Structural Holes: The social structure of competition.* Cambridge, MA: Harvard University Press.
Castiglione, D., Van Deth, J.W. and Wolleb, G. (eds) (2008). *The Handbook of Social Capital.* Oxford: Oxford University Press.

Cohen, D. and Prusak, L. (2001). *In good company: How social capital makes organizations work.* Boston, MA: Harvard Business School Press.

Coleman, J.S. (1988). 'Social capital in the creation of human capital', *American Journal of Sociology,* 94, 95–120.

Cooke, P. and Morgan, K. (1993). 'The network paradigm: New departures in corporate and regional development'. *Society and Space,* October, 75.

Cooner, K.R. and Prahalad, C.K. (1996). 'A resource-based theory of the firm: Knowledge versus opportunism'. *Organization Science,* 7, 5, 477–501.

Doz, Y.L. and Hamel, G. (1998). *Alliance advantage.* Boston, MA: Harvard Business School Press, XIII–XVIII, 137–145.

Farrell, S. and Taylor, A. (1995). *Information management for business.* Metuchen, NJ: The Scarecrow Press.

Fukuyama, F. (1995). *Trust social virtues and the creation of prosperity.* London: Hamish Hamilton.

Granovetter, M.S. (1992). 'Problems of explanation in economic sociology'. In Nhoria, N. and Eccles, R. (eds), *Networks and organizations. Structure, form and action.* Boston: Harvard Business School Press, 25–56.

Håkansson, H. (1989). *Corporate technological behaviour: Co-operation and networks.* London: Routledge.

Harrison, B. (1994). *Lean and mean.* New York, NY: Basic Books.

Hastings, C. (1995). 'Building the culture of organizational networking'. *International Journal of Project Management,* 13, 4, 259–263.

Hoffman, J.J., Hoelscher, M.L. and Sherif, K. (2005). 'Social capital, knowledge management, and sustained superior performance'. *Journal of Knowledge Management,* 9, 3, 93–100.

Järvenpää, E. and Mäki, E. (2002). 'Knowledge-sharing networked organizations' in Bontis, N. (ed.), *World Congress on Intellectual Capital Readings.* Boston, MA: Butterworth-Heinemann, 374–383.

Ketels, C.H.M. and Memedovic, O. (2008). 'From clusters to cluster-based economic Development'. *International Journal of Technological Learning, Innovation and Development,* 1, 3, 375–392.

Kogut, B. and Zander, U. (1996). 'What do firms do? Coordination, identity and learning'. *Organization Science,* 7, 502–518.

Koka, B.R. and Prescott, J.E. (2002). 'Strategic alliances as social capital: A multidimensional view'. *Strategic Management Journal,* 23, 795–816.

Kramer, R.M., Brewer, M.B. and Hanna, B.A. (1996). 'Collective trust and collective action: The decision of trust as a social decision'. In Kramer, R.M. and Tyler, T.R. (eds), *Trust in organizations: Frontiers of theory and research.* Thousand Oaks, CA: Sage, 357–389.

Lesser, E. and Cothrel, J. (2001). 'Fast friends: Virtuality and social capital'. *Knowledge Directions,* Spring-Summer, 66–79.

Manning, P. (2010). 'Explaining and developing social capital for knowledge management purposes'. *Journal of Knowledge Management,* 14, 1, 83–99.

Nahapiet, J. and Goshal, S. (1998). 'Social capital, intellectual capital, and the organizational advantage'. *Academy of Management Review,* 23, 2, 242–266.

Nhoria, N. and Eccles, R. (1996). 'Face-to-face: Making network organizations work'. InNhoria, N. and Eccles, R. (eds) *Networks and organizations. Structure, form and action.* Boston: Harvard Business School Press, 288–308.

Piore, M.J. and Sabel, C.F. (1984). *The second industrial divide: Possibilities for prosperity.* New York: Basic Books.

Porter, M.E. (1990). *The competitive advantage of nations*. New York, NY: Free Press.

Porter, M.E. and Sölvell, O. (1999). 'The role of geography in the process of innovation and the sustainable competitive advantage of firms'. In Chandler, A.D., Hagström, P. and Sölvell, O. (eds), *The dynamic firm: The role of technology, strategy, organizations and regions*. New York: Oxford University Press Inc., 440–457.

Porter, M.E. and Stern, S. (1999). *The new challenge to America's prosperity: Findings from the innovation index*. Council on Competitiveness Publications Office. Washington, D.C.

Porter, M.E., Ketels, C.H.M. and Delgado, M. (2007). 'The microeconomic foundations of prosperity: findings from the business competitiveness index', In *Global Competitiveness Report 2007-2008*, Palgrave Macmillan, London.

Prahalad, C.K. and Ramaswamy, V. (2000). 'Co-opting customer competence'. *Harvard Business Review*, Jan–Feb, 79–87.

Putnam, R.D. (1993). 'The prosperous community: social capital and public life'. *American Prospect*, 13, 35–42.

Quinn, J. B. (1992). *Intelligent enterprise: A knowledge and service based paradigm for industry*. New York: Free Press.

Ranta, J. (1998). 'Networks and network companies – Competition with time, speed and flexibility'. In Ollus, M., Ranta, J. and Ylä-Antilla, P. (eds), *Company networks – Competition using knowledge, speed, and flexibility*. Helsinki: Sitra, 8–27.

Sabel, C. (1993). 'Studied trust: Building new forms of cooperation in a volatile economy'. *Human Relation*, 46, 9, 1133–1170.

Schiele, H. (2008). 'Location, location: the geography of industry clusters'. *Journal of Business Strategy*, 29, 3, 29–36.

Smedlund, A. and Pöyhönen, A. (2005). 'Intellectual capital creation: A knowledge system approach'. In Bounfour, A. and Edvinsson, L. (eds), *Intellectual capital for communities*. Oxford: Butterworth-Heinemann, 227–252.

Spender, J-C. (1996). 'Making knowledge the basis of a dynamic theory of the firm'. *Strategic Management Journal*, 17, 45–62.

Viedma, J.M. (2004). 'Social capital benchmarking system: Profiting from social capital when building network organizations'. *Journal of Intellectual Capital*, 5, 3, 426–442.

8   Conclusions

Drucker, P. (1977). *An abridged and revised version of management: Tasks, responsibilities, practices*. Great Britain, Pan Books Ltd. in association with Heinemann, 44–45.

Garelli, S. (2002). "Competitiveness of nations: The fundamentals". Visited 8 July2011.http://members.shaw.ca/compilerpress1/Anno%20Garelli%20CN%20Fundamentals.htm

Porter, M. (2005) What is Competitiveness? IESE business School-Anselmo Rubiralta Center for Globalization and Strategy. Visited 08 july 2011.http://www.iese.edu/en/ad/AnselmoRubiralta/Apuntes/Competitividad_en.html

Index